The Mac Made Easy

The Mac Made Easy

Martin S. Matthews

Osborne McGraw-Hill

Berkeley   New York   St. Louis   San Francisco
Auckland   Bogotá   Hamburg   London   Madrid
Mexico City   Milan   Montreal   New Delhi   Panama City
Paris   São Paulo   Singapore   Sydney
Tokyo   Toronto

Osborne **McGraw-Hill**
2600 Tenth Street
Berkeley, California 94710
U.S.A.

For information on translations or book distributors outside of the U.S.A.,
please write to Osborne **McGraw-Hill** at the above address.

The Mac Made Easy

1234567890 DOC 998765432

ISBN 0-07-881773-0

Table of Contents

Acknowledgments

This book, more than most, required the help of a lot of people. First among these is Greg Hall of Apple Computer Inc.'s Bellevue, Washington office. Greg not only answered in detail several questions every day for three months (with much patience), but he substantially wrote two chapters and the installation appendix. And he did the latter over his Christmas vacation! As if that wasn't enough, Greg read every word of the book, in several cases more than once, and provided a great many excellent recommendations for improving it. This book has a lot of Greg in it.

Sandra Horwich, a writer and editor on Macintosh topics, also gave some of her holiday time to write two excellent chapters. Her willingness and capability to produce such good work in a short time while following a rigid style is both admired and very much appreciated.

Several people have influenced (positively) my thinking about the Macintosh, but foremost among them is Marsha Buxton. Marsha, a friend for over 20 years, has used the Macintosh since its birth and made it a vital part of her everyday life. Marsha read much of this book and provided many carefully thought out and in several cases heartfelt suggestions. Her time, effort, and the amount of herself that went into what she said is greatly appreciated.

After authoring or coauthoring 23 editions of 17 books, I have worked with a number of editors. None of them has put the amount of time and energy into producing a good book as has Frances Stack, the Osborne/McGraw-Hill acquisitions editor for this book. Frances not only worked very hard at real editing, something almost unheard of for an acquisitions editor, but she also agonized over the quality of the screen shots and put much effort into trying to teach an old dog a new trick or two. This book also has a lot of Frances in it.

A number of other people at Osborne/McGraw-Hill put considerable time and effort into this book. Among those who worked directly with the author, all in various phases of editing, Jill Pisoni, Laura Sackerman, and Ann Spivack stand out for their contributions to the book. Ann, who copyedited the book, not only caught many errors, but made many small additions, the sum of which materially added to the book.

Besides Greg Hall, a number of others at Apple Computer, Inc. contributed to this book. Prominent among these are Cindy Rogan, also from the Bellevue office, and Nicole Taggart from the Cupertino Public Relations office, both of whom went out of their way to make sure we had everything we needed during production of this book.

The screen shots in this book are produced with Capture 4.0 by Mainstay. It is an excellent product with many significant enhancements in the latest release. I recommend it highly.

Introduction

The Apple Macintosh has always been highly respected and desired in several segments of the market, especially the graphic arts industry. In the last several years, the ease of use, the depth and sophistication of the software available, and the power and capability of the hardware and system software have opened a much broader market to the Macintosh. It is now the computer of choice for a diverse spectrum of businesses.

As a result of this wider business audience, an increasing number of people with little or no prior Macintosh experience are being asked or decide on their own to use a Macintosh in their work. *The Mac Made Easy* is written for that group. If you are new to the Macintosh and/or want to more fully use the substantial power that is available with your Macintosh, this book is for you.

About this Book

The Mac Made Easy is the one book needed by all beginning to intermediate Macintosh users. Starting with what makes a Macintosh a Macintosh and which Macintosh is right for a given task, to exploring System 7 and trying out HyperCard, *The Mac Made Easy* covers the width and breadth of Macintosh hardware and system software. The book not only answers many how-tos and whys, but also provides numerous notes and cautions. The objective is to give you a jump start on full, and even advanced, use of your entire Macintosh system.

The Mac Made Easy is a major supplement to the reference manuals and training materials that come with the Macintosh and provides a greater depth of knowledge on how to use the Macintosh creatively and practically. *The Mac Made Easy* is written so you can follow along on your Macintosh and compare what you experience and see on the screen with what is described and shown in the book.

How this Book Is Organized

The Mac Made Easy provides the essential knowledge needed to fully and easily use this powerful computer system with the new System 7 system software. You'll get a quick overview of the hardware that is part of the system, followed by an in-depth look at how to use such important elements as the screen, mouse, and disks, as well as menus, dialog boxes, and control panels. System 7 is fully explored, as are fonts, printing, HyperCard, and communications. This information is divided into ten fast-paced chapters, which are listed here:

Chapter 1, "Meet the Macintosh," introduces the Macintosh. It discusses what makes a Macintosh a Macintosh, the importance of the Macintosh's unique graphical interface, and how the Macintosh is a system of integrated hardware and software components. The function of each of the hardware components is described, including the central processing unit (CPU), temporary (RAM) memory, disk storage, the screen, the keyboard, the mouse, and the printer, as well as how they interact with each other. The various models of the Macintosh are described, as are several Apple printers and other peripherals. The chapter ends with a discussion of which Macintosh best fits particular needs.

Chapter 2, "Using the Macintosh," explores the major features of the Macintosh: the screen, the mouse, and the keyboard, as well as windows, menus, and dialog boxes, and how each is used. You are encouraged to turn on your Macintosh and take your mouse in hand as the text describes how to hold the mouse and perform the various mouse functions such as pointing, clicking, double-clicking, and dragging. Next, the elements of windows, menus, and dialog boxes are discussed, including how to open and use a menu, how the boxes, bars, and areas of windows function, and how to use the various buttons and other controls in a dialog box. Finally, the Apple keyboards are examined, paying special attention to their non-typewriter keys, including Command (($⌘$)), (control), (option), (delete), (clear), and the arrow and function keys.

Chapter 3, "Menus," discusses the Macintosh menu system and how to use it. Opening menus and selecting options are demonstrated, as are the use of submenus and dialog boxes. This chapter reviews each of the Finder menus, including the Apple, File, Edit, View, Label, Special, Balloon Help, and Applications menus. Each menu option is described along with its function. The Desk Accessories available from the Apple menu, including the Alarm Clock, Calculator, Key Caps, Note Pad, and Scrapbook are covered in this chapter.

Chapter 4, "Files, Folders, and Disks," discusses the Macintosh hierarchical file system and how to work with files, folders, and disks. You'll see how these filing elements are used and how they relate to each other. This chapter teaches you how to create new files and folders, initialize (format) disks, and copy, duplicate, move, back up, and clear (delete) folders and files. The chapter also explores in-depth creating and using aliases, finding files, and getting around the file system.

Chapter 5, "System 7 and the Finder," describes what system software is and then looks at each of the major System 7 software components: the System, Finder, Extensions, Control Panels, Resources, Desk Accessories, and Utilities. The description of each system software component also tells how it functions, how to best use it, and why it is necessary or desirable. Next, the System folder is discussed, including how the Apple Menu Items, Control Panels, Extensions, Preferences, and Startup Items folders are used within the System folder. The chapter ends with an exploration of the Finder and how it works with several open applications using the mouse, the Applications menu, and the keyboard.

Chapter 6, "Customizing with Control Panels," describes in detail the standard control panels, including their control functions and how they are used. The standard control panels include General Controls, Color, Easy Access, File Sharing Monitor, Keyboard, Labels, Map, Memory, Monitors,

Mouse, Sharing Setup, Sound, Startup Disk, Users & Groups, and Views. Additionally, several special-purpose control panels are discussed.

Chapter 7, "Fonts, Printers, and Printing," explores the basics of fonts, including both TrueType and PostScript font technologies, and looks at how fonts are identified, stored, and used on the Macintosh. The chapter also discusses printers and printer drivers and how printers are identified with the Chooser. Finally, you'll see how the Page Setup and Print dialog boxes control printing and learn about the Print Monitor and background printing.

Chapter 8, "Applications and Transferring Data," discusses the various types of applications and how they are used; you'll see how to install, open, and work with applications. Also, you'll review the most-used menu features and the most common way that text is entered and edited. Finally, the chapter looks at how data is transferred among applications using the Clipboard, Apple Events, and the Publish and Subscribe features of the Edition Manager. Teach Text is used in demonstrating some of the standard Macintosh application features.

Chapter 9, "HyperCard," reviews HyperCard and its major features and functions, including cards, stacks, tools, and buttons, and creating, editing, and locating. Both Addresses With Audio and Appointments With Audio are used in demonstrations of HyperCard. A major part of the chapter describes the creation of a new stack.

Chapter 10, "Communications," looks at the fully integrated networking features of System 7. You'll learn how to connect to a network, turn on file sharing, identify folders to be shared, and access a file server. Other topics include direct communications between Macintoshes and between a Macintosh and an IBM PC or a compatible. The new AppleTalk Remote Access is discussed as is electronic mail and using remote communications with computer information services. Also, you'll learn about networking with LocalTalk and Ethernet, as well as how to use a modem.

The appendix, "Installing System 7," describes the process of upgrading a Macintosh with an older version of the operating system. This includes checking the compatibility of existing applications; backing up, updating, or optionally initializing your hard disk; and installing and customizing System 7. Of particular importance here are the tricks to make this go smoothly and the traps to be aware of.

Conventions Used in this Book

The Mac Made Easy uses several conventions designed to make the book easier to use and information easier to find.

- The Note, Caution, and Stop Macintosh icons, which are copywritten by Apple Computer, Inc. and used with permission, are used throughout the book to identify notes, cautions, and warnings just as they are in the Macintosh system. These icons are

Notes provide tips and information that are not of immediate importance. On the Macintosh, notes deal with situations that do not have serious effect. When finished with a note the user simply clicks OK.

Cautions alert the reader and the Macintosh user to situations that could have undesirable effects. On the Macintosh, the user is given the option of continuing or not.

Warnings alert the reader and Macintosh user to an action that, if it is carried out, will have an undesirable effect. On the Macintosh, the user is required to choose an alternative course of action.

- Terms that are relevant to your Macintosh appear in italics where they are defined, which is usually very close to, if not at, their first use.

- Text that is to be typed on your keyboard appears in boldface.

- Names of individual keys on your keyboard are presented in key-shaped graphics. For example, (option) and (shift).

- The Command key is represented by its symbol, (⌘).

- "Hard Disk" refers to whatever name you have given your hard disk. You substitute the name of your hard disk when you see "Hard Disk" in text.

1

Meet the Macintosh

The Apple Macintosh is a *personal computer*, a computer for your personal use that you can tailor to your preferences. You have a wide choice of Macintosh models to choose from, of equipment and programs to add, and of options within the computer that you can set the way you want. You can change the way the screen looks, the colors that are displayed, and the sounds that are produced. You can make your Apple Macintosh an extension of you.

The Macintosh works the way you do, with file folders, trash cans, and a desktop. To use it, you do things you would do even if you weren't working on a computer—things like opening a file folder on a desktop and discarding unwanted information into a trash can. If you want to move a drawing from one file folder to another, you do just that.

Seeing Is Believing

The Macintosh mimics your world by allowing you to actually see items—the file folder, desktop, and trash can—as small, realistic representations called icons, that look like this:

You also see the action taking place: when you put something in the trash can on screen you see the trash can expand, and you see it deflate when you empty the trash. Better yet, you manipulate what you are looking at to make the action happen. For example, to move a drawing from one file folder to another, you literally drag the drawing you see in one file folder over to the other file folder, as shown in Figure 1-1.

This ability to see and manipulate realistic representations of the entities you are working with is called a *visual interface* between you and the computer. (You will also hear this referred to as a *graphic user interface* or GUI.) The Macintosh implements this visual interface using its screen to communicate with you and the hand-held mouse for you to communicate with it.

Figure 1-1. *Moving a drawing from the open Drawings folder to the Artwork folder*

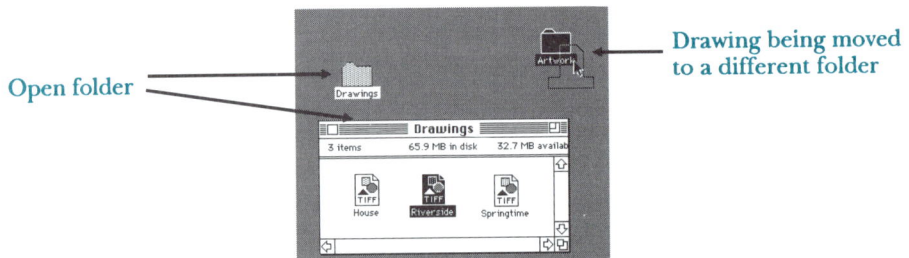

Open folder

Drawing being moved to a different folder

Figure 1-1 shows part of a Macintosh screen. At the top there are two file folders that actually look like miniature file folders named "Drawings" and "Artwork." The Drawings file folder is open and contains three drawing documents. One of the drawings, entitled "Riverside," is being dragged from the open Drawings folder to the Artwork folder. The arrow in the middle of the drawing being moved, called the *mouse pointer*, indicates that the mouse is being used to move this drawings document.

The Macintosh's visual interface is its most important attribute, and central to its design. There is more to the Macintosh, though, than the screen and the mouse.

The Macintosh System

The Macintosh is a system—a group of components that interact to perform the tasks that you want accomplished. Without any one of the components the Macintosh would, at best, be crippled and at worst unable to perform. You, the user, are an important part of the Macintosh system. That is why it is so important that you and your computer work easily together.

Besides you, there are two other major categories of Macintosh components: *hardware*, the physical computer and attachments, and *software*, also called *programs*, which directs the hardware to do specific tasks.

The remainder of this chapter is devoted to a discussion of hardware and software. You may wonder if you really need to know all this; you might compare it to driving a car: "I don't want to know how it works, I only want to use it." There are two reasons why you need to know a minimum about computers: first, you want to be able to make an intelligent decision when you buy a Macintosh, and second, you need to know something about the Macintosh in order to use it.

When you buy a new car you need to decide on an automatic as opposed to a manual transmission, the number of cylinders, and many other items. If you don't know enough about these components, you may end up with a car that doesn't fit your needs. The same is true about a computer. Also, if you don't know about the transmission in a car, you won't know how to shift it. Just as with a car, you don't need to be able to disassemble a transmission, but you do need to understand the differences between types of transmissions. In a computer, you need to know something about its components to make good use of it.

Macintosh Hardware

A wide range of equipment can be part of a Macintosh computer. Five major items make up almost every Macintosh system. Shown in Figure 1-2, these are the *computer* itself, the *screen* or *monitor*, the *keyboard*, the *mouse*, and the *printer*. Each is discussed in the following sections. A Macintosh can be used without a printer, but it must have the other four items to run.

The Computer

The "box" that houses the electronic components that tie together and direct all of the other components of the Macintosh is called the *computer*. This term can cause confusion because it is so broadly applied, but on these pages "computer" means "the box that everything connects to."

Apple offers several different models of computers, and the number of models and their characteristics change periodically. At this writing there are 11 models ranging from the Classic and Classic II on the low end to the Quadra 700 and 900 on the upper end. In the middle there are the three models of the *PowerBook* (notebook-style portable computers), the LC, and the Macintosh II family consisting of the IIsi, IIci, and IIfx. All of these computers run virtually all of the Macintosh software and they differ only in size and shape, speed, and capacity, where *capacity* is in terms of *memory*, *disk space*, and *expansion slots*. Each of these terms is explained in the following paragraphs.

Speed and the Microprocessor

Speed is one of the major factors distinguishing one computer from another. The easiest way to measure speed is by noting *clock speed*, the "heartbeat" that sets the pace for the rest of the computer. In the Macintosh Classic the clock speed is 8 *MHz* (megahertz) or eight million cycles per second. In the IIfx the clock speed is 40 MHz or five times as fast as the Classic.

Figure 1-2. A Macintosh IIsi showing the five major hardware components
(Photo courtesy of Apple Computer, Inc.)

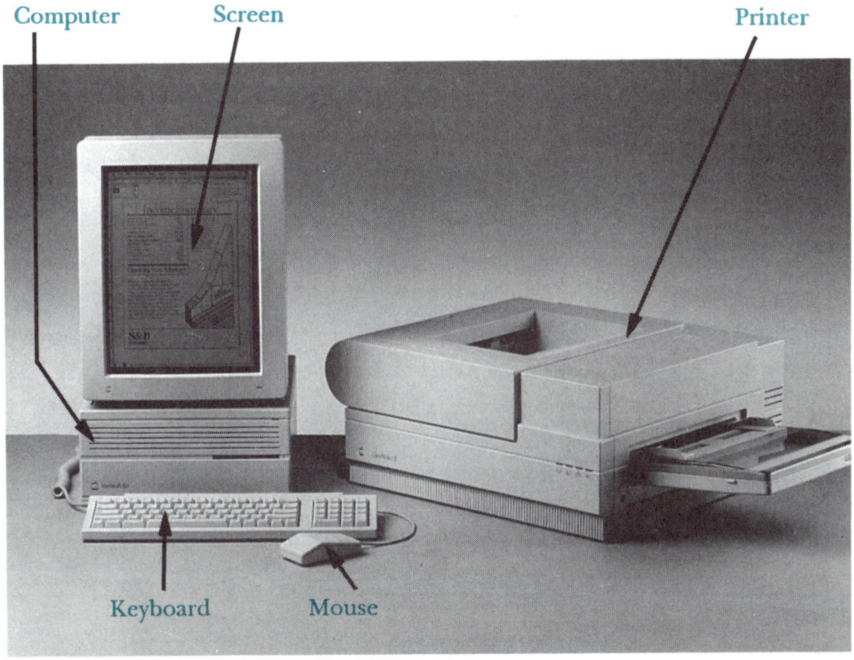

Computer   Screen   Printer

Keyboard   Mouse

This does not mean that the IIfx will run your programs five times as fast because many other factors determine how fast a program runs, but the clock speed gives you a relative measure of the various computers.

Exceptions to this are the Quadra 700 and 900, which have a clock speed of 25 MHz but, because of other factors, are about twice as fast as the 40 MHz IIfx. For this reason, speed is also measured relative to another computer. For example, a Macintosh IIsi has approximately 3 times the speed of a Classic; a IIfx has approximately 2 1/2 times the speed of a IIsi. These numbers vary depending on what the computer is doing, and are good only for rough estimates of speed.

The part inside the computer most dependent on the clock speed is the *microprocessor* or *central processing unit* (CPU). If the clock speed is the heart-beat of the computer, the microprocessor is the heart. The microprocessor is the directing component of the computer—every other component either supports or takes direction from the microprocessor. If the "computer" is the box that everything connects to, the "CPU" is the part in the box that tells everything what to do.

Macintosh computers use the Motorola 68000 series of microprocessors. The Macintosh Classic and PowerBook 100 use the 68000 itself, the LC uses the 68020, the Macintosh II family and the PowerBook 140 and 170 use the 68030, and the Quadra series use the 68040. Figure 1-3 shows a Motorola 68030 microprocessor. It is about 1 1/2 inches square and about 1/4 inch high.

Memory

Memory, which is also called *RAM* for Random-Access Memory, is temporary storage space used to hold information while it is being used in the computer. When the power is shut off or the computer is restarted, everything in RAM is lost. The more RAM you have, the more you can do and usually, the faster you can do it.

Figure 1-3.   *A Motorola 68030 microprocessor used in a Macintosh (Photo courtesy of Motorola Inc.)*

Macintosh computers range from 1 to over 64MB or 64 *megabytes* (mega means million) of RAM storage. A byte is equivalent to a character, so 64MB is roughly equivalent to 64 million characters. A page of single-spaced text is roughly equal to 5KB or 5 *kilobytes* (kilo means thousand) of memory, and many tasks require over 1MB of RAM. 2MB is considered the minimum memory needed, and 4 to 8MB is common.

You can choose from several memory levels when purchasing your Macintosh, and you can often add additional memory after purchase. Memory has become relatively inexpensive and it is hard to have too much. Memory comes in several forms. The form used in the Macintosh II series is the 1MB module called a *SIMM* (Single Inline Memory Module), shown in Figure 1-4. This is about 4 inches long and about 1 inch high.

Disk Space

Disk space is the information storage area contained on a *disk*, which is simply a circular platter that can be magnetically written on, read, and overwritten. Your disks are where information is stored when it is not being used. Once something is *stored* or written on a disk it remains there until it is erased, even when the power is shut off. Disks reside in a mechanical device called a *disk drive* that is similar to, although much smaller than, a record player. You can think of a disk drive as a file cabinet with a number of file drawers. A major question when purchasing disk drives is how much storage

Figure 1-4.   *1MB SIMM memory module used in a Macintosh IIsi (Photo courtesy of Motorola Inc.)*

space ("how many file drawers") do you need to store the information you want to keep on your computer.

Disks and disk drives come in two varieties: *floppy disks* are plastic disks that store (in current Macintosh models) up to 1.4MB; *hard disks* are metal disks that store 20 to 400MB. You can remove floppy disks from the computer using the opening on the front or right side of the computer. Floppy disks, therefore, let you transfer programs to and from your hard disk. While most Macintoshes come with both a floppy and a hard disk drive inside the computer cabinet, you may order some models without a hard disk, and you may add one after purchase. You may also add external floppy and hard disk drives. Figure 1-5 shows an external floppy disk drive used with Macintosh computers.

Having too much disk space is almost impossible. That saying about both file cabinets and computers, "information expands to fill the capacity available for it," is all too true. In a business environment, you should buy a disk twice

Figure 1-5.   *External floppy disk drive (Photo courtesy of Apple Computer, Inc.)*

as large as you think you need. With luck that will fulfill your needs for a couple of years.

Expansion Slots

The microprocessor and RAM, along with many lesser parts, are mounted on a large circuit board in the computer. This circuit board, called a *mother board*, connects to the various parts of the computer: disk drives, keyboard, mouse, screen, and printer. Some users may wish to "hook up" to other external equipment such as a musical instrument, a television, or a telephone. For this purpose some Macintosh models have one or more expansion slots. *Expansion slots* are sockets on the mother board for plugging in additional, smaller circuit boards for functions not included on the mother board. The number of expansion slots varies from none in the Macintosh Classic to six in the IIfx. The IIfx mother board is shown in Figure 1-6.

Figure 1-6.   *The Macintosh IIfx mother board (Photo courtesy of Apple Computer, Inc.)*

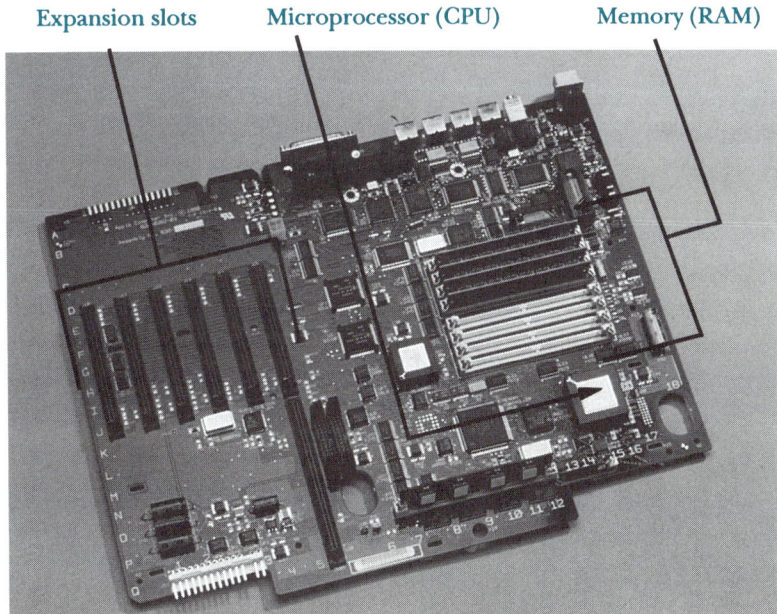

Expansion slots   Microprocessor (CPU)   Memory (RAM)

Figure 1-7 shows how the various components of the computer are connected. You can get a feel for how these components relate to each other when you install new software, with the following steps:

1. Software comes to you on floppy disks. To *install* the new program, copy the contents of the floppy disks to the hard disk.

2. When you *run* or *load* the program, the program is read from the hard disk and parts of it are copied into RAM.

3. While a program is running from RAM, instructions that are part of the program tell the microprocessor to display images and text on the screen, to accept input from both the keyboard and the mouse, and to use the printer.

4. When the program is finished or you are finished with it, you must store any resulting information on either the hard disk or a floppy

Figure 1-7.   *Macintosh computer components diagram*

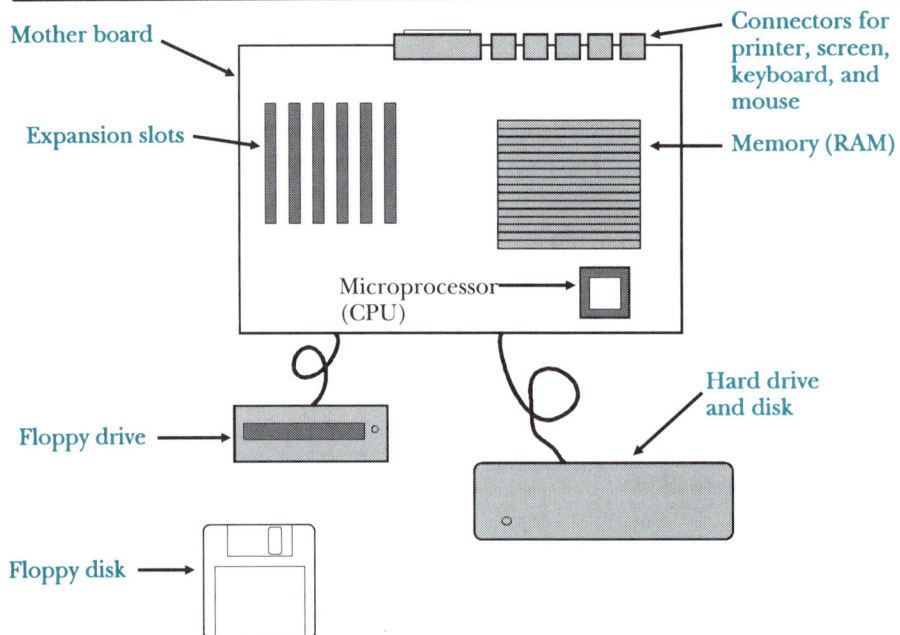

1

disk. If you wish, you can also delete the program itself from your computer's memory.

Table 1-1 compares the current Macintosh models.

The Screen

The screen or *video display* is housed in the computer cabinet of the Macintosh Classic, Classic II, and the PowerBook series. The other Macintosh models use a video display in a separate case where it is often referred to as a *monitor*. Apple makes both black-and-white and color displays in several screen sizes ranging from 12 to 21 inches (measured diagonally).

The video displays built into the Classic, Classic II, and PowerBook 100 are 9-inch black-and-white units while the PowerBook 140 and 170 are 10-inch black-and-white. Manufacturers other than Apple (called *third-party manufacturers*) also make a large variety of video displays, both color and black-and-white, in many sizes that can be attached to an LC or to any member of the Macintosh II or Quadra families. Figure 1-8 shows several models of Macintosh video displays. One third-party manufacturer, Radius Inc., makes a 15-inch display in both color and black-and-white models that can be pivoted from a vertical to a horizontal orientation.

For a video display to function, it requires special circuitry in the computer. For all Macintosh models except the IIfx, this circuitry is built into the mother board. On the IIfx, you must use one of the expansion slots for a *video adapter*, which is purchased separately. On the IIsi, IIci, and Quadra series computers you can also add a video adapter in an expansion slot for displays with higher resolution.

The Mouse

Every Macintosh except the PowerBooks comes with a mouse. It is a fundamental part of the Macintosh design philosophy. The *mouse* is used to point at and select something on the screen or to drag something across the screen. On computers without a mouse or other pointing device (see the next

Table 1-1.   *Comparison of Current Macintosh Models*

Model	Processor	Clock Speed	Speed x Classic*	Memory	Hard Disk**	Slots	Display
Classic	68000	8 MHz	1	1 to 4MB	0 or 40MB	None	Built in
Classic II	68030	16 MHz	2	2 to 10MB	40 or 80MB	None	Built in
Power Book 100	68000	16 MHz	1.9	2 to 8MB	20MB	***	Built in
Power Book 140	68030	16 MHz	2	2 to 8MB	20 or 40MB	***	Built in
Power Book 170	68030	25 MHz	5	4 to 8MB	40MB	***	Built in
LC	68020	16 MHz	1.9	2 to 10MB	40 or 80MB	1	External
IIsi	68030	20 MHz	3	3 to 17MB	40 or 80MB	1	External
IIci	68030	25 MHz	5.1	5 to 32MB	0 to 160MB	3	External
IIfx	68030	40 MHz	7.5	4 to 32MB	0 to 160MB	6	External
Quadra 700	68040	25 MHz	15	4 to 20MB	0 to 400MB	2	External
Quadra 900	68040	25 MHz	15	4 to 64MB	0 to 400MB	5	External

*Approximate speed relative to a Macintosh Classic
**All models except the PowerBook 100 have a 1.44MB floppy disk drive built in
***The PowerBooks only have modem and memory expansion slots

Figure 1-8. *Several models of Macintosh video displays (Photo courtesy of Apple Computer, Inc.)*

paragraph), these functions are accomplished by a set of keystrokes that take more effort to enter. The mouse is a very important part of the Macintosh interface.

The Macintosh PowerBook series replaces the mouse with a *trackball* built into the keyboard. You can also purchase a third-party trackball for other Macintosh models. An example of a third-party trackball from MicroSpeed is shown in Figure 1-9. A trackball performs the same functions as a mouse without requiring the same table or desk space—for example, the convenience of a trackball is obvious if you're using a computer while on an airplane. With a mouse you use your arm and wrist muscles to move the mouse around a flat surface. With a trackball, you use your fingers to move a ball around in a socket. Neither device is clearly superior. Try both to see which works best for you.

The Keyboard

The keyboard on a Macintosh is used primarily for entering text. Because the mouse is such an important part of the visual interface, you use the keyboard much less frequently to give directions to the computer. Apple has three Macintosh keyboard models—the Classic or ADB (Apple Desktop Bus) keyboard, the Apple keyboard, and the Apple Extended keyboard—but there is actually little difference among the three. The Classic keyboard comes with the Classic, Classic II, and some models of the LC. The Apple and Apple Extended keyboards can be purchased with the other Macintosh desktop models.

The Classic and the Apple keyboards have the same keys, but they are positioned slightly differently. Both keyboards have a standard *typewriter keyboard*, a *numeric keypad* as you would find on an adding machine, and a set of *arrow* or *pointer control keys* for moving the *insertion point*, which shows where you are in a block of text on screen. The third keyboard, the Apple Extended Keyboard II, has the features of the other two keyboards, the layout of the Classic keyboard, plus a set of 15 *function keys* across the top and 6 additional pointer control keys. Newer versions of Macintosh applications use the

Figure 1-9.   *A MicroSpeed trackball for a Macintosh (Photo courtesy of MicroSpeed, Inc.)*

1

function keys, so the Extended Keyboard is becoming increasingly popular. Figure 1-10 shows the Apple Extended Keyboard II.

Printers

While we are supposedly becoming a paperless society, we aren't doing it very fast; for most computer applications you'll want access to a printer. Apple sells several models of printers and many more are available from third-party vendors.

The majority of current printers used with personal computers, and the printers that Apple sells, use one of three methods to put a *printed image* on a page. The printed image can be text, a photograph, a drawing, or a combination of all three. You can compare printing methods in several ways: based on the *speed* of the printer, measured in pages per minute; on the

Figure 1-10. *Apple Extended Keyboard II (Photo courtesy of Apple Computer, Inc.)*

resolution of the printed image in terms of the *dots per inch* or dpi (this translates to resolution; more on this shortly); and on relative cost. These are the three printing methods and types of printers:

Dot Matrix   A dot matrix printer forms an image by using tiny pins to press an inked ribbon against a piece of paper. A dot matrix printer is the least expensive printing method. It has the lowest resolution but moderate speed.

Ink-Jet   An ink-jet printer forms an image by spraying tiny droplets of ink on a piece of paper. An ink-jet printer has high resolution, moderate cost, and the lowest speed.

Laser   A laser printer forms an image using a laser in a printing process similar to a copier. A laser printer is the most expensive form of printing but also has high resolution and the highest speed.

Apple printers begin, at the low end, with the ImageWriter II dot matrix printer, which allows you to print up to 2 1/2 pages per minute with a resolution of 72 dots per inch. (Because the printed image is formed by tiny dots, the more dots you have per inch, the better your image appears. Dots per inch range from under 60 to over 2500.) Next is the StyleWriter ink-jet printer that prints at 1/2 page per minute but at a resolution of 360 dots per inch. Following the StyleWriter is the Personal LaserWriter family that prints up to 4 pages per minute at 300 dots per inch. At the top is the LaserWriter II family, which prints at 8 pages per minute and 300 dots per inch. There are two models in each of the LaserWriter families. Figure 1-11 shows the Apple Personal LaserWriter LS and StyleWriter printers.

Third-party printers also cover a broad range of speed and resolution. At the top end are the professional *imagesetters* that produce images on film or paper at 1,270 to 2,500 dots per inch in both color and black and white at a very high price. On the other end there is a wide variety of dot matrix and ink-jet printers at various speeds and resolutions.

A very powerful capability is to use one of the Apple laser printers to print a document at 300 dots per inch and then, when you are satisfied, take the file to an establishment that rents time on a professional imagesetter and reprint the document at 1,270 or 2,500 dots per inch. The document will be the same except for the improved resolution.

Figure 1-11. *Apple Personal LaserWriter LS and StyleWriter printers (Photo courtesy of Apple Computer, Inc.)*

Macintosh Software

Software has two major divisions, *system software* which controls the hardware and information flow, and *application software* which performs the actual work you do such as word processing and drawing.

System Software

System software in the Macintosh provides the overall look and feel that you experience when you use the computer. The way the screen looks and the way the mouse, keyboard, disks, and printer work are all controlled by system software. System software works directly with the hardware and provides an interface for application software to accomplish hardware tasks. For example, the system software provides the means to divide the hard disk into folders and files. It also sets the rules for naming and accessing them. When you tell an application to create a new file or access an existing one, it does so through the system software using system software rules.

You might think of system software as being a cocoon around the hardware with the application software wrapped around the system software, as shown in Figure 1-12. You, the user, interact with the application software which in turn interacts with the system software to make the hardware accomplish tasks.

The current version of Macintosh system software included with new computers is System 7. Much of this book will focus on the many facets of System 7 and how to get the most from them. Besides System 7, A/UX, a Unix-related operating system, and MS-DOS, the IBM/PC operating system are available as options on some Macintosh models. MS-DOS, though, requires the use of an expansion slot and a special circuit board.

Figure 1-12.   *The user's relationship to hardware and application and system software*

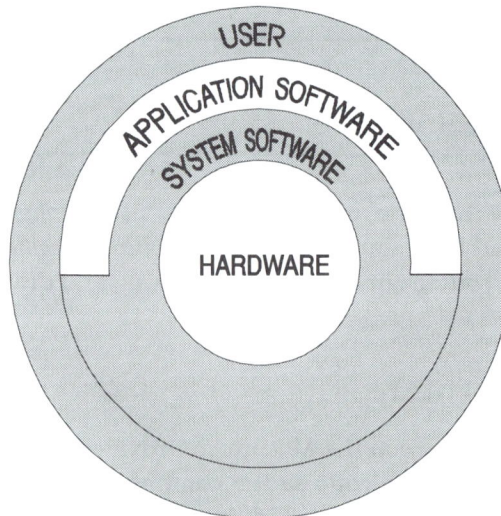

Application Software

Application software generally covers all software that isn't system software. It represents a great number of programs and even a large number of categories. Just *some* of the categories are accounting, animation, architecture, computer-aided design, computer-aided manufacturing, databases, data entry, desktop publishing, education, electronic mail, financial modeling, forms design, illustration, image processing, multimedia, networking, presentations, programming, project management, software engineering, spreadsheets, training, utilities, and word processing. For each of these categories there is a range of programs available to you that cover the spectrum of cost and capability.

Which Macintosh to Get

With all the choices in models and features, deciding which Macintosh to get might seem overwhelming. There are two obvious factors: your budget and your requirements. The requirements depend on what you want to do with your Macintosh and how sophisticated you want to get. The cost ranges from under $1,000 for a Classic with 2MB of memory and no hard disk to over $9,000 for a Quadra 900 with 4MB of memory and a 400MB hard disk.

Your requirements usually pertain to specific application software such as word processing, database, desktop publishing, or computer-aided design. Before deciding which hardware to buy, choose the specific application software you want, look at the hardware requirements of that software, and then translate those requirements into Macintosh models, memory, and disk capacities.

The Classic 2/40 (2MB memory and 40MB hard disk) is excellent for data entry, electronic mail, basic spreadsheets, and word processing. On the other end, if you are doing architectural drawing, computer-aided design, or software engineering, you probably want to get as close to the top end as your budget allows.

You know that the computer salesperson will try to sell you the most computer they can. Therefore you need to figure out which model is the smallest that will still do your job and leave room for growth. The Classic II is an excellent buy and the LC and IIsi provide a lot of capability. In choosing between the Classic II and the LC or IIsi, consider the Classic II's transport-ability and small size versus the *modularity* (your ability to purchase the keyboard and monitor separately) and the expansion capability (using expansion slots) of the LC and IIsi.

The Quadra 700 is also an excellent buy when compared to the IIci, IIfx, and Quadra 900. The Quadra 700 costs only a couple of hundred dollars more than the IIci and over $1,500 *less than* the IIfx, yet it is considerably faster and comes with more built-in capabilities such as higher resolution video and an EtherNet port. The trade-off is that the Quadra 700 has limited memory expansion and only two expansion slots.

Again, it is wise to get more memory and disk space than you think you might initially need. Also, most people trade up to larger models after using a computer for several years, so your first purchase is probably not the only one you'll make. No matter which model you get, you will have the Macintosh functions and features that make it truly easy to use a personal computer.

2

Using the Macintosh

This chapter acquaints you with the major features of the Apple Macintosh and teaches you how to use and manipulate them. You learn about the Macintosh screen, the mouse, windows, menus, dialog boxes, and the keyboard.

   This chapter is more of a tutorial than the rest of the book. It proceeds more slowly than other chapters in order to introduce you to terms and procedures that are used throughout this book. It assumes that you are sitting in front of your Macintosh and that you have System 7 and one or more applications installed. If you don't have System 7 installed, do that first (see the appendix for help). If you are already familiar with the Macintosh and using a mouse, scan the chapter to verify that you use terms and procedures the same way as they are used here.

The Macintosh Environment

The Macintosh offers a standard environment for all of the programs that run on it. This environment depends heavily on the visual interface between you and the computer. (Remember from Chapter 1 that the visual interface is simply the computer communicating with you through visual images (icons) and your communicating back through the mouse.) Once you learn to use the Macintosh environment, you'll find that working with programs written expressly for the Macintosh is much easier because they use the standard Macintosh environment. You don't have to relearn many of the primary functions with each program.

In addition to the visual interface and the mouse, the Macintosh also provides both a standard set of menus and several ways to transfer information among programs, for example to transfer a drawing from MacDraw (a drawing program) to MacWrite (a word processing program).

The quickest way to learn about the Macintosh is to start using it. The first step is to turn on your computer.

Starting the Macintosh

There are several ways to turn on a Macintosh—which way you use depends on your model. Most Macintosh models have a power switch on the back of the computer that you simply press. On the Classics this switch is located to the right of the power cord, and on the LC and Macintosh II family it is on the left, under the power cord. The other way to turn on your Macintosh (recommended if you use the Macintosh II and Quadra families) is to use the (power on) key on the keyboard. This key has a triangle on it and is located on the top center of the Classic and Apple keyboards and on the top right of the Extended II keyboard.

Turn on your Macintosh now, using the method that is appropriate for you.

After turning on your Macintosh you will almost immediately hear a tone and then, after a few seconds, you should see the "happy Macintosh" icon smiling at you. The tone and the "happy Macintosh" tell you that your

Macintosh is up and running and that, at least up to this point, everything is working correctly. If the tone should change, or if you see a "sad Macintosh" icon, something is wrong. The "happy Macintosh" and "sad Macintosh" icons look like this:

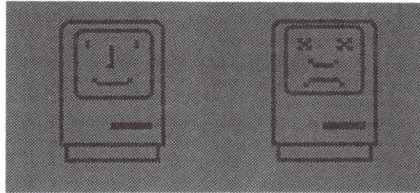

You may have gotten the "sad Macintosh" icon because you have not yet installed your system software. If this is the case, install it now (see the appendix for help). If your system software is installed and you still get the "sad Macintosh" icon, then you need to take your Macintosh to your dealer and have it checked out.

If you do not have a hard disk, you may see a Floppy Disk icon with a question mark on it. This tells you to insert a startup disk. If the floppy disk you inserted prior to starting is ejected from the floppy drive and a Floppy Disk icon with an X on it is displayed, this tells you that the floppy disk that was just ejected was not a startup disk and that you need to insert a startup disk. These Floppy Disk icons are shown here:

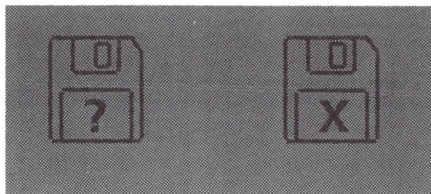

The Macintosh Screen

After getting the "happy Macintosh" icon you will see a "Welcome to Macintosh" message and the screen shown in Figure 2-1. This is the standard Macintosh screen, showing the features present in most Macintosh screens.

The top line on the screen, called the *menu bar*, contains the names of the menus that are available to you. A *menu* on a computer, just like a restaurant menu, simply gives you a list of choices, or *options*. The options allow you to direct what the computer will do next and how it will do it. The set of menus that you see in Figure 2-1 is the Finder menus. When you run an application program you will a see a different set of menus; each application has its own individual set of menus. The Finder, a part of the system software that you learn more about in Chapters 4 and 5, is the default application—it is on the screen when you aren't running an application

The area below the menu bar is called the *desktop*. The item you are currently working on is displayed here. Since you just started the computer, no work is on the desktop.

On the right side of the desktop are two icons representing the startup disk drive and the trash can in which you throw things away. You may have a Hard Disk icon, as shown in Figure 2-1, or a Floppy Disk icon.

Finally, in the center of the screen, is the mouse *pointer*. When you move your mouse, you move this arrow around the screen, a kind of remote control. By moving the mouse so that the pointer is *pointing* on an object (placing the mouse pointer on top of the object) and pressing and releasing the mouse button, you can *select* that object. You need to select an object in order to copy, move, or delete it, or to select a menu and choose an option.

Figure 2-1.   *The startup screen*

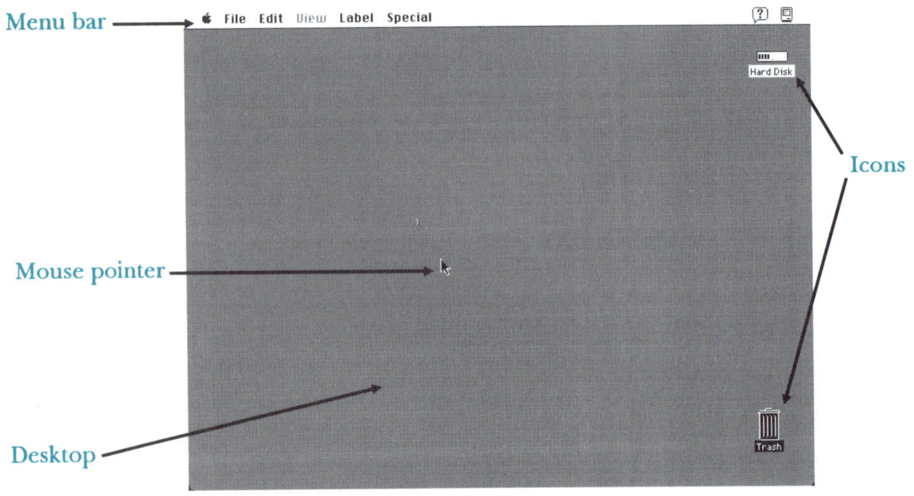

2

Using the Mouse

You use the mouse to move the pointer on the screen and you communicate your choices to the computer by pressing the mouse button. While there are alternative mouse devices on the market with more than one button, the discussion in this book will assume you use the single-button Macintosh mouse.

Because the Macintosh mouse has only one button, you can use it with either hand. Right-handed users simply plug the mouse into the receptacle on the right side of the keyboard and plug the keyboard into the computer using the keyboard receptacle on the left side. Left-handed users reverse this, plugging the mouse into the receptacle on the left side.

Familiarize yourself with the mouse by following these steps:

1. Hold the mouse so that the rectangular button is under your fingers with the cord at the top leading away from you.

2. Move the mouse across a flat surface such as a table or desk without pressing the button and watch the pointer move on the screen. If you run out of room while moving the mouse, (if you come to the edge of your desk, for example) pick up the mouse and place it where there is more room. Experiment with this now. Watch how the pointer continues from where you left it when you pick up the mouse.

This book uses the following standard terminology to guide you in using the mouse:

Term	Action
Press	Push down and hold the mouse button.
Release	Stop pressing the mouse button.
Point on	Move the mouse until the tip of the pointer is on top of the item you want to select.
Click	Point on an item that you want to select and quickly press and release the mouse button once.
Double Click	Point on an item that you want to select and press and release the mouse button twice in rapid succession.

Term	Action
Drag	Point on an item that you want to move, and press and hold down the mouse button while you move the mouse; where you move the mouse, you also move the item. When you get the item where you want it, release the mouse button.
Select	Select an item by pointing on it and pressing the mouse button. Or highlight something, such as a block of text.
Choose	Choose an option from one of the menus by pointing on the menu name, dragging down the menu until the option you want is highlighted, and then releasing the mouse button.

The drag function is used to choose an option within a menu, to move an object on the desktop, and to select (*highlight*) contiguous text. You highlight text when you want to do something to it. For example, to delete, move, or copy text, or to make it boldface or italic, you highlight the text and then choose the function to be performed on it.

Mousing Around

Practice selecting and moving the Trash icon with these instructions:

1. Point on the Trash icon by moving the mouse until the tip of the pointer is resting on it. (If the tip of the mouse pointer is not on the object you want to select or drag, the following steps will not work.)

2. Select the Trash icon by clicking it—quickly press and release the mouse button while pointing on the Trash icon. The Trash icon darkens, indicating that it is selected.

3. Drag the Trash icon to the center of the screen by pointing on the Trash icon and pressing and holding down the mouse button. Then move the mouse until the pointer and the icon are in the center of the screen, as shown in Figure 2-2.

Figure 2-2. *Trash icon moved to the center of the screen*

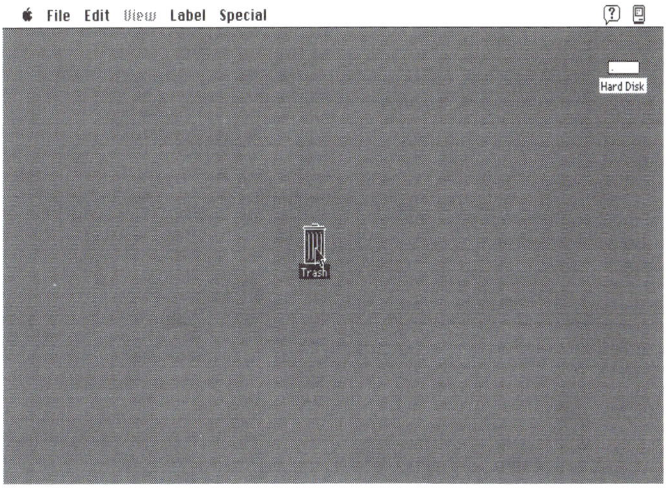

4. Drag the Trash icon back to the lower-right corner.

5. Move your mouse pointer to your Hard Disk icon and click. It becomes dark and the Trash icon lightens, indicating that you have selected the Hard Disk icon (and unselected the Trash icon).

6. Move the pointer again and double-click (click twice in rapid succession) your Trash icon. Your Hard Disk icon lightens and your Trash icon both darkens and opens, showing you its contents. In Figure 2-3, the trash is empty; at this stage yours will probably be empty, too.

It sometimes takes a couple of tries to get the rhythm of double-clicking. A general problem is that people double-click too slowly. In the control panels, discussed in Chapter 6, "Customizing with Control Panels," you can adjust the speed of double-clicking to your own comfort.

Figure 2-3.   *Trash icon selected and opened*

Using Windows

When you double-clicked the Trash icon, you opened the Trash window. A *window* is an area of the screen that you use for a specific purpose. It may momentarily display information, be your primary work space for several hours, or provide you with an opportunity to describe how you want something done. You can have one window open on the screen or many windows displayed at one time. Also, you can change the size of a window and you can move a window around the screen just as you moved the Trash icon. A window may contain one or many items such as programs, documents, or drawings. Depending on a window's size and the number of items it contains, you may not be able to see all the items it holds. In the following paragraphs you see how you can change the window size and shift the view of the window contents to see all of the items.

To view the common features of Macintosh windows, move your mouse pointer to the Hard Disk icon and double-click. The Hard Disk window will open to display the contents of the hard disk. Notice that the Hard Disk window has a dark border with lines across the title bar while the Trash

Figure 2-4. *Hard Disk window opened*

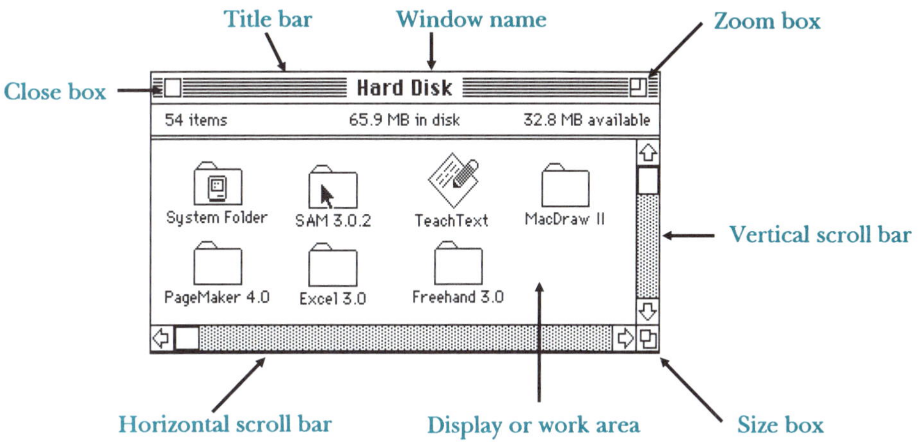

window border has become light (with no lines across the title bar)—this tells you that the Hard Disk window is now the *active window*. As shown in Figure 2-4, both windows contain features that are present in most Macintosh windows. (The contents of your hard disk are probably different from those shown in Figure 2-4.)

At the top of the window is the *title bar*. In the center of the title bar is the name of the window, generally the same as the name of the icon you clicked to open it. On the left end of the title bar is the *close box*. You can close the window by clicking the close box. On the right end of the title bar is the *zoom box*. By clicking the zoom box you can enlarge or shrink the window with a single click.

In the lower-right corner of the window is the *size box*, which lets you make windows any size you want. If you drag the size box out toward the edge of the screen you can make the window larger; drag it in and make the window smaller. Note the distinction between the zoom and size boxes: the size box allows for continuous sizing while the zoom box jumps out to the size necessary to display the contents (or the full screen) and then jumps back to the starting size.

On the right side and the bottom of the window lie the vertical and horizontal *scroll bars*, which allow you to move or *scroll* the contents of the window. The next section shows you how to use scroll bars and scroll boxes.

Practice using some of these window features now by following these steps:

1. Click the zoom box in the upper-right corner of the Hard Disk window. Usually, the window will expand to display all of its contents. If your Hard Disk window started off showing a lot more blank space than was necessary for the number of icons it held, it will shrink to be just large enough to show its contents.

2. Click the zoom box again and the window will return to its original size. This means it will shrink if the original zoom expanded the screen.

3. Drag the title bar down to move the window to the middle of the screen. (Point anywhere on the title bar except in the close or zoom boxes, press and hold the mouse button while moving the mouse toward you so that the window moves down on the screen, and then release the mouse button.) This is called *dragging* the window.

4. Drag the size box toward the lower-right corner of the screen to enlarge the window. (Point on the size box, press and hold the mouse button while moving the mouse and the window toward the lower-right corner, and then release the mouse button.) This is called *sizing* the window.

5. Drag the size box back toward the upper-left corner to make the window smaller.

6. Practice dragging the size box and sizing the window in many different sizes. Note that you can drag the size box up, down, left, and right as well as on any of the four diagonal directions. Make the window fairly small.

7. Practice dragging the window around the screen by dragging the title bar. Make the Hard Disk window partially overlap the Trash window.

8. Click anywhere in the Trash window. Notice that the series of horizontal lines disappears from the title bar of the Hard Disk

2

window and appears in the title bar of the Trash window. Also, the scroll bars disappear in the Hard Disk window and appear in the Trash window. This means that the Trash window is the active window. Also, when the Trash window is active, it will overlap the Hard Disk window and vice versa.

9. Click anywhere in the Hard Disk window. It again becomes the active window.

10. Click the close box of the Hard Disk window. The Hard Disk window closes and disappears into the Hard Disk icon.

11. Double-click the Hard Disk icon again to reopen the Hard Disk window. Notice that it appears in the exact size and location on the screen that it occupied before you closed it.

12. Click in the Trash window to activate it and then click the Trash window's close box. The Trash window closes and disappears into the Trash icon.

Using Scroll Bars

A Macintosh window is just that—an opening through which you can see the contents of the window. If a window contains only a few items, a small window adequately displays it all. If quite a few items are in a window, the largest window you can create, one that covers the entire screen, may not be large enough to display all of them. In that case, you need to be able to move or scroll through the contents of the window, either horizontally or vertically.

Imagine that you are looking through a microscope at something on a slide. You must move the slide left and right and up and down to see all of it. The scroll bars perform this function for a Macintosh window—they move the *area being displayed* (not the window) up or down (vertically), or left or right (horizontally).

Each of the two scroll bars provides three mechanisms for moving the area being displayed. These are shown in Figure 2-5. The first mechanism is the scroll arrow—note that there are four of them altogether. By clicking one of these *scroll arrows*, you move the display area in the direction of the arrow by a small amount. The second mechanism is the square *scroll box*—each

Figure 2-5.   *The reduced Hard Disk window*

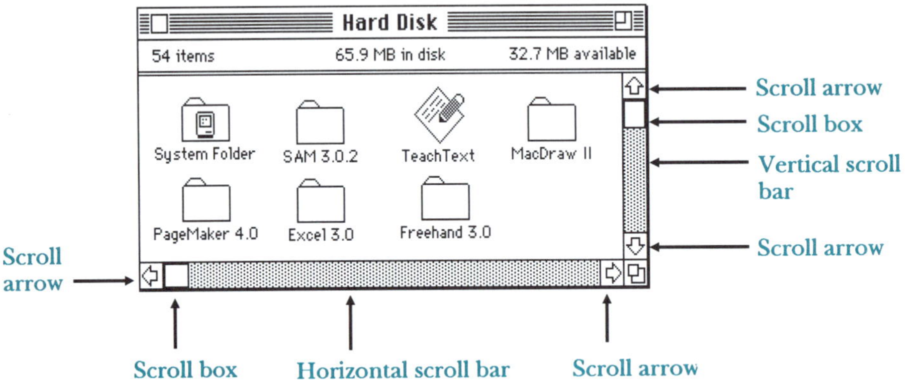

window has a horizontal scroll box and a vertical scroll box. By dragging a scroll box within its scroll bar, you move the display area by an amount proportional to the amount you dragged the scroll box. Since the scroll bar represents 100 percent of the display area's height or width, if you drag the scroll box halfway down the vertical scroll bar you will see the middle section, vertically, of your display area.

The third mechanism for moving the area being displayed in a window is the *scroll bar* itself—each window has a vertical scroll bar and a horizontal scroll bar. By clicking the scroll bar in areas other than the scroll arrows or scroll boxes, you will move the display area in the direction that you clicked by a larger amount than clicking the scroll arrows will move you.

Use the following instructions to try out the scroll bars:

1. Drag the size box for the Hard Disk window to reduce its size to that shown in Figure 2-5.

2. Click the down scroll arrow. Notice that the display area moves up, showing you the information below the section previously shown. Notice, also, that the scroll box has moved down within the scroll bar.

The position of the scroll box in the scroll bar represents the approximate position of the window display area within the overall area. When the vertical scroll box is at the top of its scroll bar, you

2

are looking at the top of the area. When the horizontal scroll box is at the left end of its scroll bar, you are looking at the left edge of the area. When both scroll boxes are in the middle of their scroll bars, you are looking at the middle of the area.

3. Click the down scroll arrow several times until the vertical scroll box is at the bottom of its scroll bar.

4. Click the right scroll arrow several times until the horizontal scroll box is at the right of its scroll bar.

5. Click the vertical scroll bar, above the scroll box, until the scroll box is at the top of the scroll bar.

6. Drag the horizontal scroll box a small amount toward the middle of the scroll bar. Note that you can move the display area in very small increments.

7. Drag the horizontal scroll box a large amount toward the left of the scroll bar. Note that you can move the display area in large increments.

The three scrolling mechanisms give you three levels of control. Clicking the scroll bar provides a large change in the display area. Dragging the scroll box usually provides the smallest and most precise increment of change while clicking the scroll arrows provides a small to intermediate amount of change.

Manipulating windows—by selecting, dragging, opening, closing, zooming, sizing, and scrolling—is one of the primary functions of the Macintosh environment. It provides the means to see easily what is in an area larger than what is currently displayed. Practice these techniques until they are second nature. You will use them often.

Using Menus

Another feature of the Macintosh environment is the use of menus. Menus are what you use to instruct your Macintosh. By choosing a menu, you give the computer a command. Different menus display depending on what tasks you are performing. Right now, you are looking at the Finder, which is the part of the system software that you see when you aren't running applications. There are eight Finder menus with System 7, as shown here:

```
 File  Edit  View  Label  Special                                    ⁇  ⌨
```

On the left is the Apple menu represented by the Apple symbol. This is followed by the five menu names: File, Edit, View, Label, and Special. On the right are the Balloon Help and the Application menu. In Chapter 3, "Menus," you will take a close look at each of the Finder menus. To learn about menus in general and how to use them, let's open the File menu and use it to create a new folder.

Using the File Menu

The File menu allows you to perform tasks related to files and the folders that contain them. Among the tasks is one to create a new folder. A *folder* is a handy way of collecting and organizing files. (The concept is the same as when you use paper file folders in old-fashioned file cabinets to separate different categories and files.) Folders give you a single place to look for a file on a given subject. Create a new folder now by following these instructions:

1. Select the File menu by pointing on the word File in the menu bar.

2. Press and hold the mouse button. The File menu will drop down from the menu bar, as shown in Figure 2-6. When a menu drops down, displaying all its options, it is said to be *open*.

3. While still holding the mouse button down to keep the File menu open, drag the mouse and, therefore, the highlight bar in the File menu, down until New Folder is highlighted, as shown here:

```
File
New Folder    ⌘N
Open          ⌘O
Print         ⌘P
Close Window  ⌘W

Get Info      ⌘I
Sharing...
Duplicate     ⌘D
Make Alias
Put Away      ⌘Y

Find...       ⌘F
Find Again    ⌘G

Page Setup...
Print Window...
```

4. Release the mouse button. A new folder, that actually looks like a file folder, will be created and placed in your Hard Disk window, as shown here (your new folder may be placed in a different location in your Hard Disk window):

```
Hard Disk
55 items        65.9 MB in disk      32.7 MB available

System Folder   SAM 3.0.2  TeachText      MacDraw II

PageMaker 4.0   Excel 3.0  Freehand 3.0   untitled folder
```

By pointing on a menu name, dragging the highlight down to a menu option, and releasing the mouse button, you have made a *menu selection*—you have chosen whatever that option does. You just chose the New Folder option of the File menu and a new folder was created for you. Generally, making a wrong menu selection is not catastrophic. Throughout Macintosh applications, if an action that you request may have catastrophic impact, your system will ask you if you really want to do what you selected. If you answer no or select Cancel, the action won't be taken.

Some options on the File menu are dark and stand out, while other options are faint and hard to read. Only the dark options are currently available. The faint options are only available under different circumstances. For example, the File menu Print option is only available when you have selected a file that can be printed.

Figure 2-6.   *The File menu opened*

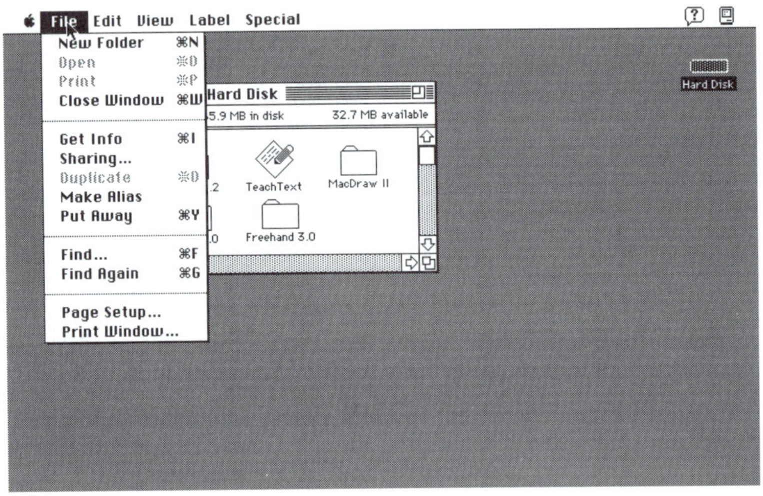

Using Dialog Boxes

Some menu options have an ellipsis (...) after them, such as Sharing... and Find... on the File menu. These options require that you enter additional information or choose from additional options. When you choose a menu option that requires additional information or has additional options, a *dialog box* opens. The dialog box provides a place for you to enter the needed information or make the choices that your system needs to receive before carrying out your command. For example, suppose you want to find a specific file but do not remember which file folder you stored it in. Follow these instructions to find your file:

2

1. Select the File menu and choose the Find option by pointing on the File menu, pressing and holding the mouse while dragging the highlight down to the Find option, and releasing the mouse button. The Find dialog box opens, as shown in Figure 2-7.

   The Find dialog box is asking what you want to find. It is a window for you to interact with your computer. The window title or dialog box name at the top of the window is the same as the menu option that opened the dialog box—in this case, Find. The Find dialog box has four items in it: a *text box* that allows you to type the name of the file you want to find, and three command buttons to tell your computer what to do next.

   You'll notice a blinking vertical bar in the text box. This is the *insertion point*. The blinking insertion point tells you that this is where text will go when you begin typing.

2. Using the keyboard, type **MYFILE** (it can be uppercase or lowercase). As you type, notice that the insertion point always shows you where the next character will go.

3. Move the mouse pointer until it is inside the text box. Note that the pointer becomes an *I-beam*, as you can see here:

Figure 2-7.   *The Find dialog box*

Insertion point   Text box

Find:

More Choices   Cancel   Find   Default command button

Command buttons

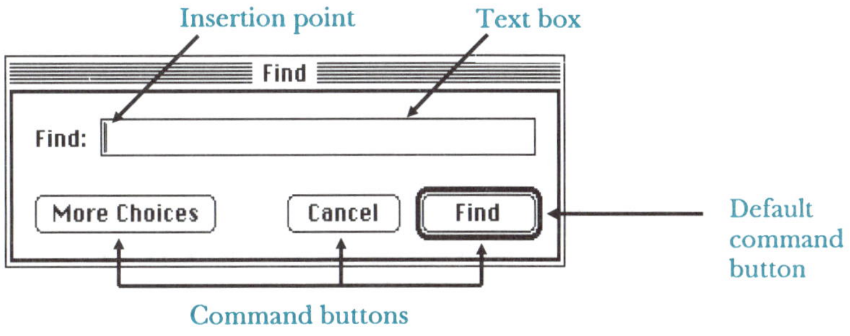

```
┌─────────────── Find ───────────────┐
│                                     │
│  Find: │MYFILE│        I◄───────────────── I-beam
│                                     │
│  ┌──────────────┐   ┌────────┐ ┌──────┐
│  │ More Choices │   │ Cancel │ │ Find │
│  └──────────────┘   └────────┘ └──────┘
└─────────────────────────────────────┘
```

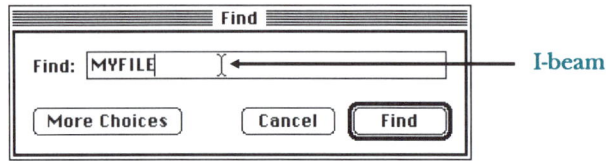

Editing in a Text Box

The I-beam will appear anytime your actions involve typing or editing words. It is uniquely shaped so you can easily place it between two letters.

1. Move the insertion point so that it is between the Y and F in MYFILE by moving the mouse to that location and clicking (pressing and releasing) the mouse button. The insertion point moves to the desired location.

2. Type **OLD**. The letters O, L, and D are inserted between MY and FILE:

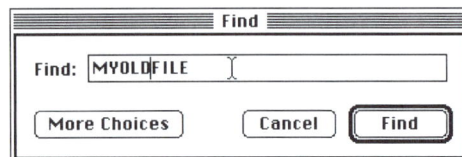

```
┌─────────────── Find ───────────────┐
│                                     │
│  Find: │MYOLDFILE      I│           │
│                                     │
│  ┌──────────────┐   ┌────────┐ ┌──────┐
│  │ More Choices │   │ Cancel │ │ Find │
│  └──────────────┘   └────────┘ └──────┘
└─────────────────────────────────────┘
```

In addition to inserting letters in existing text, you can use the I-beam to change existing letters.

3. Move the I-beam between the Y and the O, press and hold the mouse button while dragging across the O, L, and D, and then release the mouse button. OLD will be highlighted.

4. Type **NEW**. NEW replaces OLD in the Find dialog box, as shown here:

```
┌══════════════════ Find ══════════════════┐
│                                            │
│  Find: │MYNEW│FILE ⌶                      │
│                                            │
│  [ More Choices ]      [ Cancel ]  [[ Find ]] │
│                                            │
└────────────────────────────────────────────┘
```

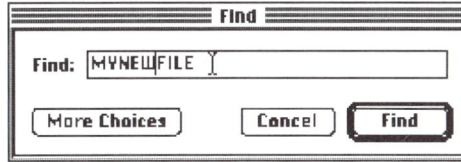

Dialog Box Controls

You have seen how you can enter and edit text in one element of a dialog box, a text box. There are several other dialog box elements that allow you to control what the computer does next. For the moment, what these control is not as important as learning how to use them.

The first control is the *command button*—there are three command buttons at the bottom of the Find dialog box. Command buttons let you choose an action from two or more alternatives. In the Find dialog box you have three alternatives: to look at More Choices, to Cancel the Find operation, or to go ahead and Find whatever you typed in the text box. You select a command button by clicking it with the mouse.

Note that the Find command button has a heavier border around it. This means that it is the *default command button* and is automatically selected if you press the (return) or (enter) key on the keyboard. Similarly, all Cancel buttons can also be activated by pressing the (esc) key rather than actually clicking the button.

For now select More Choices to look at more dialog controls.

1. Move the mouse pointer to the More Choices command button and click. A second dialog box opens, replacing the original Find dialog box, as shown in Figure 2-8.

   This second Find dialog box contains a similar set of three command buttons (Fewer Choices returns you to the first dialog box). Above the command buttons, though, are four new elements. Three of them with downward-pointing arrowheads are *pop-up menus*. Click anywhere in the boxes and a menu pops up from which you can make a choice. Try it.

Figure 2-8.   *The second Find dialog box gives you more choices*

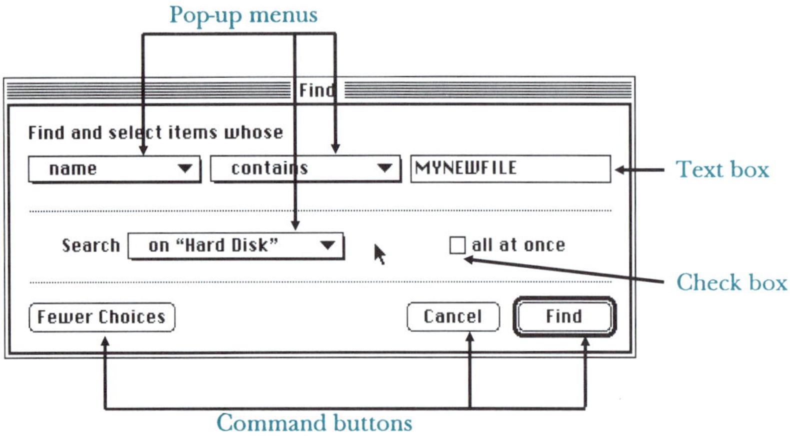

2. Move the mouse pointer until it is in the Name pop-up menu and then press and hold the mouse button. A menu of options will pop up:

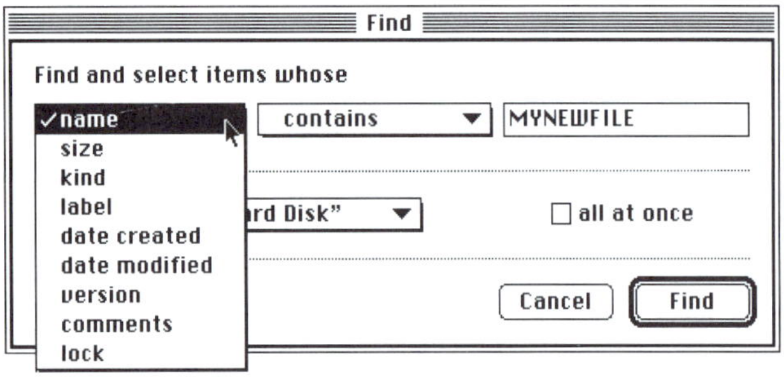

You make a selection from a pop-up menu the same way you do from a normal menu: you drag the highlight down to the option you want.

3. While still holding the Name pop-up menu open, drag the highlight down to "date created" and release the mouse button. The name of the pop-up menu changes, as does the name of the second pop-up menu.

The fourth element in this dialog box is a *check box*. A check box is a *toggle switch*—by clicking it once you turn it on, and clicking it again turns it off.

4. Move the mouse pointer to the All at Once check box and click the mouse button. An X fills the check box showing that the option is turned on, as shown here:

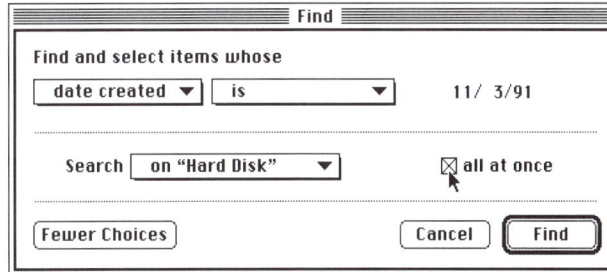

```
┌─────────────────────────────────────────────────────┐
│ ═══════════════════════════ Find ═══════════════════ │
│  ┌───────────────────────────────────────────────┐  │
│  │ Find and select items whose                    │  │
│  │   ┌─────────────────┐  ┌──────────────────┐    │  │
│  │   │ date created  ▼ │  │ is             ▼ │  11/ 3/91 │
│  │   └─────────────────┘  └──────────────────┘    │  │
│  │                                                 │  │
│  │   Search ┌──────────────────────┐   ☒ all at once │
│  │          │ on "Hard Disk"     ▼ │               │  │
│  │          └──────────────────────┘               │  │
│  │  ┌──────────────┐      ┌────────┐ ┌──────────┐  │  │
│  │  │ Fewer Choices │      │ Cancel │ │   Find   │  │  │
│  │  └──────────────┘      └────────┘ └──────────┘  │  │
│  └───────────────────────────────────────────────┘  │
└─────────────────────────────────────────────────────┘
```

5. Click the check box again to turn the option off.

6. Complete this exercise by moving the mouse pointer to the Cancel command button and clicking. The dialog box closes without carrying out the Find.

The Page Setup Dialog Box

Next, look at the Page Setup dialog box and investigate the control elements that it uses.

1. Move the mouse pointer to the File menu, press and hold the mouse button while dragging the highlight down to the Page Setup option in the lower part of the menu, and then release the mouse button. The Page Setup dialog box will open.

   If you are using an Apple LaserWriter printer, your dialog box looks like Figure 2-9. If you are using a different printer, your dialog box looks a little different but the controls are similar, as you can see in Figure 2-10. The primary difference is that the pop-up menu and text box are gone.

   In either Page Setup dialog box, the command buttons are in the upper-right section instead of across the bottom as you saw in the previous dialog boxes. Command buttons may be in either of these positions in your dialog boxes. The default command button, the one with the additional heavy border, is the OK command button.

Figure 2-9.   *The LaserWriter Page Setup dialog box*

Pop-up menu

LaserWriter Page Setup   7.0   OK

Paper: ⊙ US Letter   ○ A4 Letter   Command
       ○ US Legal   ○ B5 Letter   ○ [Tabloid ▼]   Cancel   buttons

       Reduce or [100]%   Printer Effects: Options
       Enlarge: □ Font Substitution?
Radio   ⊠ Text Smoothing?
buttons   Orientation   ⊠ Graphics Smoothing?
            [⬆🖼] [⬆📄]   □ Faster Bitmap Printing?

            Picture buttons   Check boxes

                      Text box

Clicking this button or pressing (return) or (enter) tells the computer
that you are finished making changes in the dialog box and are ready
to close it.

Toward the top of the dialog box in Figure 2-10 are five small
circular radio buttons that let you select the size of the page you are
setting up. *Radio buttons*, like the buttons on a car radio, are mutually
exclusive—that is, you can only select one at a time. To select one
means any other that was selected will no longer be active. This

Figure 2-10.   *The ImageWriter Page Setup dialog box*

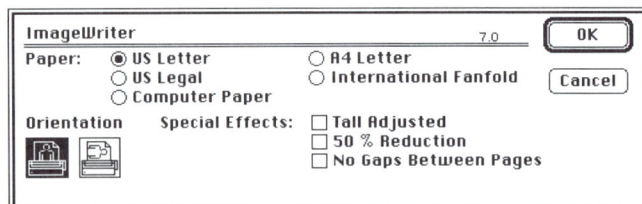

ImageWriter   7.0   OK

Paper: ⊙ US Letter   ○ A4 Letter
           ○ US Legal   ○ International Fanfold   Cancel
           ○ Computer Paper

Orientation   Special Effects: □ Tall Adjusted
[🖼] [📄]   □ 50 % Reduction
                                 □ No Gaps Between Pages

2

contrasts with check boxes, three or four examples of which are shown in the middle of the dialog box. You can select as many check boxes as you want—they can all be active at the same time.

In the bottom-left section are two picture buttons. *Picture buttons* are like radio buttons in that you can only select one at a time. Above the picture buttons in the LaserWriter dialog box is a small text box and above the check boxes is a pop-up menu (you have seen both of these before).

2. Move the mouse pointer to the Cancel button and click to close the Page Setup dialog box.

There are other dialog box control elements but they don't exist in the Finder menus so discussion of them will wait until you encounter them. What you have seen are the primary elements of dialog boxes: text boxes for entering text, radio buttons for making exclusive choices, check boxes for selecting options, pop-up menus for choosing alternatives, and command buttons for deciding what step to take when you are ready to leave the dialog box. Taken all together, these dialog box elements give you a lot of control over what your Macintosh does.

Using the Keyboard

Your mouse and your keyboard are the primary means of communicating with your computer. While the Macintosh is very mouse oriented, the keyboard is necessary, obviously, for entering text.

As you saw in Chapter 1, "Meet the Macintosh," the Apple Macintosh line offers three keyboards; which you use depends on the computer you have and your preference. Figures 2-11, 2-12, and 2-13 show the three keyboards.

All three keyboards have standard keys just like a typewriter, with the alphabetic and numeric keys in their normal positions. All three keyboards, though, have a number of additional keys that are unique to computer keyboards. Since you are probably familiar with a typewriter keyboard, focus now on these unique keys. They are on the periphery of the keyboard and are identified in Figures 2-11, 2-12, and 2-13.

Figure 2-11. *The Apple ADB or Classic keyboard*

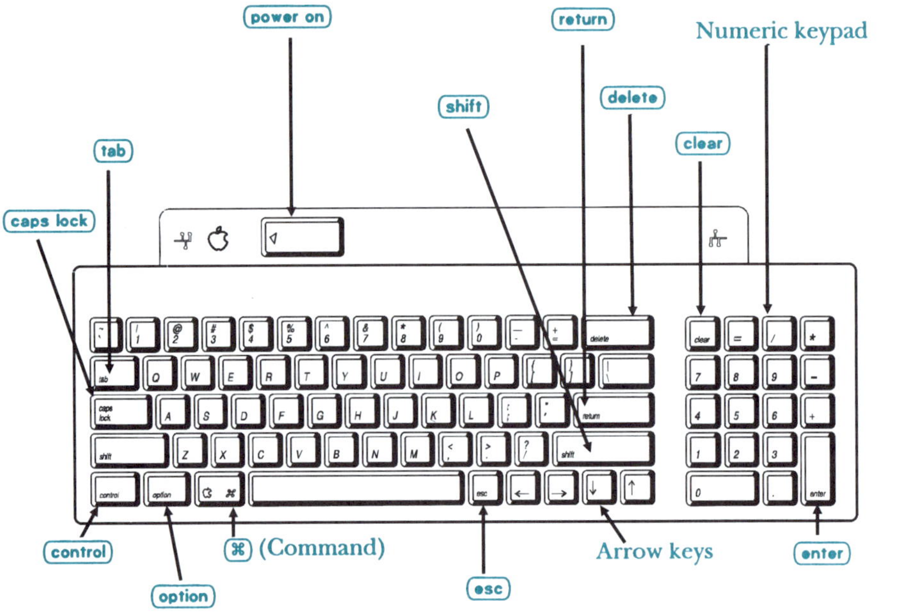

Key	Function
(control)	Modifies the function of other keys when pressed with them. The result depends on the application you are running when you press the keys.
(option)	Produces foreign and other special characters when pressed with alphabetic and numeric keys. Also used to modify the function of other keys when pressed with those keys. The result depends on the application you are running when you press the keys.

Figure 2-12. *The Apple keyboard*

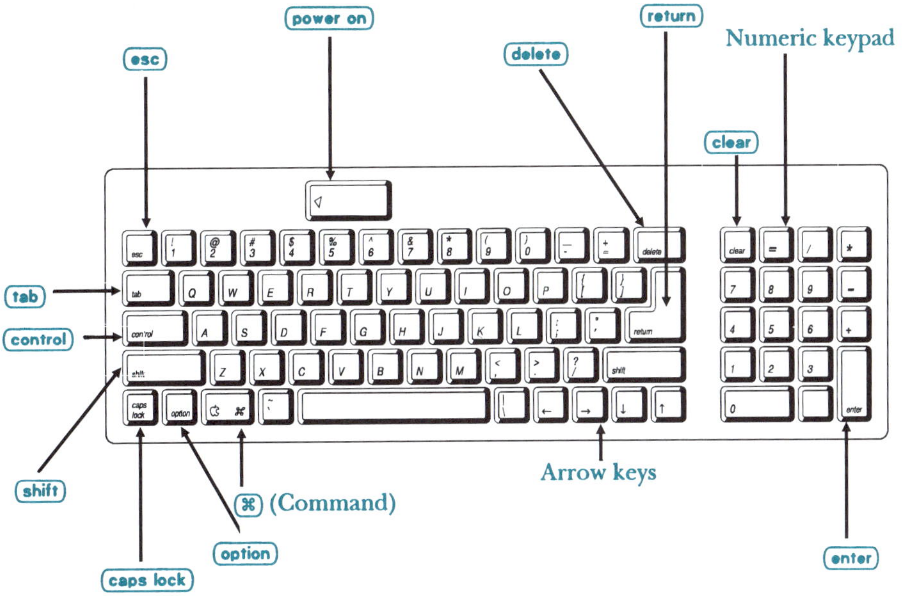

Key	Function
Command key or ⌘	Substitutes for menu commands when pressed with alphabetic and numeric keys. Also used to modify the function of other keys when pressed with alphabetical keys. The result depends on the application you are running when you press the keys. This key is usually referred to with the ⌘ symbol and will be in this book.
return	Completes and closes most dialog boxes or performs the default dialog box command with the additional heavy border around it. Also used to start a new paragraph in text by forcing the insertion point to move to the beginning of the next line.

Figure 2-13.   *The Apple Extended keyboard II*

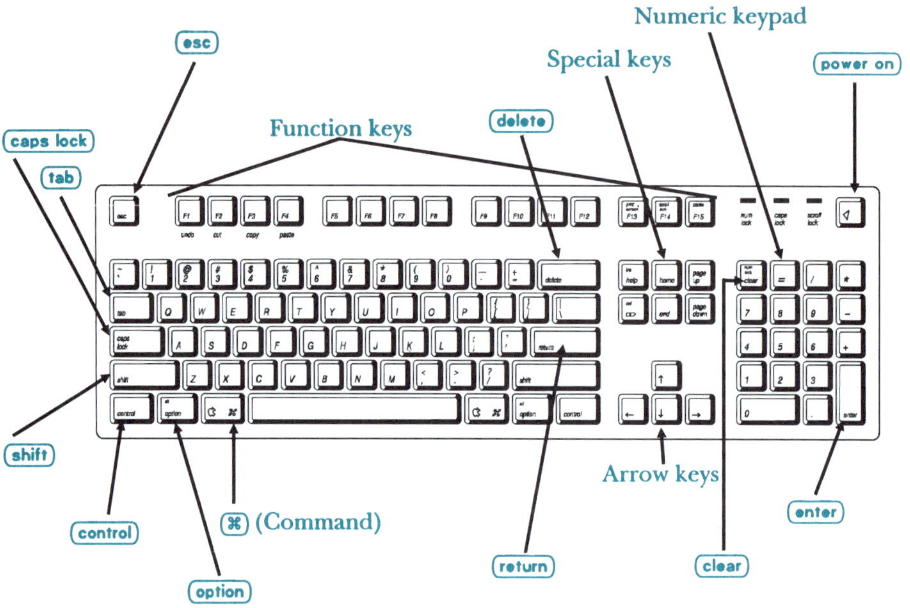

Key	Function
Arrow keys	Move the insertion point in text or occasionally the pointer in some applications.
(enter)	Completes and closes most dialog boxes or performs the default dialog box command with the additional heavy border around it. Usually the same as the (return) key, although some applications treat it differently.
Numeric keypad	Provides for numeric entry similar to a ten-key adding machine. May be used as pointer movement keys ("Mouse Keys") in some applications.

Key	Function
(power on)	Turns on the computer in some Macintosh models.
(clear)	Deletes whatever is currently selected or, in some applications, the character to the right of the insertion point.
Special keys	Move the insertion point or pointer in some applications and operating systems, or perform other functions.
(delete)	Deletes the character to the left of the insertion point (like a Backspace key on a typewriter) or whatever is currently selected.
Function keys	Substitute for menu commands in some applications, or may perform functions you specify with third party utility programs.
(esc)	Cancels and closes many dialog boxes or operations depending on the application in use.

You can see that a lot of what the keys do depends on the application you are running at the time. There are two exceptions to this—the (option) key and the (⌘) key.

The (option) Key

The (option) key allows you to enter foreign and special characters by pressing and holding it while pressing an alphabetic or numeric key both with and without the (shift) key. You can find out which characters each key gives you by using the Key Caps desk accessory found in the Apple menu. The Key Caps desk accessory puts an image of your keyboard on the screen and allows you to type or click a key with the mouse and see the results in a display line above the keyboard. This allows you to see how to produce special or international characters. Try that and see how it works.

1. Move the mouse pointer to the Apple menu at the left of the menu bar. Press and hold the mouse button while dragging the highlight

down to Key Caps and then release the mouse button. An image of a keyboard, as shown here, appears if you are using an Extended keyboard II:

If you are using a different type of keyboard, the image will be of your keyboard.

This keyboard image is *interactive*, which means it reflects typing on the keyboard as well as clicking the keys with the mouse. If you press and hold the (option) key, the alphabetic and numeric keys change to foreign and special characters.

2. Press (option). The keyboard image changes to this:

The actual characters you see may differ from what is shown here because of the font you are using. You can change the font using the Key Caps menu.

Notice that when you press a key, the key is darkened in the Key Caps image. Also, when you press or click an alphanumeric key, the character of the key pressed appears in the display line above the keyboard image. The display line also shows appropriate characters when you press a key while holding (shift), (control), or (option).

When you press (option), notice that the grave or backward accent key above (tab), and the (E), (U), (I), and (N) keys all have borders around them. This tells you that when you press and hold (option) while pressing one of these keys you can release (option) and then press a third key to form a compound character like the international characters ò, é, ä, î, and ñ. When you release (option) before pressing the third key, you will see the keys that can be used for the third key have a heavy border around them, as shown here for the key above (tab) (the grave or backward accent):

You can use Key Caps in two ways. First, just by looking at the image when you press (option) you can see the key that produces the special character you want. When you go back to your application you can use that key combination by pressing and holding the (option) key while pressing the key with the special character on it. Second, you can type the special characters in Key Caps and then copy those characters into the application you are using. (You'll learn how to copy in Chapter 3, "Menus.")

The ⌘ Key

The ⌘ key allows you to use the keyboard to choose many menu options. These are called *keyboard shortcuts* and are particularly useful when you are typing on the keyboard for some other reason and don't necessarily wish to move to your mouse. The actual key combination used for a particular menu option may vary from application to application, so you need to watch for differences. There is, though, a lot of similarity among the more common applications.

Some frequently used keyboard shortcuts with their menu options are given here:

Menu Option	Keyboard Shortcut
File New	⌘-N
File Open	⌘-O
File Close	⌘-W
File Save	⌘-S
File Print	⌘-P
File Quit	⌘-Q
Edit Undo	⌘-Z
Edit Cut	⌘-X
Edit Copy	⌘-C
Edit Paste	⌘-V
Edit Select All	⌘-A

Once again, these are not universal in all applications. For example, WriteNow from T/Maker uses ⌘-T for File Print and both Aldus PageMaker and Adobe Illustrator do not have a shortcut for File Close; ⌘-W is used for another purpose. Also, almost all applications have many more keyboard shortcuts than those shown here. You can find the keyboard shortcuts by looking at the right side of most menus. The shortcuts are next to the options they replace.

In Chapter 3, you'll look at menus and their options in more depth.

3

Menus

The Macintosh provides a host of tools to make using the computer easy. One tool is basic to the functioning of the Macintosh and is used much more frequently than any other. This tool is the Macintosh menuing system.

The Menuing System

The *Macintosh menuing system* consists of the menu bar at the top of your screen, a series of pull-down menus that descend from the bar, a list of menu options on each menu, and dialog boxes and submenus that are opened when you choose certain menu options. This system is central to your use of the Macintosh; the following sections look at each of its components.

The Menu Bar

As you have already learned, the menu bar contains the symbol or name of each of the menus that is available in a particular application or with the system software. The Finder menu bar contains the eight Finder menus starting with the Apple menu on the left through to the Application menu on the right, as shown here:

⊞ File Edit View Label Special   ⑦ ▣

Later in the chapter, we'll examine each of these eight menus in depth.

Opening Menus

You open a menu by moving the mouse pointer to the menu name and pressing and holding the mouse button down. Do that now:

1. Select the Edit menu by moving the mouse pointer so that it is on top of the word Edit in the menu bar at the top of the screen, as shown here:

   ⊞ File Edit View Label Special

2. While still pointing on the word Edit, press and hold the mouse button. The menu will open, showing these options:

Edit	
Undo	⌘Z
Cut	⌘K
Copy	**⌘C**
Paste	⌘U
Clear	
Select All	**⌘A**
Show Clipboard	

Menu Options

Each menu has two or more options from which you can choose. You choose an option by continuing to hold down the mouse button while dragging the mouse pointer and a highlight bar down to the option you want and then releasing the mouse button. Do that next:

1. While still pointing on the Edit menu and holding down the mouse button, choose the Select All option by dragging the mouse pointer and the highlight bar down to Select All, as shown here:

2. Complete the selection by releasing the mouse button. Depending upon what you have on the screen, all icons or folders are selected (highlighted). To deselect everything, click any blank space on the desktop (not on an icon or in a window).

Submenus and Dialog Boxes

One of three things happens when you select a menu option:

- An immediate action takes place. For example, something you have selected is duplicated as a result of your choosing Duplicate from the File menu.

- Another menu (a *submenu*) opens as a result of choosing an option with a ▶ to the right of the option name. To select an option from a submenu, drag the mouse to the right after highlighting the main menu option, and then down to highlight the submenu option you want before releasing the mouse button, as shown here:

3

```
Type
 Font           ▶
 Size           ▶
 Leading        ▶    Other...
 Set width      ▶   ✓Auto ⇧⌘A
 Track          ▶    11
 Type style     ▶    11.5
                     12
 Type specs... ⌘T    12.5      ▸
 Paragraph...  ⌘M    13
 Indents/tabs...⌘I   13.5
 Hyphenation...⌘H    14
                     18
 Alignment      ▶    24
 Style          ▶    36

 Define styles... ⌘3
```

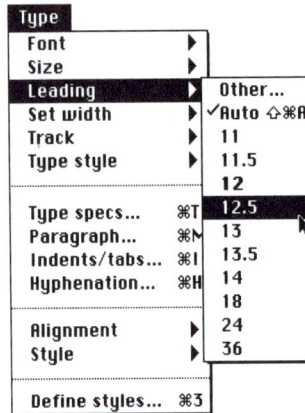

- A dialog box opens as a result of choosing an option with an ellipsis (...) to the right of the option name. A dialog box, you'll remember, allows you to enter information such as a filename as well as make additional choices, as shown in this dialog box for opening an existing file:

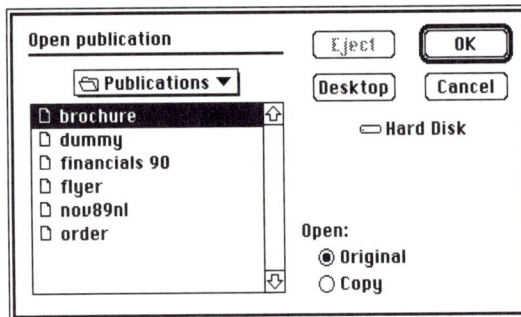

```
Open publication                    [ Eject ]   (   OK   )

   [🗀 Publications ▼]              [ Desktop ] [ Cancel ]

 D brochure          ⇧                ⊏ Hard Disk
 D dummy
 D financials 90
 D flyer
 D nov89nl
 D order                           Open:
                     ⇩               ◉ Original
                                     ○ Copy
```

The Finder Menus

When you first turn on the Macintosh the only thing that is running is the Finder, a part of the system software. The initial set of menus is the Finder menus. The following sections look briefly at each of these menus and the options they contain. Most of these menus and options are discussed further in later chapters.

The Apple Menu

The Apple menu, the first menu on the left of the menu bar with the , is shown open here:

The Apple menu is a catchall for the accessories that come with the system software as well as three other functions for which the Apple menu provides a handy home.

The accessories or *desk accessories* (DAs) are small applications that you can use at any time, independent of what else you are running. The standard desk accessories are the Alarm Clock, Calculator, Key Caps, Note Pad, Puzzle, and Scrapbook. The three other functions are About This Macintosh, the Chooser, and the Control Panels. Each of the accessories and facilities is discussed here.

About This Macintosh

About This Macintosh provides some information about the Macintosh you are using. It tells you the type of Macintosh (Classic, IIsi, or another type), the version of system software that is running (such as System 7.0), the total amount of memory in the computer and how much is unused, and what is using memory. The About This Macintosh screen is shown here for the computer used to write this book. Yours probably looks different.

```
┌──────────────────────────────────────────────────┐
│ ▤☐▤▤▤▤▤▤  About This Macintosh  ▤▤▤▤▤▤ ▣▤      │
│                                                    │
│                        System Software 7.0         │
│       ┌─────┐                                      │
│       │▱▱▱▱▱│ Macintosh IIci  © Apple Computer, Inc. 1983-1991 │
│       └─────┘                                      │
│                                                    │
│      Total Memory :   5,120K  Largest Unused Block :  3,002K │
│      ▣ System Software  1,770K  ████████████████████   ⇧  │
│                                                        │
│                                                    ⇩  │
│                                                    ▣  │
└──────────────────────────────────────────────────┘
```

The Alarm Clock

The Alarm Clock allows you to display and set a digital clock on the screen and to set the time when an alarm will go off. When you change the time and date in the Alarm Clock window, you are changing the *system time and date*, the time and date that is maintained in your computer with a battery, even when you turn the computer off. Try out the Alarm Clock with these instructions:

1. Select the Apple menu and choose the Alarm Clock option. The digital clock opens:

```
                              ╱ Lever
        ┌──────────────────┐ ╱
        │ ☐  4:31:02 PM ♦ │
        └──────────────────┘
```

2. Expand the Alarm Clock window by clicking the lever on the right (move the mouse pointer to the lever and then press and release the mouse button):

```
        ┌──────────────────┐
        │ ☐  4:31:24 PM ♦ │
        │     11/ 3/91     │
        ├──────────────────┤
        │  ◷    ▦    ◔    │
        └──────────────────┘
```

The expanded Alarm Clock window has three layers. The top layer looks the way it did when it originally popped up on the screen. The bottom layer provides three picture buttons that you can click to determine what appears in the middle layer. The left button in the bottom line, which looks like a clock, puts the current time in the middle layer and allows you to change the current time. By clicking a number in the time, for example, the minutes, and then clicking the up and down arrows in the middle layer you can set the time, as shown here:

3

The middle button in the bottom line, which looks like calendar pages, displays the date in the middle layer. This can also be changed by clicking a number, for example, the day of the month, and clicking the up and down arrows.

The right button in the bottom line, the alarm clock, displays in the middle layer the time the alarm is set to go off. Again, you change this time by clicking a number and then clicking the up or down arrow. Try that by following these steps:

1. Click the lower-right button—the one that looks like an alarm clock. The time the alarm is set to go off appears in the middle layer.

2. Click the number representing the hour. The hour becomes highlighted and a pair of arrows appears:

3. Click the up or down arrow or type a number on the keyboard to change the hour the alarm is set to go off.

4. When you have set the time you want, click the switch on the left of the middle layer to turn on the alarm. Note that the icon in the bottom-right button changes:

5. Click the lever to the right of the time in the upper layer to compress the window and activate the alarm.

The alarm will only go off if you compress or close the Alarm Clock window or activate another window. It does not go off if the full Alarm Clock window is still open or expanded. When the alarm does go off, you will hear a single tone from your computer and see a flashing Alarm Clock icon alternate with the Apple symbol on the left of the menu bar. To turn off the flashing icon, open or activate the Alarm Clock window and turn off the switch in the middle panel by clicking it. This is the same switch you used to activate the alarm clock.

The Calculator

The Calculator desk accessory is similar to a small hand-held calculator that adds, subtracts, multiplies, and divides. You can use it either by clicking the keys with the mouse or by using the numbers and math symbols on your keyboard. Note that if you are using an Apple Classic or Extended keyboard, the numeric keypad on the right of the keyboard is functionally the same as the Calculator shown here (the keypad (clear) key does the same thing as the C on the calculator and the (enter) key works in calculator mode as a second (equals) key):

If you have an Apple keyboard, the plus and minus keys are reversed from what you see here.

Once you have developed a result on the calculator, you can use the commands in the Edit menu to copy the result to a document you are working on. The copy function is discussed in Chapter 8, "Applications and Transferring Data."

The Chooser

The Chooser is where you identify the printer you want to use and where you connect or disconnect to an AppleTalk network. The Chooser is discussed and demonstrated in Chapter 7, "Fonts, Printers, and Printing."

3

Control Panels

Control Panels is a folder that is opened either by clicking the Control Panels option of the Apple menu or by opening the Control Panels folder in the System folder. (Chapter 4, "Files, Folders, and Disks" talks about folders and how to open them.) Within this folder there are at least 15 control panels that are standard with System 7, and possibly others that are part of software that you have added. With these control panels, you can vary the double-click speed of the mouse, vary the type and the volume of the sound your Macintosh makes, vary the colors on the screen with a color monitor, and vary many other options that allow you to customize your Macintosh to your preferences. The use of the Control Panels folder is described fully in Chapter 6, "Customizing with Control Panels."

Key Caps

Key Caps provides a keyboard in a window that displays the normal and special characters you produce when you press (option), (control), or (shift) with the normal typewriter keys. You can type a particular set of characters and then copy them to a document in another window in case you can't remember the placement of special characters. Chapter 2, "Using The Macintosh," provides several illustrations of the Key Caps window and further discusses its use.

The Note Pad

The Note Pad allows you to make and keep text notes. You can have up to 8 pages of notes, and each page can have up to 12 lines of 25 characters. You may type information directly on to the Note Pad, or copy information to the Note Pad from another document. The Note Pad is shown here:

When you first open the Note Pad, you see a blinking vertical line in the upper-left corner. This is the insertion point—where the text you next type begins. When you reach the end of a line, the text automatically wraps to the next line without your pressing (return). If you want to end the text before the end of a line, press the (return) key.

When you want to go to a new page, you need to click one of the two triangles you can see in the lower-left corner of the previous illustration. If you click the "top" triangle pointing to the upper-right, you will turn the pages in their normal order: 1, 2, 3. If you click the "bottom" triangle pointing to the lower-left, you will turn the pages in reverse order: 3, 2, 1.

Information in the Note Pad stays there until it is deleted or cleared, even after you turn off the computer. You can erase a page with either the (delete) key or one of two Edit menu options. You will learn more about the Edit menu options in "The Edit Menu," later in this chapter.

The Puzzle

The Puzzle is a game with 15 pieces and 1 empty position into which you can move an adjacent piece by clicking it. The objective is to move the pieces in such a manner so as to end up with the Apple logo, similar to what you see in the upper-left corner of your screen. You can practice your mouse clicking while solving the puzzle.

The Scrapbook

The Scrapbook stores *graphics* (drawings, charts, and images) and sounds as well as text. In the very near future (probably by the time you read this book), you will also be able to store and play back a movie with the Scrapbook. You can only copy text to the Scrapbook, not type in it like you can in the Note Pad, but you can store as many items as your disk space will allow.

To go from one graphic, sound, or text item to another, click the scroll bar beneath the item. This scroll bar works like the horizontal scroll bar on a window, with the scroll arrow and scroll box tools. These scroll bar features are discussed in Chapter 2, "Using the Macintosh." Here is an example of a graphic image in the Scrapbook window:

3

At the bottom left of the window are two numbers representing the current item number and the total number of items in the Scrapbook. This tells you where you are within the total Scrapbook. (The example just shown is on page 2 out of 8 pages in the Scrapbook.) Text on the bottom right tells you what type of item is being displayed—text, picture, or sound. (The example shown says "PICT" for picture.) When the item is a sound, a button appears in the middle of the bottom area with the label "Play Sound." Click this button to hear the sound.

Like the Note Pad, the Scrapbook Edit menu options allow you to copy and move items from the Scrapbook to other documents and to remove items from the Scrapbook.

The File Menu

The File menu, shown here, allows you to perform tasks related to files and the folders that contain them:

```
┌─────────────────────────┐
│ File                    │
├─────────────────────────┤
│ New Folder          ⌘N  │
│ Open                ⌘O  │
│ Print               ⌘P  │
│ Close Window        ⌘W  │
├─────────────────────────┤
│ Get Info            ⌘I  │
│ Sharing...              │
│ Duplicate           ⌘D  │
│ Make Alias              │
│ Put Away            ⌘Y  │
├─────────────────────────┤
│ Find...             ⌘F  │
│ Find Again          ⌘G  │
├─────────────────────────┤
│ Page Setup...           │
│ Print Desktop...        │
└─────────────────────────┘
```

You can create new folders with the File menu, as discussed in Chapter 2, "Using The Macintosh." In addition, the File menu has 12 other options. The functions of all of the File menu options are discussed in the following paragraphs.

In the File menu option descriptions, the phrase *currently selected* is used with files, folders, icons, and windows. Currently selected refers to the item that is currently active, generally darker than other objects, because you have clicked it or in some other way selected it. Also, remember that the discussion in this chapter is an introduction only. Files, folders, and related topics will be discussed in depth in Chapter 4, "Files, Folders, and Disks." Here are brief descriptions of each File menu option:

Menu Item	Function
New Folder	Creates a new, untitled folder in the currently selected window, or on the desktop if no window is open.
Open	Opens the currently selected file, folder, or icon. Choosing Open is the same as double-clicking a file, a folder, a disk, or the Trash icon. When you open a folder, a disk, or the Trash icon, you create a window with the same name as the icon, and the contents of the icon are displayed. When you open a file, the computer tries to *execute* the file. If the file is a program, such as MacWrite, the program is started and you can do things unique to that program. If the file is a data file associated with a particular program, such as a MacWrite document, the associated program starts and it opens the data file and allows you to work with it.
Print	Prints the currently selected file. If the currently selected file cannot be printed, this menu option is dim. This is the same as starting the application that created the file, loading the file, and then choosing the Print option in the application. The Finder Print option is much simpler. Before using Print, look at the File menu's Page Setup option to see if it is right for the printing you want to do.
Close Window	Closes the currently selected window. This is the same as clicking the Close button of a window.
Get Info	Provides information on the currently selected disk, folder, or file. The information includes the kind of item, the size, the folder and disk where it is located, the creation date, and when it was last modified, as you can see here:

3

```
┌─────────────────────────────────────────────┐
│ ▦  ▦▦▦ ══ Special Keys Info ══ ▦▦▦           │
├─────────────────────────────────────────────┤
│                                               │
│      ▨   Special Keys                         │
│                                               │
│      Kind : Microsoft Word document           │
│      Size : 4K on disk (4,096 bytes used)     │
│                                               │
│     Where : Hard Disk :                       │
│                                               │
│                                               │
│   Created : Sat, Aug 17, 1991, 8:48 AM        │
│  Modified : Wed, Sep 18, 1991, 11:24 AM       │
│   Version : n/a                               │
│                                               │
│  Comments :                                   │
│   ┌───────────────────────────────────────┐   │
│   │                                       │   │
│   │                                       │   │
│   │                                       │   │
│   └───────────────────────────────────────┘   │
│   □ Locked              □ Stationery pad       │
└─────────────────────────────────────────────┘
```

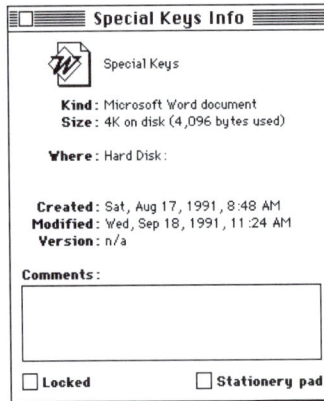

Menu Item	Function
Sharing	Establishes the network sharing status of folders, files, and applications. See Chapter 10, "Communications."
Duplicate	Makes a copy of the currently selected folder or file on the same disk.
Make Alias	Allows you to create another name for a file, a folder, or a disk. This creates another icon with the new name for the original item, *not* a copy of it. The new icon takes very little memory (less than 2KB) and can be placed anywhere on the computer, allowing you to easily get to a frequently used file from different locations.
Put Away	Returns icons (usually files and folders) that have been dragged out onto the Desktop, and replaces them in their original folders. If a floppy disk is selected, Put Away will eject the disk and remove its icon.
Find	Allows you to locate files and folders by their names based on text that you supply. When the first match is found, it is highlighted and displayed along with the folder it is contained in. Using a secondary dialog box, you can change the search criteria and search pattern. Chapter 2, "Using the Macintosh," demonstrates the Find option.

Menu Item	Function
Find Again	Repeats the last Find.
Page Setup	Allows you to specify the size of paper, the orientation, and the effects to be used on the currently selected printer. Chapter 7, "Fonts, Printers, and Printing," discusses this in more detail.
Print Desktop	Prints what you see on the screen. If a window is selected, the name of this option is Print Window. This allows you to get a printed copy of the contents of the currently selected window. Depending on how you are viewing a window, the printout varies from the normal icon view to a list of files and folders in the window with their name, size, and so on.

3

The Edit Menu

The Edit menu, shown here, provides the means of working with the Clipboard:

The *Clipboard* is a holding place for text or graphics that you want to *copy* from one document to another or that you want to remove (*cut*) from one document and place (*paste*) in another document. The Cut, Copy, and Paste options on the Edit menu provide these functions:

Menu Item	Function
Cut	Deletes the currently selected text, graphic, or sound from the document that contains it, and places that text, graphic, or sound on the Clipboard. The original document no longer contains the cut object.

Menu Item	Function
Copy	Copies the currently selected text, graphic, or sound and places that copy on the Clipboard. The original document still contains the copied object.
Paste	Places a copy of the current contents of the Clipboard into the currently open document. After pasting an object, the Clipboard still retains a copy of it.

The Clipboard can hold one piece of text, one graphic, or one sound. Therefore, if you try to place two things on the Clipboard, the second item replaces the first. You can delete or clear an item without affecting the contents of the Clipboard using the Edit Clear option or the (delete) key.

*Should you make a mistake with the (delete) key or the Cut, Copy, Paste, or Clear options, you can usually undo the effects of those operations with the Edit menu Undo option, if the operation you want to undo **was the last thing you did**.*

The functions of the remaining Edit menu options are as follows:

Menu Item	Function
Undo	Reverses the most recent edit operation, including Cut, Copy, Paste, and Clear. Also, the most recent press of the (delete) key can be undone, and Undo can reverse itself (you can undo Undo) if you do it immediately.
Clear	Deletes the currently selected text, graphic, or sound from the document that contains it, *but does not* place it on the Clipboard. The contents of the Clipboard remain unchanged.

Once you clear an object, there is no way to retrieve it after the immediate Undo.

Menu Item	Function
Select All	Selects all of the items in a set, for example, all of the files in a folder, or all of the folders in the Hard Disk window.
Show Clipboard	Displays the Clipboard window, showing the contents of the Clipboard:

```
┌─────────────────────────────────────┐
│▤□════════ Clipboard ═══════▱▤│
├─────────────────────────────────────┤
│ Clipboard contents :  none           │
│                                  ┌─┐ │
│                                  │⇧│ │
│                                  ├─┤ │
│                                  │ │ │
│                                  │ │ │
│                                  ├─┤ │
│                                  │⇩│ │
├──┬────────────────────────┬──┬───┤
│⇦│                        │⇨│▱│ │
└──┴────────────────────────┴──┴───┘
```

3

The View Menu

The View menu allows you to vary the way the contents of a folder or a disk are displayed. Open the View menu and look at the options by following these steps:

1. Make sure that your Hard Disk window is opened and active. Then select the View menu. It will be displayed, as shown here:

```
┌──────────────────┐
│ View             │
├──────────────────┤
│   by Small Icon  │
│ ✓ by Icon        │
│   by Name        │
│   by Size        │
│   by Kind        │
│   by Label       │
│   by Date        │
└──────────────────┘
```

The default view is By Icon (note the check mark on it in the screen just shown). By Icon represents files and folders as icons in a window just as you have seen in the previous figures and illustrations in this book. There are two other methods of display. The first, By Small Icon, puts the icon and its name on the same line, as shown here:

```
┌────────────────────────────────────────────────────┐
│▤□═════════════ Hard Disk ═══════════════▱▤│
├────────────────────────────────────────────────────┤
│ 58 items          66.3 MB in disk      32.4 MB available│
├────────────────────────────────────────────────────┤
│ 🖿 System Folder   ▱ SAM 3.0.2      ✐ TeachText   ⇧│
│ 🗀 PageMaker 4.0   ▱ Excel 3.0      🗀 Freehand 3.0   │
│ 🗀 Art Work        ▱ WriteNow 2     🗀 Screens        │
│ 🗀 Illustrator     ▱ Chap3 Scr      🗀 Drawings       ⇩│
├────────────────────────────────────────────────────┤
│⇦□░░░░░░░░░░░░░░░░░░░░░░░░░░░░░░░░░░░░░░░⇨▱│
└────────────────────────────────────────────────────┘
```

The second alternative display is a text listing sorted in one of five ways: by name, by size, by kind, by label, and by date last modified, which provide the remaining entries in the menu. Look at the listing by name now.

2. With the View menu still open, choose By Name. The currently selected window will change to a list sorted alphabetically by name, as shown here:

Name	Size	Kind	Label	Last Modified
▷ ☐ ArtWork	—	folder	—	Sun, Nov 3, 1991, 7:16 PM
▷ ☐ Chap2scr	—	folder	—	Sun, Nov 3, 1991, 7:16 PM
▷ ☐ Chap3scr	—	folder	—	Sun, Nov 3, 1991, 7:16 PM
▷ ☐ Drawings	—	folder	—	Sun, Nov 3, 1991, 7:16 PM
▷ ☐ Excel 3.0	—	folder	—	Sun, Nov 3, 1991, 7:16 PM
▷ ☐ FreHand3.0	—	folder	—	Sun, Nov 3, 1991, 7:16 PM
▷ ☐ Illustrator	—	folder	—	Sun, Nov 3, 1991, 7:17 PM
▷ ☐ MacDraw II	—	folder	—	Sun, Nov 3, 1991, 7:17 PM
▷ ☐ Pagemaker 4.0	—	folder	—	Sun, Nov 3, 1991, 7:17 PM

You may want to choose each of these views and look at them on your own. Each of the views serves a purpose; over time you will probably find that you will use most of them. For example, you might want to look at application programs, which are a kind of a file. To do this choose By Kind from the View menu. Or you could look at your most recent files by selecting By Date from the View menu. The By Date option sorts files and folders with the most recent dates at the top.

3. If you wish, return the view to By Icon by again selecting the View menu and choosing By Icon.

The Label Menu

You may have noticed in the View menu that you can sort a list of files and folders by labels, as well as by name, size, kind, and date. The Label menu, shown here, allows you to attach one of seven labels and, if you have a color monitor, apply one of seven colors to the icon:

The purpose of this is to be able to group all folders and files that relate to the same category or project. Once a label is attached to a group of files and folders, you can use the View menu to sort them by that label.

To apply a label to an icon, first select the icon by clicking it, then select the Label menu and choose the label you want. The label will be attached and, if you have a color monitor, the icon's color will change to the color associated with the label you choose. You can see the color in all views, but you can see the label only in one of the list views.

The seven labels in the Label menu and their associated colors can be changed to any phrase and color that you like. To do this you need to open the Control Panels folder from the Apple menu and select the Labels icon. The Labels window will open, as shown here:

Using this window you can edit the labels and select a new color for each of the seven labels. Chapter 6, "Customizing with Control Panels," will discuss this in more detail.

The Special Menu

The Special menu provides the system-related options shown here:

```
Special
 Clean Up Desktop
 Empty Trash
 ┄┄┄┄┄┄┄┄┄┄┄┄┄
 Eject Disk        ⌘E
 Erase Disk...
 ┄┄┄┄┄┄┄┄┄┄┄┄┄
 Restart
 Shut Down
```

The functions of each of the Special menu options are as follows:

Menu Item	Function
Clean Up Window	Rearranges icons in a window. If a window is not open, the option reads "Clean Up Desktop" and it rearranges icons on the desktop. If you hold down the (option) key when choosing Clean Up Window, the icons are sorted by name or by the most recent list view used on the window, and the icons are lined up in the upper-left corner. If you hold down the (option) key when choosing Clean Up Desktop, the icons are arranged down the right side of the screen. If you hold down (shift) with either clean-up option, only the selected items are rearranged.
Empty Trash	Deletes the contents of the Trash icon. When you put something in the trash, for example by dragging an unwanted file to the Trash icon, the icon's sides will bulge out, like this:

Menu Item	Function
	Whatever you put in the trash will stay there and take up disk space until you empty the trash. When you choose Empty Trash, you are given a warning asking if you really want to permanently delete what is in the trash, as shown here:

3

> ⚠ The Trash contains 4 items, which use 71K of disk space. Are you sure you want to permanently remove these items?
>
> Cancel   OK

If you click OK in response to the warning, the trash is permanently removed.

⚠ *Once you have deleted the contents of the trash, you cannot easily get it back.*

Menu Item	Function
Eject Disk	Ejects the floppy disk currently in the computer. This is not quite the same as choosing Put Away from the File menu since the Eject Disk option leaves the Floppy Disk icon on the desktop after the disk is ejected.

Using Eject Disk and leaving the icon on the desktop can be a hassle. If you happen to double-click the icon, the computer will display a message asking you to reinsert the floppy disk you just ejected. If you can't find the disk, you must press ⌘-period.

The purpose of Eject Disk's leaving the icon on the desktop is to allow copying one floppy disk to another. You do this by putting the first floppy disk—the one to be copied—in the disk drive and then immediately choosing Eject Disk. Next, put the second floppy—the one that will be a copy—in the drive and drag the first disk's icon to the second disk's icon. You will then be guided in swapping disks until the copy is accomplished.

Menu Item	Function
Erase Disk	Initializes a disk and erases everything on it. Once you have done this, you cannot retrieve any information that was previously on the disk. Initializing is also done when you put a new disk in the drive and the computer asks if you want to initialize it. To *initialize* means to prepare the disk to receive data. You must initialize a new disk, and it is a good idea when you recycle a disk from one use to another. Chapter 4, "Files, Folders, and Disks," discusses this further and provides an example of initializing.

Once you initialize a disk, any information on the disk is permanently erased in most cases.

There are utility programs such as Norton Utilities for the Macintosh that in some cases can recover information from an initialized disk or a deleted (placed in the trash and the trash emptied) file. These programs may not always be able to accomplish their objective and they may require that you install them before the accident for them to work. Even though they are imperfect, you may be more comfortable knowing you have one more possible "escape route."

Menu Item	Function
Restart	Completely clears the memory of the computer and reloads the system software. Information in memory that you have not saved on disk will be lost. This is the same as shutting down the computer and then turning it back on. The purpose of this is to clear an error condition that may exist. Occasionally, while you are using your computer you'll see a message, sometimes with a bomb icon, saying that you must restart your computer because of some error. When you see this, use the Restart option.

Menu Item	Function
Shut Down	Turns off your computer in an orderly fashion. If some application is still running or if some file has not been saved, you will be warned and given a chance to save any open files, then the applications will be shut down, and finally the computer turned off. The Shut Down option is very strongly recommended over using the on/off switch on the back of most Macintosh computers because the Shut Down option makes sure everything is completed and put away before the power is turned off.

3

The Balloon Help Menu

Balloon Help allows you to point on something and get a quick statement about what it does. The statement is enclosed in a comic strip-like balloon that looks like this:

The Balloon Help menu, shown here, primarily provides the means of turning Balloon Help on or off:

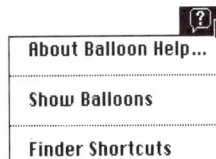

Balloon Help is particularly useful in learning about the objects on your screen. All you need to do is point on them to find out what they do. Try that now:

1. Select the Balloon Help menu and choose Show Balloons.

2. Point on your Hard Disk icon and you should get the message shown in the screen you just saw.

3. Point on several other objects such as parts of a window, other menus, and the Trash icon to get a feel for the type of information available.

4. Turn off Balloon Help by again selecting the Balloon Help menu and choosing Hide Balloons.

The Balloon Help menu has two other options. The first of these is About Balloon Help. It gives you a quick statement on how to use Balloon Help. The other option, which only appears if an application is not running, is Finder Shortcuts. This provides a series of keyboard shortcuts that can be used when you are working with icons and windows.

The Application Menu

System 7 allows you to have multiple application programs in memory at the same time. The Application menu provides the means to switch among applications and the Finder. The Finder, a part of the system software, keeps track of the applications and is the default application that runs when no other application is running. Applications that are in memory are listed along with the Finder in the lower part of the menu. By clicking one of the alternatives, you can switch to that application. The application currently running is shown by a check mark, as you can see here:

If you see an application in the Application menu that has a diamond where the checkmark usually is, it means that that application needs attention.

The top part of the menu has options that let you hide the application that is currently running, hide everything but the current application, or display all hidden applications. To hide an application means to remove it from visibility on the desktop. Hidden applications are still loaded in memory and are available for immediate use. Chapter 5, "System 7 and the Finder," will discuss the Finder in more depth.

3

4

Files, Folders, and Disks

Your Macintosh principally handles *information.* As technology improves, this information will include sound and full-motion video, but today it is still largely *text* (letters, financial reports, or lists) and *graphics* (drawings or photographs). Despite the differences in the types of information, the Macintosh treats them similarly; for the purposes of this chapter the term information is meant to cover any type of information handled by your Macintosh. Also, in this book, the terms *data* and *information* are synonymous.

In *handling* information, the Macintosh performs one of the following tasks, as shown in Figure 4-1:

- Brings information in from a floppy disk, keyboard, or other device
- Stores and retrieves information to or from the hard disk
- Manipulates information—changing it in some way or creating new information based on the existing data
- Sends information to a floppy disk, a printer, or some other device

As information is moved to, within, and from a computer, the normal unit of information is a *file.* When you bring information into the computer

Figure 4-1.   *Handling information*

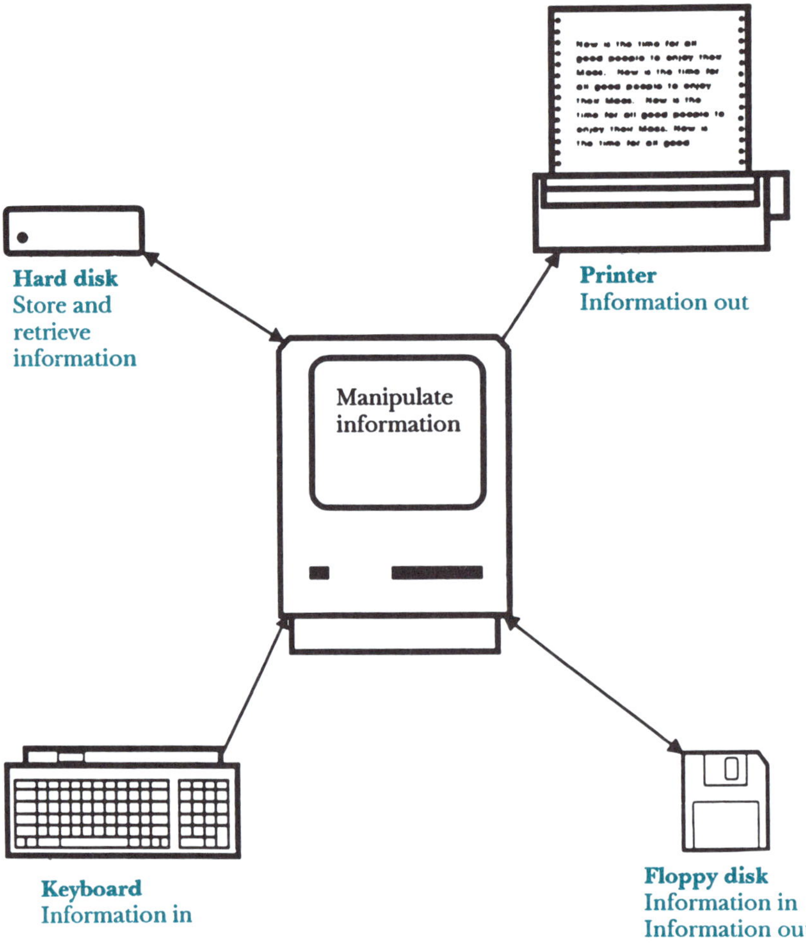

Hard disk
Store and
retrieve
information

Printer
Information out

Manipulate
information

Keyboard
Information in

Floppy disk
Information in
Information out

from a floppy disk, you bring in a file; when you type information in and save
it, it is stored in a file; when you print out information, you print out part or

all of a file. Files are the units in which information is transferred with your Macintosh.

As files are transferred to a disk (either floppy or hard), they are said to be *written* on the disk; when files are taken from the disk they are said to be *read*. Since disks are magnetic recording devices, these terms are literally true.

The File System

Both floppy and hard disks can hold many files (hard disks of course can hold many more files than can floppies). If you are looking for a particular file, you may have to search through many files to find the one you want. Grouping similar files will narrow your search—you can look through the group of files related to the file you want instead of going file by file through everything on your disk.

The Macintosh provides the ability to group files using *folders*, which are simply units that hold related files (just like the folders in a file cabinet). These folders can contain other folders—or *subgroups*—(like a paper-clipped set of papers inside the folders in a file cabinet). By dividing a group into subgroups you have even fewer files to search.

This structure of disks that contain folders that contain other folders that contain files is called a *hierarchical file structure* (HFS). Each of the open windows in Figure 4-2 represents a subgroup of the window behind it on screen. The hard disk contains a folder named PageMaker 4.0. PageMaker 4.0, in turn, contains a folder named Publications that contains a folder named Newsletter 2/92 that contains all of the files related to an issue of a newsletter.

The number of folders you place within folders in a path to a file is up to you. (Think of the *path* as being a list of the folders followed by the filename.) Some people believe that with three or more levels it is easy to lose track of where you put a particular file, while others find files faster in multilevel paths. You need to determine which method works for you by trying both over a period of time.

4

Figure 4-2.   *The hierarchical file structure (files within folders within folders)*

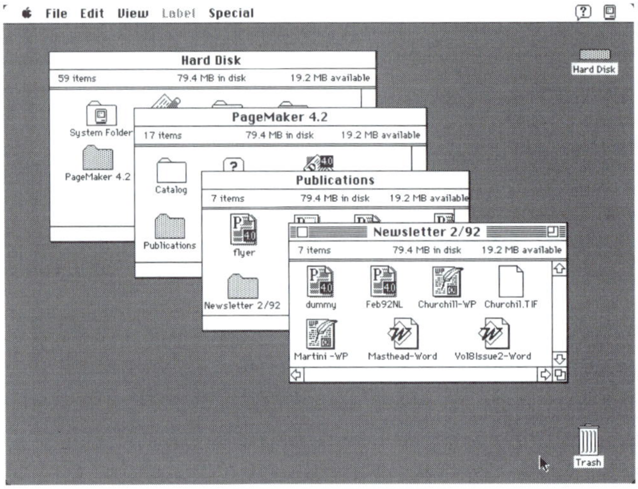

Working with Files and Folders

As you have seen, files and folders provide a handy way to move and store information. The Macintosh icons make this even easier by giving you a familiar visual reference, as shown here:

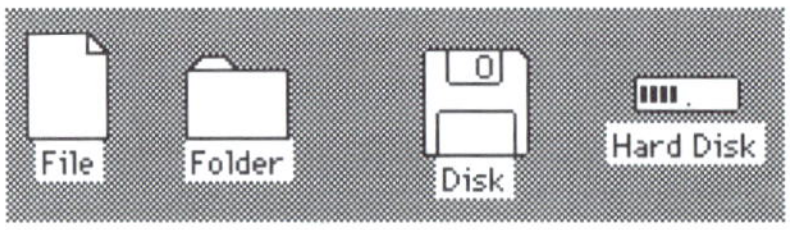

To move a piece of information, you simply drag the file, folder, or disk icon that contains it. You saw this demonstrated in Chapter 1, "Meet the Macintosh." Later in this chapter you will practice moving both files and folders.

Types of Files

Files contain many different types of information: system software programs, application programs, drawings, text, and other information. While the contents of these files may be different, you treat the files the same way. You drag, copy, and delete graphic files the same way you do text files, for example. Most files can be *activated*, or opened, in the same way (you'll see how in a minute).

A useful distinction can be made between program files and document files. Program files can be activated without another file whereas document files require that a program file be activated first.

While there is little difference among files, software publishers have created many customized icons to represent their application programs and related document files, as you can see in Figure 4-3. Despite this diversity in icons, all these files are treated the same way.

4

Creating Folders

You saw in Chapter 2, "Using the Macintosh," how to create a new folder with the File menu. You should still have that folder, titled "untitled folder." Create another folder now so you have two folders to use in the following exercises. If you no longer have the folder you created in Chapter 2, create two folders with the following instructions:

1. If your Hard Disk window is not open, double-click its icon. If your Hard Disk window is open but not currently selected, click the Hard Disk window to select it.

2. Select the File menu and choose New Folder. A second new folder should appear, as shown here:

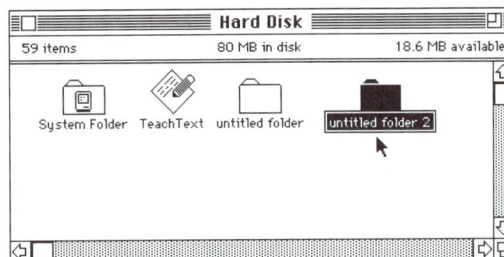

Figure 4-3.   *Examples of document and program icons*

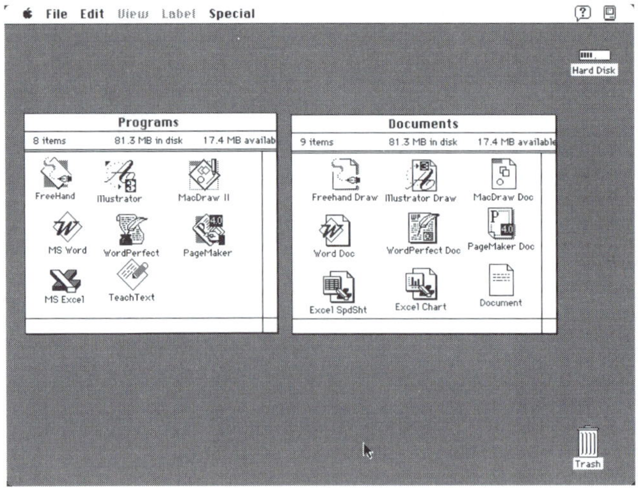

New folders are easy to create. You may want to create many to organize your files. Create the hierarchical structure within folders that works best for you.

Creating Files

You create files with application programs. Drawing files are created with drawing programs, word processing files are created with word processing programs, and spreadsheet files are created with spreadsheet programs. Therefore, to create a new file, you must first start an application program, such as a word processing or drawing program.

Activating a Program File

The system software that you get with a Macintosh includes an application program for simple text editing called TeachText. You can see its icon between the System folder and the first untitled folder in the last illustration. Since you can create files with this application, you'll use it in the following exercise.

When you turn on a Macintosh, the system software is automatically started. When the start-up process is complete you can use the Finder menus to perform the functions described in Chapter 3, "Menus," but for other capabilities such as word processing or drawing you must start an application program. This means activating the program file by double-clicking its icon. Follow these steps:

1. Double-click the TeachText icon.

    The TeachText window opens with the insertion point blinking in the upper-left corner, as you can see in Figure 4-4.

2. Type any text. For instance: **Now is the time for all good people to enjoy their Macintoshes.**

3. Select the File menu and choose Save. The Save dialog box opens, as shown here:

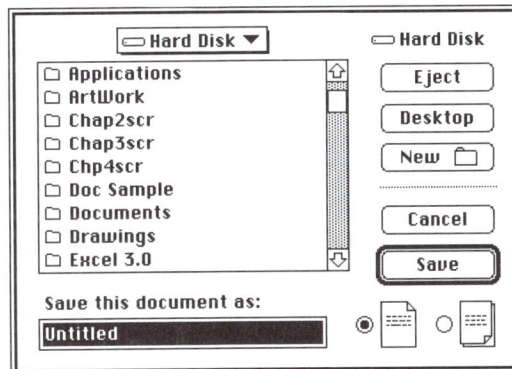

```
┌──────────────────────────────────────────────────┐
│   ┌── Hard Disk ▼───┐        ⊂⊃ Hard Disk          │
│   │ ☐ Applications  │ ⇧    ┌──────────┐            │
│   │ ☐ ArtWork       │      │  Eject   │            │
│   │ ☐ Chap2scr      │      └──────────┘            │
│   │ ☐ Chap3scr      │      ┌──────────┐            │
│   │ ☐ Chp4scr       │      │ Desktop  │            │
│   │ ☐ Doc Sample    │      └──────────┘            │
│   │ ☐ Documents     │      ┌──────────┐            │
│   │ ☐ Drawings      │      │ New  ☐   │            │
│   │ ☐ Excel 3.0     │ ⇩    └──────────┘            │
│   └─────────────────┘      ┌──────────┐            │
│                            │  Cancel  │            │
│   Save this document as:   └──────────┘            │
│   ┌─────────────────────┐  ┌──────────┐            │
│   │ Untitled            │  │   Save   │            │
│   └─────────────────────┘  └──────────┘            │
└──────────────────────────────────────────────────┘
```

4. Type **TestDoc1** and click Save.

    You have just created a new file and saved it on your hard disk. Next create a second file and save it also. Follow these steps:

5. Select the File menu and choose Save As. The Save As dialog box opens looking almost exactly like the Save dialog box you just saw.

6. Type **TestDoc2** and click Save.

You now have two new files. Their contents are the same, but they are two separate and independent files.

Figure 4-4.   *The TeachText window*

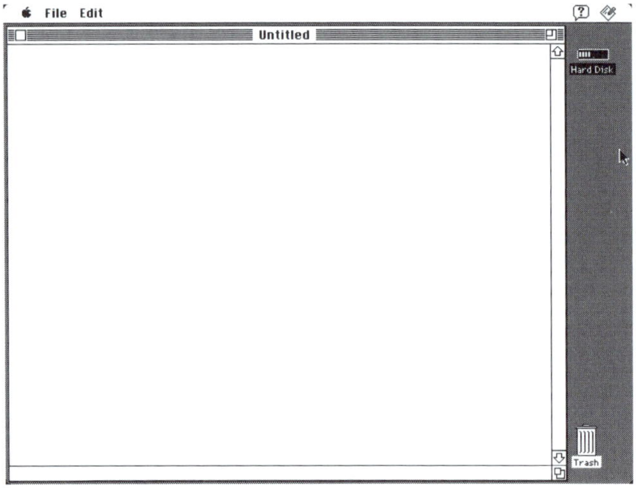

You used Save As instead of Save when creating the second file because if you had used Save a second time you would not get a dialog box for entering the filename; instead, the file is simply saved again with the same name. A second Save replaces the copy of the file on disk with the copy of the file in memory. The Save As option allows you to change the name and create a new file as a result.

Using the File Save option after you have created and saved a file replaces the copy of the file on disk with the copy of the file in memory. The original copy of the file on disk is lost. Use Save As to create a new file and avoid overwriting the original file.

Quit TeachText and look at your handiwork in the Hard Disk window.

1. Select the File menu and choose Quit.

   The TeachText application closes and you can again see the Hard Disk window, which should look something like this (you probably have other applications showing as well):

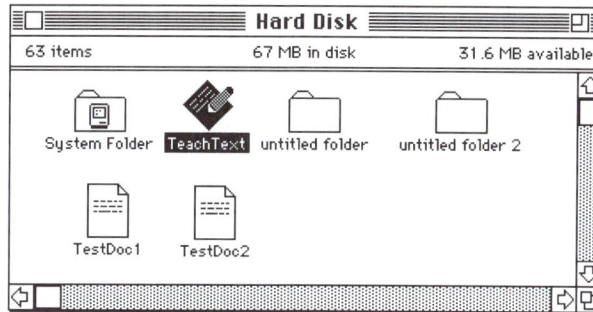

4

Changing the Folder Names

The automatically created folder names ("untitled folder" and "untitled folder 2") are not very informative and need to be changed to more specific titles. Follow these steps:

1. Click the words *untitled folder* in the text box beneath the icon for the first new folder so the text box is selected. It may take several seconds, but the text box should be a lighter color than the rest of the icon and the mouse pointer should become an I-beam—as you can see here:

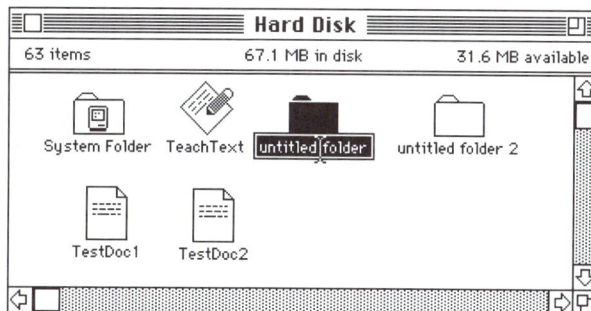

Figure 4-5.   *The first new folder is renamed Documents*

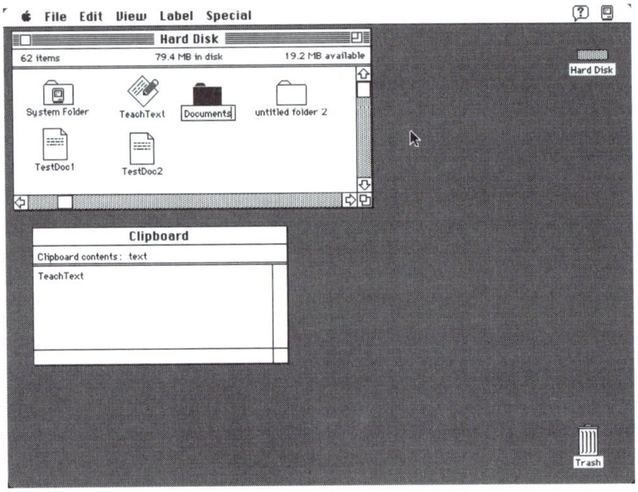

2. Type **Documents** and see how the characters replace the original contents. Your screen should now look like the one shown in Figure 4-5.

3. Press (return) and then click the words *untitled folder 2* in the text box for the second folder so all the text is selected. Type **Other Stuff** for the new name and press (return).

You can replace text by selecting or highlighting the old text and typing the new. You do not have to clear or delete the old text first.

Moving Files and Folders

To move a file or a folder from one window or folder to another on the same disk drive, drag the file or folder to where you want it. The file or folder disappears from the original folder and reappears in the new folder. Try that with the following instructions:

1. Drag the TestDoc2 file so that it is over the Other Stuff folder and the Other Stuff folder is highlighted, as shown here:

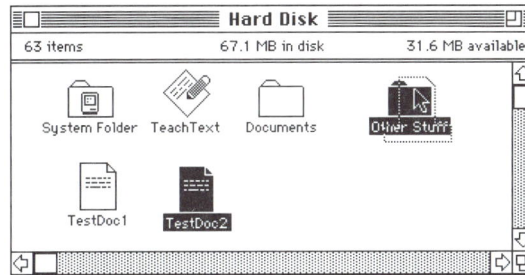

Release the mouse button and the TestDoc2 file will disappear into the Other Stuff folder.

2. Drag the TestDoc1 file to the Other Stuff folder so that it too disappears.

3. Drag the Other Stuff folder to the Documents folder and it will disappear in the Documents folder. Your Hard Disk window should now look like this (you probably have some additional files and folders):

4. Double-click the Documents folder to open it so you can see the Other Stuff folder and then double-click the Other Stuff folder so you can see the two files. Your screen should look like the one shown in Figure 4-6.

Moving either a file or a folder within a disk is nothing more than dragging the file or folder to where you want it. You'll see later in this chapter that dragging a file or folder between disks gives you a different result.

Figure 4-6.   *Files and folder moved to new locations*

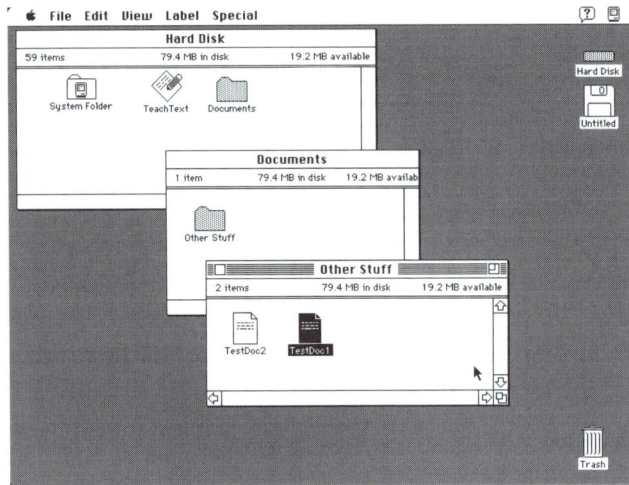

Moving Multiple Files and Folders

When you have multiple files and/or folders to move you can move them one at a time as you just did or you can select several files and move them all at once. You can select several files using one of two methods. The first method is to hold down (shift) while clicking each of the objects you want to select. This is called *shift-clicking*. The second method only works if all the objects are near each other. It entails drawing an imaginary rectangle, called a *marquee* or a *selection box*, around all of the objects. You move the pointer to one of the corners of the imaginary rectangle outside one of the icons. Then press and hold the mouse button while dragging the pointer diagonally to the opposite corner. Practice each of these methods with these steps:

1. Press and hold (shift) while clicking first TestDoc1 and then TestDoc2. Release the (shift) key. Both files should be highlighted when you are finished.

2. Point on one of the files and drag it to the Documents folder. The other file will move to the Documents folder also, as shown in Figure 4-7.

3. Close the Other Stuff folder by clicking its Close box.

Figure 4-7. *Two files being moved at once*

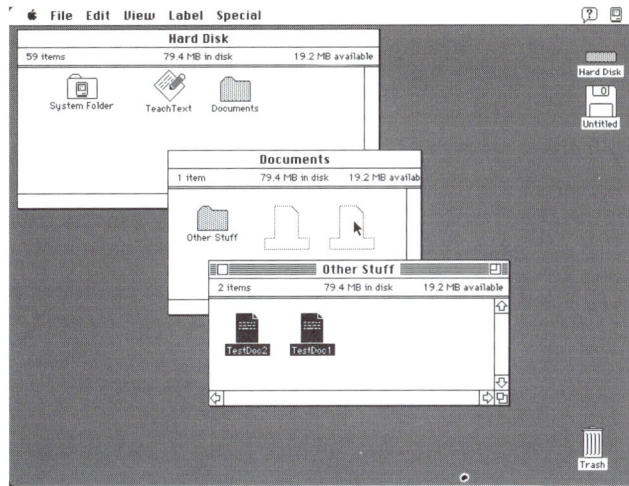

4. Select the three objects in the Documents folder by moving the pointer above and to the left of the object on the far left; then press and hold the mouse button while moving the pointer diagonally below and to the right of the object to the far right to encircle all three objects with the marquee, as shown here:

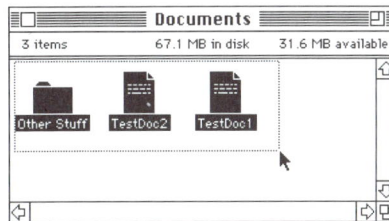

5. Release the mouse button to complete selecting the three objects. Then drag one of the objects to the Hard Disk window. The other two objects will follow along, as you can see in Figure 4-8.

Figure 4-8.   *Moving three objects back to the Hard Disk folder*

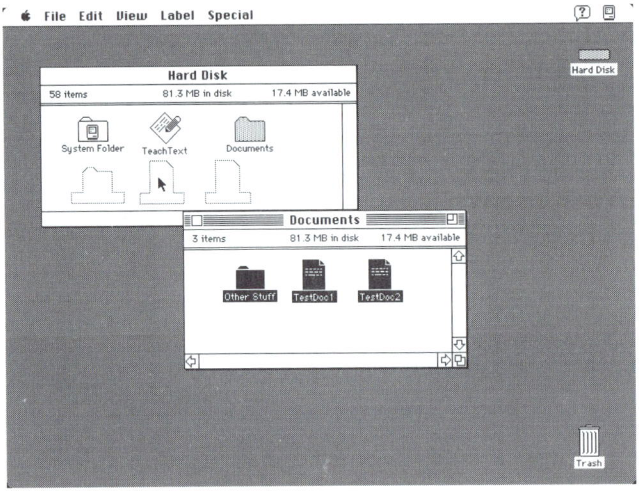

In Macintosh system software prior to System 7, the marquee had to completely enclose the objects you were selecting. If any part of the object was outside of the marquee, the object was not selected. With System 7 this is no longer true. Now, if any part of the object is in the marquee, it is selected.

6. Close the Documents window by clicking its Close button.

Copying Files and Folders

Copying files and folders is very similar to moving them if you are copying from one folder to another—you simply hold down the (option) key while you drag. See how that works with these instructions:

1. Press and hold (option) while dragging the TestDoc1 file to the Document folder. When you are finished, you will get a brief message that copying is in progress, as shown here,

```
═══════════════ Copy ═══════════════
 Items remaining to be copied:      1
 Writing:    TestDoc1
 ████████▌_____   [ Stop ]
```

and you should hear a sound from your disk. Notice that the original file is still in the Hard Disk window.

2. Select both the Other Stuff folder and the TestDoc2 file using either the shift-click method or by drawing a marquee around them as you did in the previous exercise.

3. Press and hold (option) while dragging the TestDoc2 file to the Documents folder. The Other Stuff folder will follow along. Again you will see the message about copying and you'll hear a sound from your disk.

4. Double-click the Documents folder to open it. Your screen should resemble Figure 4-9.

   Notice how the copies have the exact same names. You can do this if the files are in separate folders, but you can't have two files with the same name in the same folder. Try moving one of the new files back to the Hard Disk window and see.

5. Drag the TestDoc1 file back to the Hard Disk folder. When you release the mouse button to complete the move you will get the Caution message shown here:

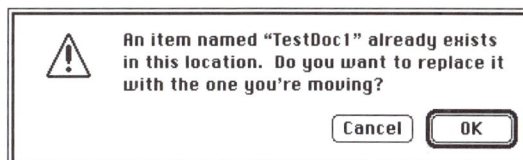

```
┌──────────────────────────────────────────┐
│  ⚠   An item named "TestDoc1" already exists │
│  /!\  in this location. Do you want to replace it │
│       with the one you're moving?            │
│                                              │
│              [ Cancel ]  [  OK  ]            │
└──────────────────────────────────────────┘
```

Figure 4-9.   *Copies in the Documents folder*

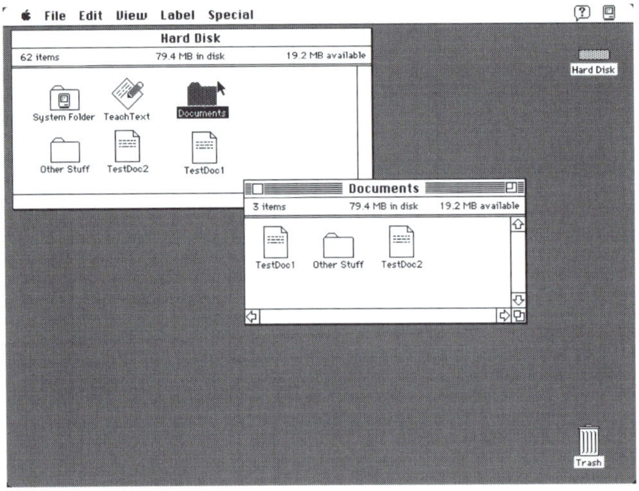

6. Click Cancel to close the message box and cancel the move.

7. Close the Documents folder by clicking its Close box.

Duplicating Files and Folders

In the last exercise you copied the files and the folder. The copies, though, had to be in a different folder because they had the same names as the originals.

Duplicating is making a copy of a file or folder in its current folder but giving it a different name. You duplicate using the Duplicate option of the File menu. Try duplicating now with these steps:

1. Click the TestDoc1 file to select it. Then select the File menu and choose Duplicate. Another file is created and named TestDoc1 copy, as you can see here:

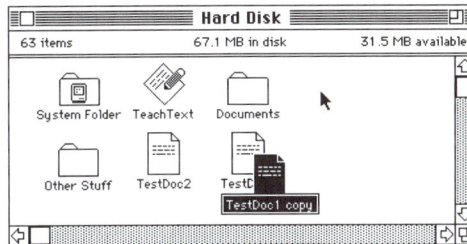

2. Select the Documents folder and press ⌘-D (the shortcut keys for Duplicate). You will briefly see a message indicating that the files inside the folder are also being copied. Then a new folder called Documents copy will appear.

3. Open the Documents copy folder. Inside are the same three objects you have been using in the last several exercises, as shown in Figure 4-10. Note that they do not have *copy* in their name because they are in a separate folder.

4. Close the Documents copy folder.

You will use both copying and duplicating. Choose which you'll use in a specific situation by deciding whether you want to keep the copy in the same folder. If you do, you must use Duplicate. Otherwise either command can be used.

Deleting Files and Folders

Your Hard Disk window is getting cluttered; it is time to start throwing away some files and folders. Throwing something away—*deleting* a file or folder from your hard disk—is a two-step process. First, you drag the object you want deleted to the Trash icon. This puts it in the trash but it doesn't remove it from your hard disk. To do that, you must empty the trash. As you saw in Chapter 3, "Menus," Empty Trash is an option on the Special menu. So to complete the process, you select the Special menu and choose Empty Trash.

With System 7, the only way to empty the trash is to choose the Empty Trash option. In earlier versions of the system software, the trash was automatically emptied when you started an application program or restarted

Figure 4-10.   *The Documents Copy window*

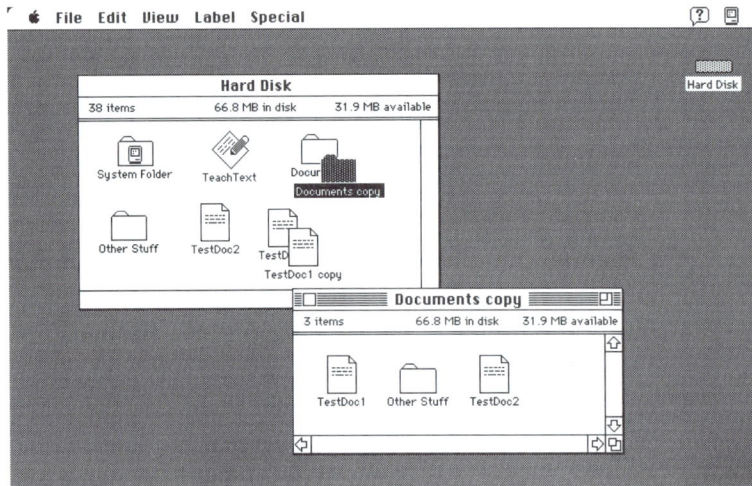

or shut down the computer. Now, with System 7 you must take an action before the trash is gone. This is a definite plus, because it means emptying the trash is under your control, not the computer's. The negative side is that if you don't empty the trash the files still take up room on the hard disk. (There is no harm in leaving something in the trash for a while if you have plenty of room on your hard disk. Your Macintosh will tell you if you can't do something unless you empty the trash first.)

Get rid of some of the clutter in the Hard Disk window and practice deleting a file and a folder, next. Follow these steps:

1. Drag the TestDoc1 copy file to the Trash icon. Before releasing the mouse button, make sure the Trash icon is highlighted. The file disappears into the Trash icon and the Trash icon bulges out, as you saw in Chapter 3, "Menus."

2. Drag the Documents copy folder to the Trash icon. It too will disappear.

3. Open the Trash window by double-clicking the icon. It should look like this:

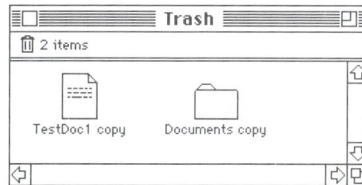

```
┌─────────────────────────────────────┐
│ ≣□≣════════ Trash ════════⊡≣         │
├─────────────────────────────────────┤
│ 🗑 2 items                        │⇧│ │
│                                  ├─┤ │
│      ┌───┐        ┌────┐         │ │ │
│      │≈≈≈│        │    │         │ │ │
│      └───┘        └────┘         ├─┤ │
│   TestDoc1 copy  Documents copy  │⇩│ │
│  ◁──────────────────────────▷ ▷◁┘   │
└─────────────────────────────────────┘
```

4. Select the Special menu and choose Empty Trash. The following Caution message will appear:

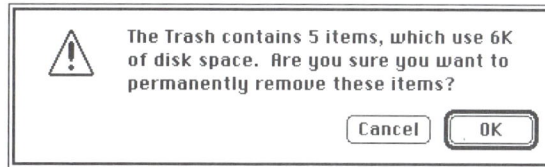

```
┌─────────────────────────────────────────────┐
│                                             │
│   ┌──┐   The Trash contains 5 items, which  │
│   │/!\│  use 6K of disk space.  Are you     │
│   └──┘   sure you want to permanently       │
│          remove these items?                │
│                                             │
│                      ┌────────┐ ┌────────┐  │
│                      │ Cancel │ │   OK   │  │
│                      └────────┘ └────────┘  │
└─────────────────────────────────────────────┘
```

5. Click OK. The Trash window will empty and the Trash icon will slim down. What you threw away is now gone from your disk.

Choosing Empty Trash from the Special menu and clicking OK to the Caution message permanently deletes everything in the trash.

If you want to retrieve something from the trash *before* choosing Empty Trash, you can do so by opening the Trash window and dragging the items from the Trash window to the desktop or another window or folder.

6. Close the Trash window.

If you are sure enough of yourself that you do not want to see the Caution message after choosing Empty Trash, you can disable the message appearance. You can do this on a case-by-case basis by holding down the (option) key while choosing Empty Trash. The trash is gone as soon as you empty the trash.

You can turn off the Caution message in all cases by selecting the Trash icon and choosing Get Info from the File menu. In the bottom of the Get Info dialog box is a check box that says "Warn before emptying," as shown here:

```
┌───────────────────────────────────────────────┐
│ ▤□▤▤▤▤▤▤▤ Trash Info ▤▤▤▤▤▤▤▤▤▤ │
├───────────────────────────────────────────────┤
│   ╔═══╗                                        │
│   ║║║║║  Trash                                  │
│   ╚═══╝                                        │
│                                                │
│   Where : On the desktop                       │
│                                                │
│   Contents : 3 files and 2 folders are in the  │
│              Trash for a total of 6K.          │
│                                                │
│                                                │
│   Modified : Fri, Nov 15, 1991, 8:29 AM        │
│                                                │
│   ☒ Warn before emptying                       │
└───────────────────────────────────────────────┘
```

If you click the check box to turn it off, the Caution message will not appear until you turn on the check box again.

Under most circumstances, turning off the Trash icon warning message is not a wise choice. Clicking OK in the Caution message is not that onerous a task and it allows you one last opportunity to change your mind about what you are throwing away.

Creating and Using Aliases

When you copy or duplicate a file, you get two full copies. If the original file takes 100KB of disk space, the file and its copy will take 200KB. Therefore, it is usually not practical to have multiple copies of a file in several locations just to make that file more easily available. Also, you don't want multiple copies of a data file because of the problem of keeping all copies current.

System 7 has solved this problem by allowing you to attach another icon and name, an *alias*, to a file without duplicating the file itself. You can add as many aliases to a single file as you want. You can then move the aliases anywhere you want them and only use 1KB to 2KB of disk space for each alias. An alias is not a file. It's just another way to access an existing file—like adding another door into a house. It makes life simpler by allowing you to put icons where you need them.

Why Use Aliases?

There are several reasons why you might want to use aliases. When you install an application program, the normal procedure is to create a new folder for that application and put all associated files in that folder. That way you know where to go to find something related to that application. To start the application, though, you must first open the application folder. A better approach is to create an alias and keep the alias either out on the desktop, in a folder of just application aliases, or in the Apple Menu folder. The last alternative will be discussed further in Chapter 5, "System 7 and the Finder." An example of a separate applications folder with aliases (the italicized filenames are aliases) is shown here:

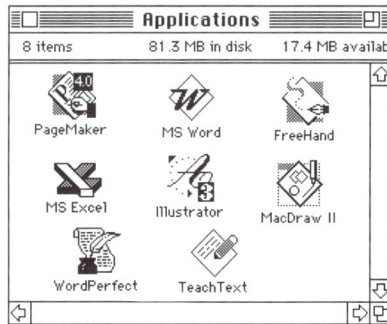

Having an application alias on the desktop, in a special folder, or in the Apple menu lets you reach a file faster with fewer steps than if you had to find and open the application-specific folder.

A good use of aliases with data files is for sales information. The original file might be in an accounting folder, the first alias in a marketing folder, a second alias in a sales commission folder, and a third alias in a folder used for sales tax matters. In this example, the original file resides in the accounting folder, but the data can be easily accessed from any of the other folders without having to find the original folder.

One of the best reasons to use an alias is to move the original file off the hard drive to a floppy disk for archival storage and still maintain the link between the original file and the alias. When you use the alias, you will be reminded to load the floppy disk. This saves a lot of space on your hard drive for infrequently used data and programs and yet gives you a reminder of where you stored a file. Of course, you need to remember to label your floppy disks and have a good filing system for them.

If you use aliases for files on floppy disks and try to open the file, you will get a message asking you to insert the disk. If you cannot find the disk the file is on, press ⌘-(period) to close the message and return to the desktop.

Working with Aliases

Create several aliases now and watch their behavior with the following steps:

1. Select both of the Test files in the Hard Disk window.

2. Select the File menu and choose Make Alias. Two new document icons appear with their names in italics and the word alias at the end, as you can see here:

3. Drag the two alias files (they should already be selected) to the Other Stuff folder.

4. Open the Other Stuff folder.

5. Select the View menu and choose "by Name" to see the information on the alias files that is shown here:

```
┌────────────────────────────────────────────────┐
│ ▤☐▦▦▦▦▦▦ Other Stuff ▦▦▦▦▦▦▦▦ ◱▤ │
├────────────────────────────────────┬──────┬─────┤
│      Name                          │ Size │ Kind│
├────────────────────────────────────┴──────┴─────┤
│  ▯  TestDoc1 alias               2K   alias   ⇧ │
│  ▯  TestDoc2 alias               2K   alias      │
│                                                  │
│                                                  │
│                                               ⇩ │
├──┬───────────────────────────────────────┬──────┤
│⇦ │▒▒▒▒▒▒▒▒▒▒▒▒▒▒▒▒▒▒▒▒▒▒▒▒▒▒▒▒▒▒▒▒▒▒▒▒▒▒▒│ ⇨ ⊡ │
└──┴───────────────────────────────────────┴──────┘
```

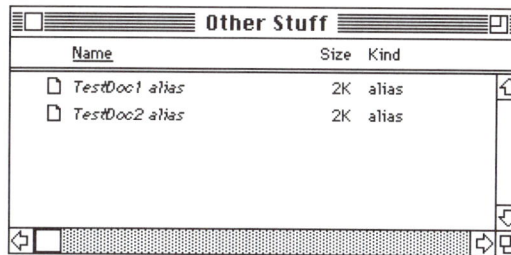

Note that the aliases' sizes are only 1KB each and that they are labeled as alias under Kind. Because the name is italicized, you don't have to leave the word *alias* in the name after you move the icon to a different folder.

6. Select the TestDoc1 alias file. Then select the File menu and choose Get Info. The Get Info dialog box will open, as shown here:

```
┌──────────────────────────────────────┐
│ ▤☐▦▦▦ TestDoc1 alias Info ▦▦▦▦ │
├──────────────────────────────────────┤
│  ┌────┐                                │
│  │▤▤▤▤│   TestDoc1 alias               │
│  └────┘                                │
│                                        │
│    Kind: alias                         │
│    Size: 2K on disk (515 bytes used)   │
│                                        │
│   Where: Hard Disk :                   │
│                                        │
│                                        │
│ Created: Fri, Dec 6, 1991, 7:50 PM     │
│ Modified: Fri, Dec 6, 1991, 7:50 PM    │
│ Original: Hard Disk : TestDoc1         │
│                                        │
│ Comments:                              │
│  ┌──────────────────────────────────┐ │
│  │                                  │ │
│  │                                  │ │
│  └──────────────────────────────────┘ │
│                                        │
│ ☐ Locked          ( Find Original )    │
└──────────────────────────────────────┘
```

The Get Info dialog box tells you that this file is an alias. More importantly, this dialog box helps you find the original file should you want to do that. The line headed Original describes where the original is. The Find Original button takes you right to the original file or tells you it's on a floppy disk.

7. Click the Find Original button in the Get Info dialog box. The Hard Disk window is brought forward, and the original TestDoc1 file is highlighted, as you can see in Figure 4-11.

4

Figure 4-11.   *The original TestDoc1 file found*

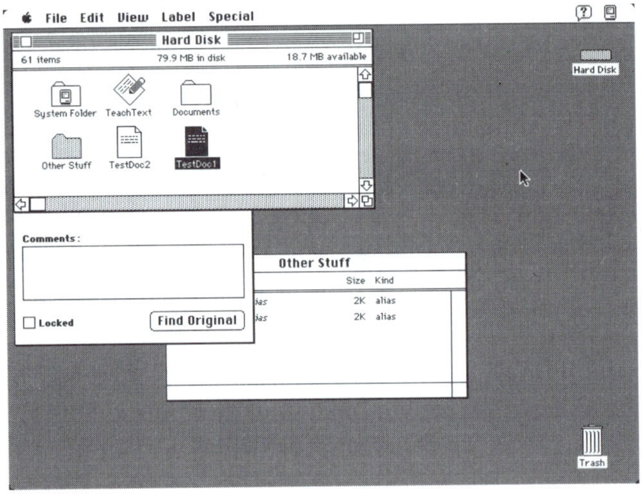

Next, test the Find Original option again after moving the original file.
Follow these steps:

1. Open the Documents folder and then select and drag all of its
    contents to the Trash icon. This allows you to move the original
    TestDoc1 and TestDoc2 files to the Documents folder without a
    name conflict.

2. Close the Documents folder, select the two original Test files, and
    move them to the Documents folder.

3. Select the Get Info dialog box that is open and then click the Find
    Original button. The Documents folder will open and the TestDoc1
    file will be highlighted, as shown in Figure 4-12.

    You can see that moving the original files does not affect the link
    with the aliases.

4. Close the Documents folder, the Get Info dialog box, and the Other
    Stuff folder to clean up the desktop. Also select the Special menu,

Figure 4-12.   *Original files found again*

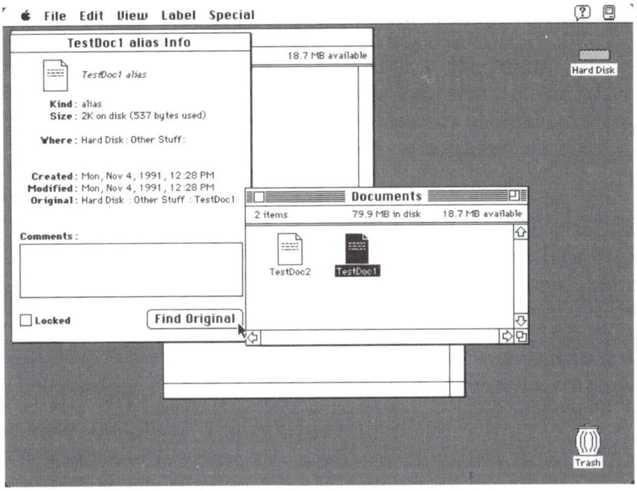

choose Empty Trash, and click OK to remove the unwanted files in the trash.

Other Alias Considerations

Aliases are a simple concept, but they have some not so simple ramifications. The more important of these are discussed in the following sections.

Folder Aliases   Folder aliases are just another doorway to the original folder. They are not a folder themselves. If you try to place a file or folder in a folder alias, the object will go into the original folder, not the alias. When you double-click the alias you will open the original folder, not the alias.

Trash Icon Alias   If you have folders in which you are creating and throwing away a lot of files, make an alias of the Trash icon (select the Trash icon and choose Make Alias from the File menu) and drag it to the folder in which you want it. (This is like bringing a trash can into your office when cleaning your desk.) You will have a shorter distance to drag items being thrown away and you can still dispose of items when the window you're using has covered the original Trash icon.

The Trash alias works like a folder alias. To put an object in the trash, drag it to the alias. It is exactly the same as dragging an object to the Trash icon. You can also double-click the alias to see what is in the trash. To delete everything in the trash, you must still select the Special menu and choose Empty Trash.

Aliases of an Alias   All aliases of a given file should be created from that file, not from another alias. This prevents a chain of aliases that could be broken by deleting an intermediate alias.

Deleting Aliases and the Original Files   You can delete an alias without affecting the original file; however, deleting the original file, even after copying the file, breaks the links to the aliases. A broken link cannot be rebuilt except by creating a new alias. Also, the old aliases will remain until you delete them even though they no longer refer to an original file.

Finding Files

As you build a more complex file system of folders within folders, and add more files, you will probably find that you sometimes forget where you placed a file. System 7 has come up with a solution for this—the File menu Find option. You read a little about this option in Chapter 2, "Using the Macintosh." Prior to System 7, Apple provided a desk accessory called Find File that was harder to use, not as readily available, and much less sophisticated in its search techniques.

The File menu Find option or the shortcut keys (⌘)-(F) open the Find dialog box, shown here:

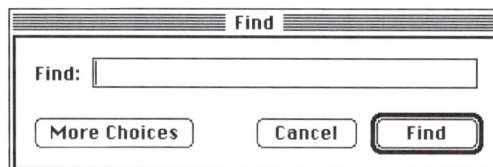

```
╔══════════════════ Find ══════════════════╗
║                                           ║
║  Find: │                               │  ║
║                                           ║
║  ┌─────────────┐    ┌────────┐ ┌───────┐  ║
║  │ More Choices│    │ Cancel │ │ Find  │  ║
║  └─────────────┘    └────────┘ └───────┘  ║
╚═══════════════════════════════════════════╝
```

To find a file, enter all or part of a filename in the text box and click the Find command button or press ⟨return⟩. It is usually better to enter the first three or four letters of the filename and then, if necessary, repeat the search if you don't find the file the first time. It is easy to make a mistake if you enter the full filename.

Using Find

Find a file now with these steps:

1. Select the File menu and choose Find. The Find dialog box opens.

2. Type **Test** in the text box and click Find. Unless you have other files containing the word *Test* in their names, either the Documents folder or the Other Stuff folder will open and one of the Test files will be highlighted, as shown in Figure 4-13.

Figure 4-13. *TestDoc1 found*

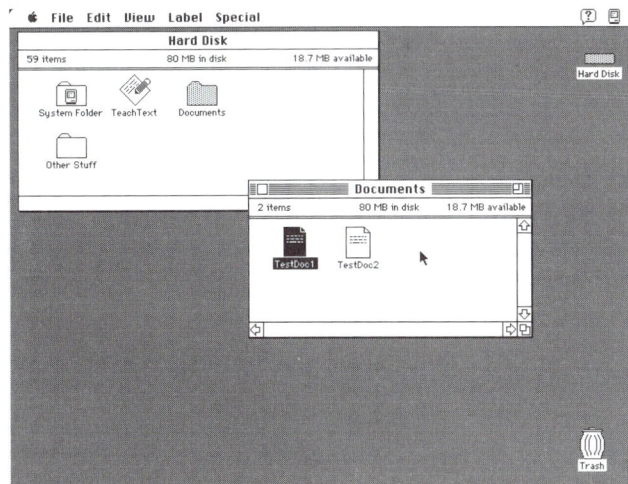

3. Press ⌘-Ⓖ to repeat the search (you could also select the File menu and choose Find Again). Again, unless you have other files beginning with *Test*, another of the Test files will be highlighted.

If you repeat the Find two more times you'll find the other two Test files.

Complex Searching

The Find option as just demonstrated is a very good way of finding a file if you know part of its name, which you will in probably 80 percent of your searches. For the other 20 percent where you don't know the name, there is a second Find dialog box that gives you a number of ways to vary the search. Open the second dialog box now and look at its alternatives. Follow these steps:

1. Choose File Find or press ⌘-Ⓕ and after the first Find dialog box opens, click the More Choices button. The second Find dialog box opens, as shown here:

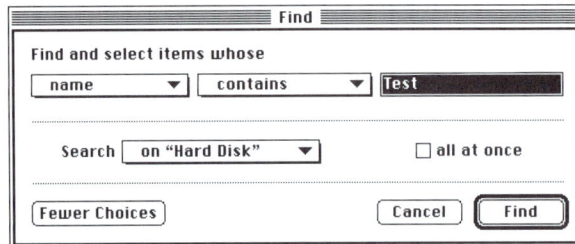

2. Hold the mouse button down on each of the three pop-up menus to see their initial contents. Then choose each of the options in the top-left pop-up menu and see how the choices in the top-middle pop-up menu change and how the text box in the top right also changes.

As you can see, there are a large number of options against which you can search. The full set of these options is shown in Table 4-1.

Items Searched

The disks and folders you want searched are controlled by the Search pop-up menu in the lower left of the second Find dialog box. The contents

Table 4-1. *Find Options*

Search On	Constraints	Enter
name	contains starts with ends with is is not doesn't contain	text
size	is less than is greater than	a number (KB)
kind	contains doesn't contain	text "alias" "application" "document" "folder" "stationary"
label	is is not	"None" a label
date created	is is before is after is not	a date
date modified	is is before is after is not	a date
version	is is before is after is not	a number text
comments	contain do not contain	text
lock	is	"locked" "unlocked"

4

Figure 4-14.   *Search options with one disk and nothing selected*

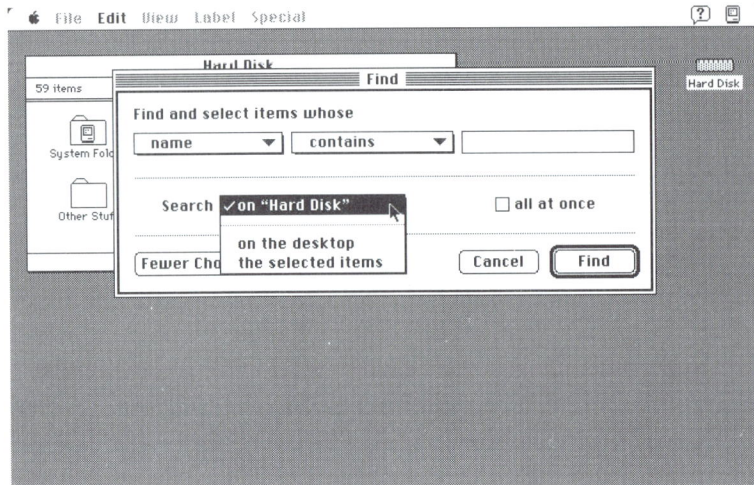

Figure 4-15.   *Search options with one disk and a folder selected*

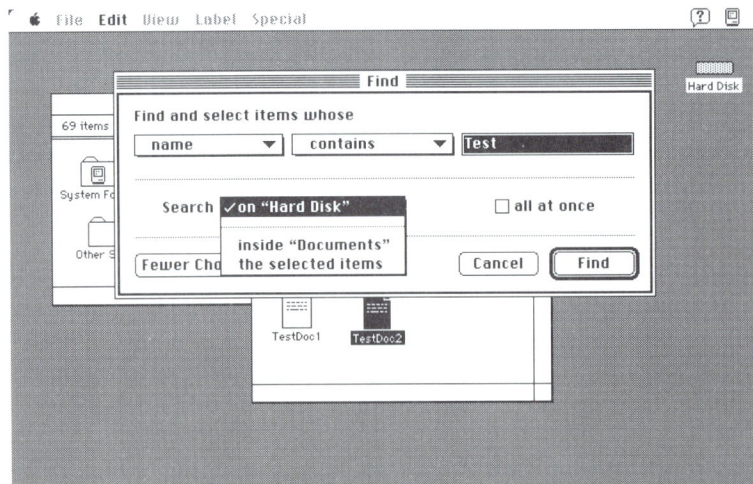

Figure 4-16. *Search options with two disks and a folder selected*

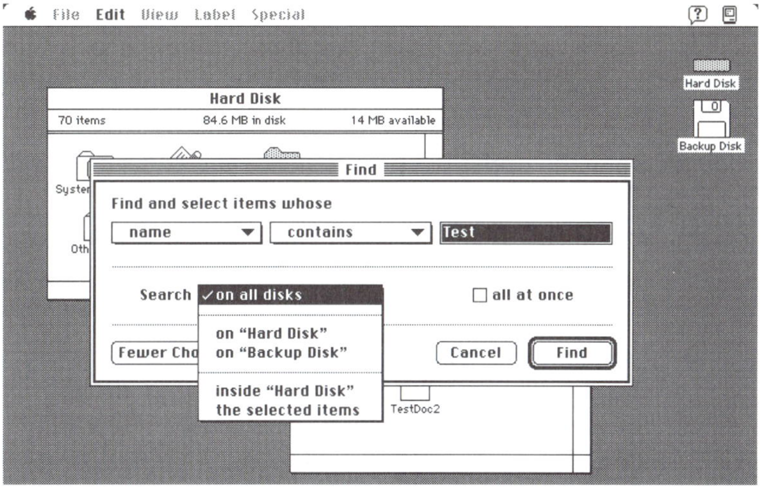

of the Search pop-up menu vary depending on the number of disks on your computer and whether a disk and/or folder is selected. Figures 4-14, 4-15, and 4-16 show the alternatives with one and two disks and with and without something selected.

The Search options run from searching all folders on all disks, to searching a single selected folder. The difference between the options "on Hard Disk" and "in Hard Disk" is that in the latter case the Hard Disk is selected. Also, "on the desktop" results from having nothing selected and is the same as searching all files on all disks.

Viewing Found Files All at Once

The All At Once check box gives you a choice of looking at one found object or a list of all found items. Up to now you have been looking at the "one at a time" view, as was shown as Figure 4-13. This displays both the object that was found and the window for the folder that contains the object. By clicking the All At Once check box you get a list of all the folders in the items that were searched. The folders that contain files that match the criteria are opened and display a list all of their files. Finally, all of the files that match the criteria are highlighted. See this for yourself with this exercise:

1. The second Find dialog box should be open as you left it from the last exercise. If it isn't, select the File menu, choose Find, and then click the More Choices command button.

2. Open the upper-left pop-up menu and choose "date created." Also, choose "is after" from the middle pop-up menu.

3. Pick a date after which you know several files were created (say the day before you created the two Test files). Then click the day number in the date on the right and click the down arrow until the day you want is displayed.

4. Check to see that the Search pop-up menu shows your hard disk as the item to search and then click the All At Once check box to turn it on. Although your date will differ, the rest of your Find dialog box should look like this:

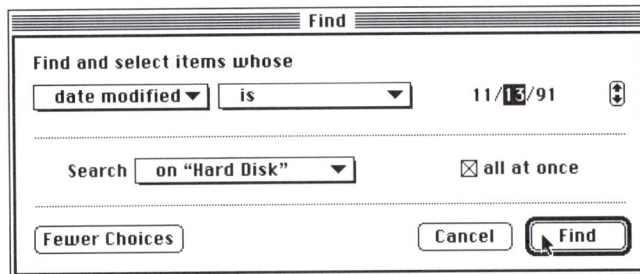

```
╔═════════════════════════ Find ═══════════════════════╗
║                                                        ║
║  Find and select items whose                           ║
║    ┌─────────────────┐   ┌──────────────┐              ║
║    │ date modified ▼ │   │ is        ▼ │  11/13/91  ⬍  ║
║    └─────────────────┘   └──────────────┘              ║
║  ....................................................  ║
║                                                        ║
║    Search │ on "Hard Disk"   ▼ │      ⊠ all at once    ║
║  ....................................................  ║
║    ┌──────────────┐           ┌────────┐ ┌─────────┐   ║
║    │ Fewer Choices │           │ Cancel │ │  Find  │   ║
║    └──────────────┘           └────────┘ └─────────┘   ║
╚════════════════════════════════════════════════════════╝
```

5. Click Find. You next get a brief message about items being found and displayed, as shown here:

```
╔═════════════════════════ Find ═══════════════════════╗
║                                                        ║
║  Items found on "Hard Disk":                    100    ║
║  ┌──────────────────────────────┐   ┌──────────┐       ║
║  │▨▨▨▨▨▨▨▨▨▨▨▨▨▨▨│   │   Stop   │       ║
║  └──────────────────────────────┘   └──────────┘       ║
╚════════════════════════════════════════════════════════╝
```

Figure 4-17. *List view with matching items highlighted*

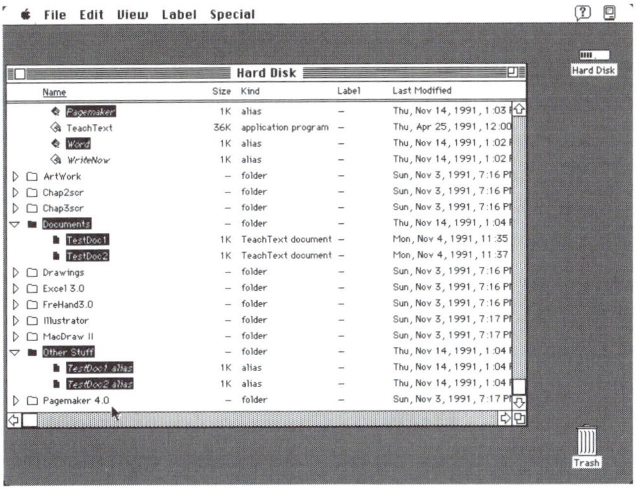

Then you get a list of the Hard Disk window. Folders that have files that match the criteria are open and display their files; the folders and files that match the criteria are highlighted, as shown in Figure 4-17. You may want to enlarge your window to see all of the information. If you do, simply drag the size box in the lower-right corner for this purpose.

Ways to Use Find

Find is useful for a variety of searches. Several of these are listed here:

- By searching on the date created or the date modified, you can find files that need to be erased or files that need to be *backed up* (files that should be copied to a floppy disk for safekeeping off the computer).

- By searching on the kind of file, you can find all the files that were created by a given application or all the aliases.

- By searching on the size you can find all of the files that are above a certain size and therefore are candidates to be removed from the hard disk to provide room for new files.

- By searching on the name you can find all the files that have a common element in a name, possibly for a certain project. Another way to do this is to use the Label menu as described in Chapter 3, "Menus," to attach a common label to all files that relate to a project and then search on a label (use the More Choices dialog box and select Label from the top-left pop-up menu) to find all of these files.

You can also do multiple searches to find exactly what you want. Say you want to find the MacWrite files you created on a certain day. First you search on Kind with "MacWrite" in the top-right field. The item searched is your hard disk and the All At Once check box is checked. After that search is complete, all of the MacWrite files are selected (highlighted). Then you do another Find, searching on the date created equal to ("is") the date you are searching for. The items searched are "the selected items" (the MacWrite files you just found) and All At Once should still be checked. The resulting selected files will be the MacWrite files you created on a certain day.

Getting Around the File System

Except for the just completed Find exercise and a brief mention in Chapter 3, "Menus," all of your work in this book has been "by Icon" view. The icon view is very intuitive and easy to use. If you have even a moderately sophisticated file system, though, of folders within folders, the icon view does not lend itself to finding files that are several folders deep. For this you need to use the hierarchical properties of the list view.

The *hierarchical properties* of the list view, which are new to System 7, allow you to go easily from one folder to another within it, and from there to a third or even a fourth folder within the previous one to see a list of files. It also provides an easy means of moving back up the chain of folders to the first folder or any one in between. Use the following exercise to see how this works:

1. If necessary, adjust what you have on your desktop so that your Hard Disk window is the only one open and you are in icon view.

2. Select the Other Stuff folder, select the File menu, choose Duplicate, and rename the new folder **More Stuff**.

3. Drag More Stuff to Other Stuff so More Stuff disappears inside. Similarly, drag Other Stuff to Documents so it too disappears. You now have a folder within a folder within a folder.

4. Select the View menu and choose "by Name." Your Hard Disk window should look like this:

Name	Size	Kind	Label
▷ ☐ ArtWork	—	folder	—
▷ ☐ Doc Files	—	folder	—
▷ ■ Documents	—	folder	—
▷ ☐ Drawings	—	folder	—
☐ File	37K	TeachText document	—
▷ ☐ PageMaker 4.2	—	folder	—
▷ ☐ SAM 3.0.2	—	folder	—

5. Click the right-pointing triangle next to the Documents folder. The triangle turns downward and the folder and files within the Documents folder are displayed, as shown here:

Name	Size	Kind	Lab
▷ ☐ ArtWork	—	folder	
▷ ☐ Doc Files	—	folder	
▽ ■ Documents	—	folder	
▷ ☐ Other Stuff	—	folder	
☐ TestDoc1	1K	TeachText document	
☐ TestDoc2	1K	TeachText document	
▷ ☐ Drawings	—	folder	

6. Click the right-pointing triangle opposite the Other Stuff folder and then do the same to the right-pointing triangle opposite the More Stuff folder.

Each folder will open in turn showing the hierarchical (stair-stepped) listing of files and folders at each level, as shown here:

```
╔════════════════ Hard Disk ═══════════════╗
║ ▽  ▪ Documents                    6K  folder  ║
║ ▽      ☐ Other Stuff             4K  folder  ║
║ ▽          ☐ More Stuff          2K  folder  ║
║                 ☐ TestDoc1 alias  1K  alias   ║
║                 ☐ TestDoc2 alias  1K  alias   ║
║             ☐ TestDoc1 alias      1K  alias   ║
║             ☐ TestDoc2 alias      1K  alias   ║
╚═══════════════════════════════════════════╝
```

You can close each folder by clicking the downward-pointing triangle so that it again points to the right. You do not have to close files in order; you can jump directly to the Documents folder and close it without closing the folders within it. Using the list in this way you can quickly go through a complex file system and find just what you are looking for.

Closing Windows While Opening Others

If you are working in a window several folders down, you can quickly move to a higher level folder, and either close or not close the folder you are leaving. Follow these steps:

1. In the listing in the Hard Disk window, press and hold the (option) key while double-clicking the More Stuff folder. The More Stuff window opens and the Hard Disk window closes.

The Hard Disk window closed because you held down the (option) key while opening another window. This is a general facility. Whenever you go from one window to another, if you hold down (option), the window you are leaving closes. This also works when you are starting an application. If you hold down (option) while you double-click an application icon, the window you are leaving will close. Finally, if you hold down (option) and click a window's Close box, all open windows will close.

With the Hard Disk window closed, the only way to move to another folder above the current folder, prior to System 7, would have been to reopen the Hard Disk window. With System 7, you hold down the (⌘) key while pointing on the window title and holding the mouse button down. A pop-up menu opens with the folders between the current folder and the Hard Disk as options.

2. Move the mouse pointer to the More Stuff window title, and press and hold both ⌘ and (option) while pressing and holding the mouse button. A pop-up menu of folders will open, as shown here:

Note that the folder icons look like each folder will slip into the folder below it.

3. Choose the Documents folder and release all buttons. The More Stuff window will close and the Documents window will open.

4. Double-Click the Other Stuff folder to open it while leaving the Documents window open. Then press and hold (option) while clicking the Close box on the Other Stuff window. Both the Other Stuff and the Documents window will close as described in the last Note.

Knowing how to easily move around your file system is vital to your effectively using your Macintosh. System 7 has provided several new tools toward that end. If you practice them until they are second nature, file management will be a snap.

Working with Disks

Disks are the principal means of storing information on your computer. Disks store information by writing it on a magnetic surface. Turning off your computer will not affect information on a disk. Once written onto a disk the information stays, regardless of whether the computer is turned on, until the information is erased or written over, either on purpose or by accident. The information can be read from a disk at any time (when the computer is turned on) without removing or erasing the information on the disk.

As you learned in Chapter 1, "Meet the Macintosh," there are two kinds of disks in most Macintoshes: removable floppy disks that store up to 1.44MB, and fixed hard disks that store from 20MB to 400MB or more. (MB stands for *MegaBytes* and can be thought of as one million characters.)

Floppy disks are the principal means of transferring information between computers. New application programs come to you on floppy disks, which you then use to transfer the information to your hard disk. You can also use a floppy disk to transfer information to another computer, even a computer that is not a Macintosh if you have a newer computer with a SuperDrive. A *SuperDrive* allows you to use a *high-density* floppy disk, marked "HD" on its case, that stores up to 1.44MB. A SuperDrive also allows you to read and write disks that can be read or written on an IBM PC.

In addition to the 1.44MB high-density floppy disks, there are two other kinds of floppy disks: 800KB (*KiloBytes* or thousand characters) normal-density double-sided disks, and 400KB normal-density single-sided disks that were used on the original Macintosh and are seldom used any more.

Using a Floppy Disk

A floppy disk has a flexible plastic disk inside a hard plastic case. As shown in Figure 4-18, at one end of the case there is a shutter or sliding door, often made of metal, that, when opened, exposes the flexible disk inside. At the other end of the case, in one corner, is a small, rectangular hole that can be covered with a plastic tab. This is called the *write-protect* or *locking* tab and is used to prevent accidentally writing over something on the disk. On the bottom of a floppy disk is a hub, again often metal, that is used to spin the disk inside the case. On the other side of the disk there is space for a label.

Never touch the flexible plastic disk inside the hard case. The oil from your skin can prevent reading and writing on the disk. Also keep magnets and smoke away from all disks and do not leave floppy disks in the sun or where liquids can spill on them.

Write-Protecting a Floppy Disk

The write-protect tab slides back and forth. When the tab is toward the center of the disk, covering the hole, you can write on the disk. When you slide the tab toward the closest edge of the disk, opening the hole so you can

Figure 4-18. *Top view of a floppy disk*

see through it, the disk becomes write-protected—you can no longer write on it.

Take a look at a disk of your own now and move the tab back and forth. Notice how it clicks into each of its two positions. If the tab does not click, it is not firmly in place.

A floppy disk is write-protected only when you can see through the write-protect hole and the tab has clicked firmly into the open position.

Inserting a Floppy Disk into the Computer

As you saw in Chapter 1, "Meet the Macintosh," the slot on the front of the computer (on the right side for the PowerBooks), is for inserting a floppy disk. To do this, hold the disk so you can see the label on top with the shutter pointing away from you. Also you should see an arrow pointing away from you on most disks. You then slide the disk into the drive, lightly pushing it until the disk snaps into place. When this happens, you hear the disk being accessed and either a dialog box or the Floppy Disk icon shown here appears:

Backup Disk

Don't worry a lot about putting the disk in the wrong way. If you use only moderate pressure, the disk will not go all the way into the drive unless it is properly aligned. Practice inserting a disk into the computer with the following instructions. If possible, use a new, unused floppy disk or one that you know can be erased in preparation for the exercise after this. Follow these steps:

1. Take a new, unused floppy disk or one that you know can be erased. Hold it so the label is on top and the shutter and the arrow on the left are pointing away from you.

2. Slide the disk into the slot on the front or right of your computer. Keep lightly pushing the disk until it snaps into place. You then hear some noise (a whirring sound) from the drive and, after a few seconds, see something on your screen.

   What you see depends on the disk you put in the drive. If you put in a new normal-density (800KB) disk, you will see the message shown here:

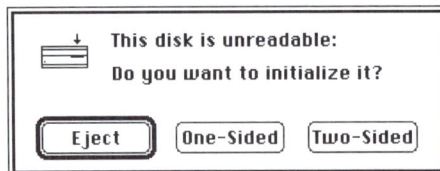

   This disk is unreadable:

   Do you want to initialize it?

   [Eject]   [One-Sided]   [Two-Sided]

   If you put in a new high-density disk you will see a similar dialog box with an Initialize button replacing the One-Sided and Two-Sided buttons. If you put in a disk that has already been initialized you will see the Floppy Disk icon.

3. If you have one of the initialize messages on the screen, click Eject. If you have a disk icon on your screen, select the File menu and

choose Put Away. In either case the floppy disk will be ejected from the computer.

4. Using only light pressure, carefully try to put the disk in the computer every way but the right way. Notice that the disk does not go in more than at most two-thirds of the way when you are abruptly stopped.

5. Slide the disk back into the computer the correct way and notice how the disk is pulled in the last quarter inch just before it clicks into place.

   The feel of this is so different from the feel of putting the disk in wrong that it is almost impossible to make a mistake so long as you use only light force in inserting the disk. (Floppy disks inserted into the PowerBook notebook computers are not pulled in the last quarter inch. You must firmly push them in all the way.)

Initializing or Formatting Disks

Both initializing and formatting mean exactly the same thing—to erase a disk completely and prepare it for use. For a new disk this means dividing up the disk into *sectors* or standard-size areas used to hold information. For a used disk, initializing means erasing all data on the disk and then re-creating the sector division. The key point to remember is that any data on the disk will be lost. While there are several utilities for repairing a mistakenly initialized disk (for example, Norton Utilities for the Macintosh has one), they normally require that the utility be installed before the error occurs and even then they do not always work.

Do not initialize a floppy disk that contains information you want to keep. All your information will be lost.

Use the following instructions to initialize a floppy disk. You should still have the Initialize dialog box or Floppy Disk icon on your screen. If you don't, insert a new floppy now that can be erased.

1. If you have the Initialize dialog box on your screen, click Initialize or Two-Sided depending on the type of disk you are using. If you

have the Floppy Disk icon on your screen, select the Special menu and choose Erase Disk. In any case you will get a message reminding you that you are about to erase everything on the disk, like this one:

```
┌─────────────────────────────────────────┐
│                                         │
│      ⚠    This process will erase all   │
│      !    information on this disk.     │
│                                         │
│                                         │
│   ┌──────────┐          ┌──────────┐    │
│   │  Cancel  │          │  Erase   │    │
│   └──────────┘          └──────────┘    │
└─────────────────────────────────────────┘
```

2. For a new disk, click Erase; for a used disk, click either Initialize or Two-Sided depending on the type of disk you are using.

3. For a new disk you will next get a dialog box asking you to enter a name for the disk. This can be any name up to 27 characters long and can include spaces. Type it now and then press (return).

   In all cases, you will get three messages in succession: "Formatting Disk," "Verifying Format," and "Creating Directory." (Creating a directory sets up an area on the disk that will be used for a list of the disk's contents.)

When the formatting is done, a Floppy Disk icon appears with the name you gave it. You are now ready to copy information to the disk.

Copying Files Between Disks

Copying folders and files from one disk to another is exactly the same as *moving* folders and files within a disk—you simply drag the item between the disks. You don't have to press (option) like you did to copy within a disk. Also, this process prevents you from directly moving items between disks: you must first copy them and then delete the original items.

Practice copying between disks now, by copying some items to your newly initialized floppy disk with these instructions:

1. Double-click the Hard Disk icon to open its window. The window opens in list view sorted by name, as you left it in the last exercise that used the Hard Disk window.

2. Drag the Other Stuff folder icon to the Floppy Disk icon and release the mouse button. As you drag the Other Stuff folder, all of the folders and files that are within it come along, as you can see in Figure 4-19.

   When you release the mouse button you will see a Copy dialog box telling you the status of copying all of the items in the Other Stuff folder, as shown here:

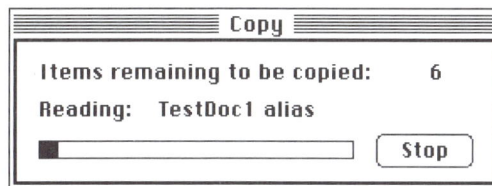

   ```
   ══════════════ Copy ══════════════

   Items remaining to be copied:       6

   Reading:   TestDoc1 alias

   [▓▓░░░░░░░░░░░░░░░░░]    [ Stop ]
   ```

3. When the copying is complete, select the TestDoc1 and TestDoc2 files and drag them to the Floppy Disk icon.

4. Double-click the Floppy Disk icon to open it. Inside you see copies of the items dragged to it, as shown in Figure 4-20.

Figure 4-19.   *Copying items to a floppy disk*

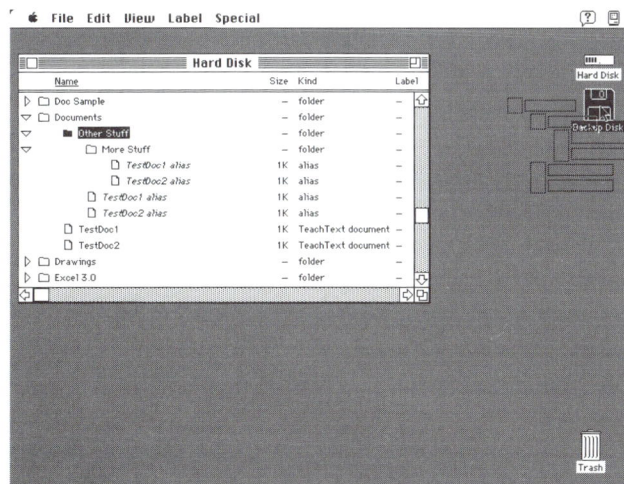

Figure 4-20.   *Items copied to the floppy disk*

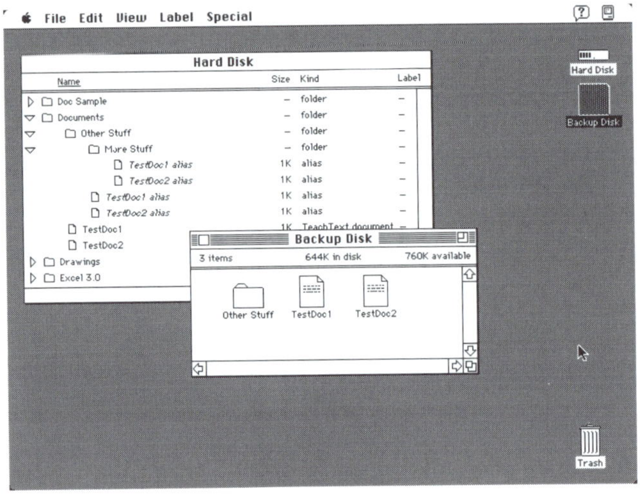

You copy items from the floppy disk to the hard disk in exactly the same way—you simply drag them. Transferring items between a floppy disk and the hard disk and vice versa could not be easier. It is one of the Macintosh's more appealing features.

Backing Up Files and Floppy Disks

Backing up means to make a copy of files and folders so you can remove them from the computer and put them in safe, archival storage. Hard disks and some floppy disks should be backed up to protect their contents from erasure. One way to do this is to use the file copy process you just performed. For hard disks this is rather tedious since they are so much larger than floppy disks. For that reason a number of third-party commercial products are available to speed up and simplify backing up hard disks.

For backing up floppy disks, though, the system software has an shortcut that makes the procedure painless. This process is to take a floppy disk that is the same size (800KB or 1.44MB) as the original, that can be used as a backup disk (all of its current files will be written over) and insert it in the computer. Then eject this disk using the Eject Disk option of the Special menu, which leaves the icon of the ejected disk on the desktop. Next, insert the disk to be backed up and drag its icon to the backup disk's icon. If you have a full floppy disk, you may have to swap the disks several times (go back and forth between the disks), but other than the disk swapping it is a fully automated process. Try it now with these steps:

1. Put a floppy disk whose contents can be copied over in the computer (call this the "new disk"). Don't use the disk that you initialized and copied to earlier.

2. Select the Special menu and choose Eject disk. The floppy disk will eject but the disk's icon will remain on the desktop.

3. Put the floppy disk you formatted and copied to in the previous exercise (call this the "first disk") into the computer. (You may be asked to reinsert the new disk. If this happens, reinsert it, eject it again using the Special menu, and then reinsert the first disk.)

4. When the icon for the first disk appears on the desktop, drag it to the icon for the new disk. A dialog box will appear that looks like this:

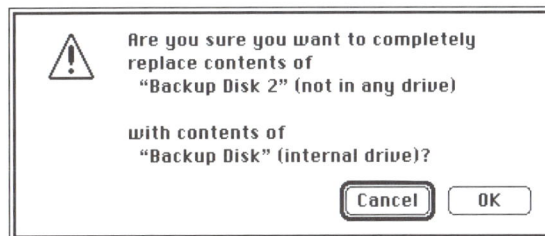

> ⚠ Are you sure you want to completely
> replace contents of
> "Backup Disk 2" (not in any drive)
>
> with contents of
> "Backup Disk" (internal drive)?
>
> [Cancel] [OK]

5. If you are sure the contents of the new disk can be replaced with the contents of the first disk, then click OK. If you are not sure, click Cancel.

6. You will be asked to exchange the disks several times and will be kept informed of the copy process with messages that look like this:

> 🖪🖪 Please insert the disk:
> Backup Disk 2

After a few minutes the backup will be done. It is not the most efficient of processes nor the best use of memory, but it is fully automated. Again, third-party commercial backup products do this better. Among these are Norton Utilities for the Macintosh, and SUM II, both produced by Symantec.

Ejecting Floppy Disks

There are five methods of ejecting a floppy disk from the computer. You have already used two: Put Away from the File menu and Eject Disk from the Special menu. The only difference between these two is that Eject Disk leaves the Floppy Disk icon on the desktop while Put Away does not.

The third way is a shortcut: simply dragging the Floppy Disk icon to the Trash icon. This shortcut is similar to using Put Away in that no icon is left on the desktop.

The fourth and fifth methods are only for emergencies of increasing severity. Method four is to shut down or restart your computer (select Special and choose either Shut Down or Restart). That almost always will eject your disk. The final method, if everything else fails, is to shut down your computer, straighten out a large paper clip and push it gently, using mild force into the small hole on the right of the floppy disk slot. Try the shortcut and shut-down methods now to eject the floppy remaining in your computer and end this chapter. Follow these steps:

1. Select both Floppy Disk icons and drag them to the Trash icon. The floppy disk still in your computer will be ejected.

2. Reinsert the floppy disk into your computer. When its icon appears, select the Special menu and select Shut Down. The floppy disk should again be ejected. If it isn't, turn on and shut down your computer again. If the disk still doesn't eject, use the paper-clip technique.

This chapter has covered the basic tools to easily handle files, folders, and disks. This is a good place to pause. The next chapter will explore the components of System 7 and the Finder.

5

System 7 and the Finder

System 7 is the current version of system software used on Macintosh computers. *System software* allows you to communicate easily with your computer. It provides the visual interface and gives you the ability to perform tasks on your computer via icons instead of typing in difficult-to-remember command names. System software is what makes a Macintosh a Macintosh. The icons on the screen and the way you move them, and the menus and the way they open are just two of the many facets of the Macintosh produced by the system software, which is also called an *operating system*. The two terms are synonymous, but system software is primarily used in association with the Macintosh.

If you have installed System 7 as described in the appendix, "Installing System 7," you know that System 7 is not just one program. Rather, System 7 is a set of programs as well as other items such as screen and printer fonts that are required by the system software. This chapter introduces the system software components and discusses select portions of it. The next two chapters: Chapter 6, "Customizing with Control Panels" and Chapter 7, "Fonts, Printers, and Printing," further discuss other components of system software.

System Software Components

The system software has two major components and five supporting components. The System itself and the Finder are the two primary components, and the five groups of supporting components are extensions, control panels, resources, desk accessories, and utilities. While this list is roughly in order of importance, it doesn't mean that desk accessories and utilities are unimportant. When you need them nothing else can take their place.

The following sections cover each of the seven components or groups of components.

The System

The *System* is the nucleus of the system software. It provides the central core and the structure around which the rest of the system software operates. It provides all of the functionality of menus—how they open, how you choose an option, and how submenus and dialog boxes work. *However*, it does not provide the actual menus. The Finder provides the set of start-up menus and each application provides its own set of menus. The System provides the structure for storing and retrieving information on disks, but the Finder initializes new disks and copies information to and from disks, and the Finder or one of the applications sends information to and from disks. The System provides the basic mechanisms by which the menu and disk capabilities are made available but the Finder or an application lets you actually use them.

The System is the interface between the hardware and all other software. It provides a buffer around the hardware, as pictured in Figure 1-12 in Chapter 1, "Meet the Macintosh." The System provides the mechanism for hardware to perform various functions such as writing on a disk. The Finder and application software use the mechanism to actually accomplish the task.

The application software does not need to know very much about the hardware. Whether you are writing to a floppy disk, a hard disk on your computer, or a hard disk on a computer across a network does not really matter to the application you are using. Similarly, the type of printer you are using does not matter to the application. The application sends the information to be printed to the System and the System, with some help from the appropriate Extension (as you will see in a moment), takes care of making the printer print.

The System has several pieces that operate together to perform its functions. When you first start the computer, you activate a piece of the System that is resident in hardware. This hardware is *read only memory* (ROM) chips on the motherboard or main circuit board and is referred to as *System ROM*. ROM retains its contents even when the power is turned off. When you start the computer, the System ROM is what is controlling the computer. It produces the initial tone you hear and checks the hardware. The System ROM then begins the process of reading in the System from your hard disk.

5

The Finder
Finder

The *Finder* performs two primary functions: being the default application and managing other applications. At the same time, the Finder is an integral part of the System; one cannot run without the other. The Finder's first function—standing in as the default application—makes the Finder the application your Macintosh automatically returns to when you are not using another application. As an application, the Finder provides the basic disk and file management functions that you saw in Chapter 4, "Files, Folders, and Disks." The Finder initializes disks, copies and moves files, and displays, prints, and maintains the file structure that you create.

The Finder also manages other applications as they run, especially when you have multiple applications running. The Finder provides the set of menus and gives you the power to switch among applications. The System side of the Finder provides the means to start applications, put them away when you are finished using them, and to handle their needs for printers and disk files. You'll see some other roles that the Finder plays later in this chapter.

Extensions

The icons used by many *extensions* look like pieces of a puzzle, as shown in Figure 5-1. This is an excellent visual image of what extensions are—add-on pieces (or extensions) of the System. They provide the specific information needed to handle a particular device, such as a printer. The System knows about printers in general, but not the specific details of how a LaserWriter IIf differs from an ImageWriter. To print to a specific printer you must have an extension for that printer.

Included with the system software are a number of extensions for Apple hardware devices and Apple software modules that extend what your Macintosh is capable of doing. Examples include using a particular printer, implementing file sharing, and working with multiple-frame (movie) video.

Figure 5-1. *Extensions icons look like puzzle pieces*

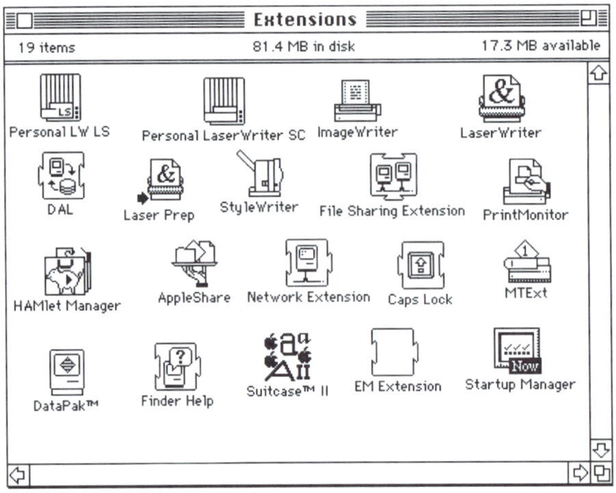

Third-party manufacturers who sell printers and other devices for use with the Macintosh either make their devices *emulate* (operate the same as) Apple devices, or they supply an extension for their device.

There are three major types of extensions included with System 7: those related to printing, to networking, and to communications. The following sections provide a brief look at the extensions in each of the three types.

Printing Extensions

System 7 provides a printing extension for each of the current Apple printers. Printer extensions, which are also called *printer drivers*, give the System the specific information needed to use a particular printer. Chapter 7, "Fonts, Printers, and Printing," discusses the printing extensions in greater detail and tells how to use them.

Networking Extensions

Networking is the exchange of information among computers connected by cables, usually in a local area like a building. The computers are said to be on a *local area network* or *LAN*. The networking extensions, or *networking drivers*, that come with System 7 allow you to connect to a LocalTalk, EtherNet, or Token Ring network and tell the System about your networking plans much as you use a printer extension to tell the System about your printing plans. Chapter 10, "Communications," will go into networking and communications in much greater depth.

Communications Extensions

Communications is the exchange of information between computers, usually over longer distances, using telephone lines and a device called a *modem*. A modem connects your computer to phone lines. To use any of the communications extensions, you typically need a third-party communications application program like Microphone II. The extensions are used to tell the System you are using a modem or alternately just a serial cable for communications, to control how the screen looks, to facilitate mainframe database queries, and to establish the protocol or rules by which data is transmitted. Chapter 10, "Communications," will provide greater depth on communications.

5

Extensions Not Included with System 7

Many software publishers and hardware manufacturers include extensions that provide the necessary information about their products to the System. These extensions come on a disk packaged with the product along with instructions on how to use them. Most of the third-party extensions fall into one of the three types just covered—printing, networking, and communications.

Control Panels

Control Panels

Control panels are the means by which you customize the system to your tastes. As you see in Figure 5-2, there are control panels for just about everything from the color of the screen, to the speed of the mouse double-click, to the sound you hear when the computer beeps at you. Each of these control panels is discussed and its use demonstrated in Chapter 6, "Customizing with Control Panels."

System 7 currently comes with 17 control panels. Some of these are only for special purposes and so are not automatically installed. Others are only for certain Macintosh models. You, therefore, may have more or fewer control panels than those shown in Figure 5-2. Also, there are third-party application programs that are automatically installed when you start up the computer, called *inits*, that have control panels for their settings. You may have one or more of these.

Resources

Resources are data files used by the System that primarily contain fonts and sounds. You may have noticed that the icon for the System is a suitcase. If you double-click the System icon, it opens and displays a number of fonts and several sounds, as shown in Figure 5-3. These are the System's resources. The fonts support System 7's new *TrueType* font technology and are for both the screen and printers. The sounds are alternatives for the standard sound made by the computer. The only other resource file might be a keyboard file to change the key layout. Such a file would come with a foreign or special purpose keyboard. Fonts and TrueType are discussed more fully in Chapter 7,

Figure 5-2. *Control panels for almost everything*

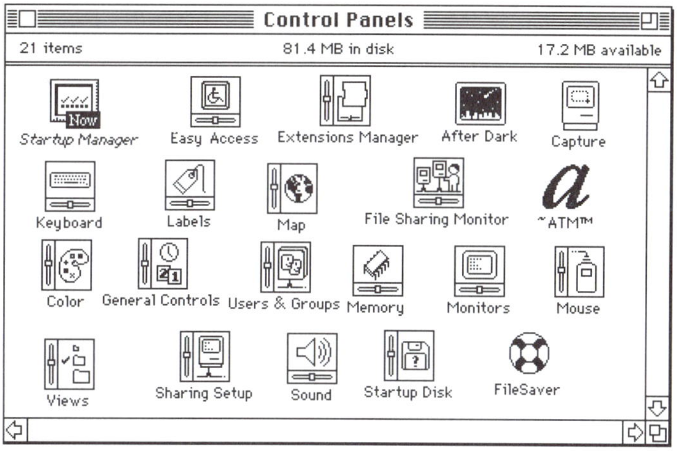

Figure 5-3. *System resources: fonts and sounds*

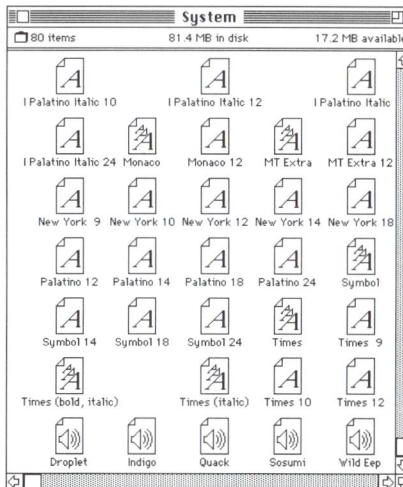

"Fonts, Printers, and Printing," and changing the sound is discussed in Chapter 6, "Customizing with Control Panels."

If you double-click a sound icon you will hear the sound; if you double-click a font icon you will see samples of the font.

Desk Accessories   Apple Menu Items

Desk accessories are small application programs. Seven or eight of these are included with System 7. Like any other application, you can start them by opening their folder and double-clicking the application icon. To make this easier, the desk accessories are kept in the Apple Menu Items folder, shown in Figure 5-4. As you saw in Chapter 3, "Menus," the Apple Menu is available at virtually any time, whether you are using the Finder or another application. Therefore, the desk accessories and any other application or *alias* (the Control Panels folder in Figure 5-4 is an alias, which you learned about in Chapter 4, "Files, Folders, and Disks") that you put in the Apple Menu Items folder is readily available. This is discussed further in "The Apple Menu Items Folder," later in this chapter.

Utilities

There are several application programs that come with System 7 that fulfill some utilitarian function but are not otherwise easily classifiable. These are the *utilities*. They perform such functions as initializing the hard disk (something you *do not* want to casually do), translating files from IBM PC format to Macintosh format and vice versa, looking for and correcting errors on your hard disk, and printing while you are performing other tasks.

The System Folder

The various components of System 7 are usually kept in the System folder. The icon looks like this:

System Folder

Double-click your System folder now to open it and see its contents.

Your System folder may display many, but not all, of the components the System folder shown in Figure 5-5 contains, but probably in a different order. Your folders and files will reflect the applications you have on your computer, and will not match exactly the System components shown in Figure 5-5.

The application files that exist in the System folder are the settings or defaults used by the applications plus the common files shared by several applications such as dictionaries and thesauruses. Folders and files are placed in the System folder because every Macintosh computer has a System folder and the System always knows where it is. Therefore an application can usually find a folder or file it placed in the System folder.

Using the System Folder

From many standpoints the System folder is like any other folder. You can move and copy files and folders to and from other folders in the System folder, and you can make aliases of any of the files and folders in the System folder. Several folders in the System folder, though, have a special use, and

Figure 5-4. *Desk accessories in the Apple Menu Items window*

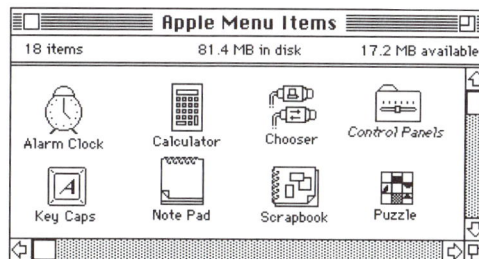

Figure 5-5. *The System folder opened*

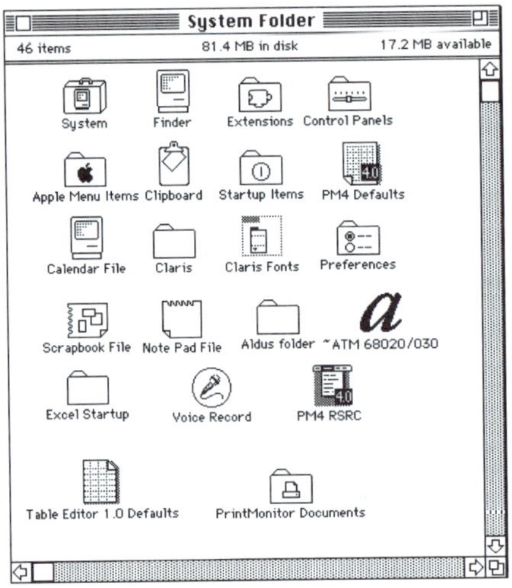

files or folders placed in these special folders are treated in a particular way. The most obvious example of this is the Apple Menu Items folder. Files placed in the Apple Menu Items folder are displayed in the Apple menu which, as discussed previously in the "Desk Accessories" section of this chapter, can be opened at virtually any time.

Letting the System Add Items to the Extensions and Control Panels Folders

The Extensions and Control Panels folders are meant only for files that are extensions or control panels. While you can drag files to these folders, you should let the System do this automatically. That way the appropriate items will get to the right folders. If you close the System folder and then drag the files on top of the System folder, the System will place the files in the right folder for you. You will get a message, similar to the one shown next, that tells you where the System has decided to place the files and asking you to confirm the placement.

> ⚠ Control panels need to be stored in the
> Control Panels folder or they may not
> work properly. Put "Capture" into the
> Control Panels folder?
>
> [Cancel] [**OK**]

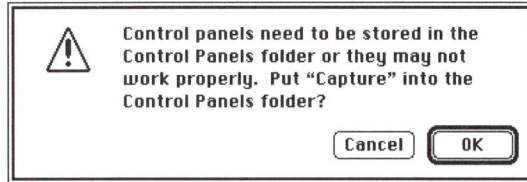

To have the System automatically place an item in the correct folder within the System folder, close the System folder, and drag the item to the System Folder icon.

Applications programmed to work with System 7 automatically place their appropriate files in the correct folder in the System folder during their installation. Older programs simply put their files in the System folder. The older program's files will still work, even inits, but you will have a more cluttered System folder. It's better to live with this than to try and fix it, because the application program may become confused if you drag the file to the folder where it belongs.

The Preferences Folder

The Preferences folder was created specifically to clean up the System folder. The settings or default (preferences) files placed by applications in the System folder are quite numerous on many computers. As new versions of these programs come out, their preferences files will be placed in the Preferences folder automatically.

You should not try to clean up the System folder by dragging older preference or settings files to the Preferences folder. The older applications may not be able to find the files.

Files and folders are added to the Extensions, Control Panels, and Preferences folders automatically. You should not have to worry about them. However, you must add items to and maintain the Apple Menu Items and the Startup Items folders.

The Apple Menu Items Folder

When you are using an application and need to make a note, you can reach the Note Pad quickly by opening the Apple menu and highlighting the

5

Note Pad option. The Note Pad is on the Apple menu because it is in the Apple Menu Items folder. In other words, anything that is in the Apple Menu Items folder is placed alphabetically on the Apple menu. This can include applications as well as documents.

To put an item in the Apple Menu Items folder, you simply drag it there. Although the actual program can be placed in the Apple Menu Items folder, it is probably best to make an alias of an application or a document that is correctly stored with its associated files in its own folder. Then drag the alias to the Apple Menu Items folder and the application will be available on the Apple menu.

One point to keep in mind is that the items in the Apple Menu Items folder are displayed *alphabetically* in the Apple menu. If this becomes a problem, say if you want all your applications before the desk accessories, then place a leading character in the name of each file, such as "a" for applications, and "d" for desk accessories. To carry this a step further, if you want the applications in some order other than alphabetical, then precede them with "a1," "a2," and so on. An example of an Apple menu built in such a way is shown here:

```
About This Macintosh...
  1 Chooser
  2 Control Panels
  a1 Word
  a2 PageMaker
  a3 Excel
  a4 MacDraw II 1.1
  a5 Illustrator
  a6 WordPerfect
  c1 Apple Menu Items
  d1 Alarm Clock
  d2 Note Pad
  d3 Calculator
  d4 Scrapbook
  d5 Key Caps
  d6 Puzzle
```

The Startup Items Folder

Some application programs are meant to be started automatically when you start your computer. These are called inits, as mentioned in the "Control Panels" section earlier in this chapter. Examples of these are Pyro and After Dark screen savers and SAM the Symantec Antivirus Manager. Inits are placed in the Control Panels folder if they have a control panel for setting options or in the Extensions folder if they do not. You often see the icon of one or more inits when you start up a Macintosh.

Other "normal" applications such as word processors, drawing programs, and spreadsheets are usually started only when you need them. However, suppose that you are a writer, a graphic artist, or a financial analyst who frequently uses one or two of these programs every time you use the computer. Why not have these programs started when you start the computer so you don't have to go through the added steps each time?

This is the purpose of the Startup Items folder. If you put an alias of an application or the application itself in this folder, the application will start every time you start your computer. You can put two or more applications in the Startup Items folder, as shown next, and, if you have enough memory, the applications will start and be immediately available to you.

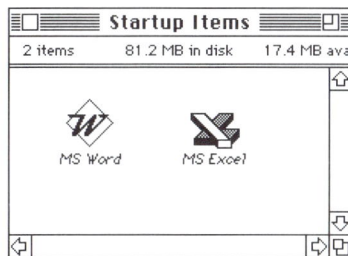

When you put two or more applications in the Startup Items folder, they are started in alphabetical order. The order of appearance of the icons has nothing to do with the startup order. In the preceding example, Excel is started before Word. You can change this by preceding the application name with some other characters, such as 1, 2, and 3 as you did in the Apple Menu Items folder.

Using the Finder

Chapter 4, "Files, Folders, and Disks," discussed the application side of the Finder, the side that initializes, copies, moves, and keeps track of files, folders, and disks. Now take a look at the other side of the Finder, the part that handles applications as they are started and allows you to switch among multiple running applications.

Multitasking—Handling Multiple Applications Simultaneously

Running multiple applications at one time, called *multitasking*, is a standard feature of System 7. In earlier versions of the system software, a separate system program, called MultiFinder, had to be started to do multitasking. In System 7 multitasking is always available.

There are a number of reasons to run more than one application at a time. First, if you have one application working on some process that the computer can run by itself, such as printing or sorting a large file, you can have your computer complete this process while you work on another application that requires your attention, saving yourself some time.

Multitasking is also convenient when you have to switch often among two or more programs. Suppose you need to transfer several tables and charts from Excel to Word using the Clipboard. Without multitasking you must load Excel, open the file, select the table or chart, copy it to the clipboard, close the file and Excel, load Word, open its file, select a location, paste the clipboard contents, and close the file and Word—and you must do this whole routine for each item being transferred. With multitasking, while both applications are running, you need only to click first one and then the other application window to switch back and forth—a significant savings in effort.

Another reason for multitasking is the ability to halt one application and immediately begin another without losing your work in the first application. For example, say you are running one application and you get interrupted by a phone call that requires a second application. With multitasking you start the second application, answer the request, close the second application, and go back to the first without having to put away and then reload the first application and its files.

The penalty for multitasking is that it takes a lot of memory. To run both Excel and Word, depending on the version of each, you need to have 3MB to 5MB of memory. But with the cost of memory dropping considerably, this is not a large penalty and well worth the cost. All Macintosh computers can utilize a minimum of 4MB and most can be expanded to at least 8MB.

Starting Multiple Applications

Starting multiple applications is very easy if the applications are in the Apple menu (as discussed in the "Apple Menu Items Folder" section earlier in this chapter). One of the major reasons for the Apple menu is multitasking. To start multiple applications that are on the Apple menu, you simply need to open the menu and highlight the option for each application you want to start. Try that now with the following steps:

1. Select the Apple menu and choose the Alarm Clock option.
2. Select the Apple menu and choose the Note Pad option.
3. Select the Apple menu and choose the Calculator option.

You now have three applications running, as shown in Figure 5-6. These could just as well be applications such as Word, Excel, or PageMaker as long as you have enough memory to handle them and as long as they or their aliases are in the Apple Menu Items folder.

If the application that you want to start is not on the Apple menu, then you must start it in the normal manner by double-clicking its icon or an alias. If the icon is not visible, you must switch to the Finder (discussed in the next

5

Figure 5-6.   *Three applications running at the same time*

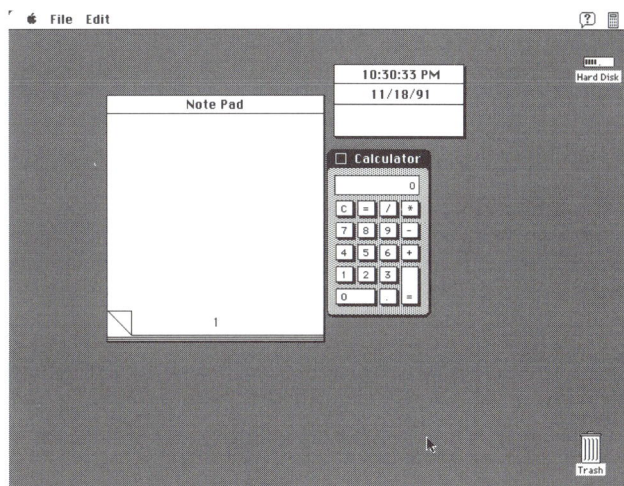

section) and do what is necessary to locate the icon. You can see why the Apple menu is so valuable.

Switching Among Several Running Applications

Once you have started several applications, you need to be able to switch among them. Since you started the Calculator last, it is currently the *active application*. If you type on the numeric keypad, the numbers will go into the Calculator. If you want to switch applications and place a note on the Note Pad, you have only to click the Note Pad and begin typing. The characters will go on the Note Pad. Try that with these steps:

1. With the three desk accessories on your screen and the Calculator as the active application, type some numbers from either the numeric keypad or the shifted numbers across the top of the typewriter keyboard. The numbers go into the calculator.

2. Click the Note Pad and type anything. The Note Pad is now the active application and the characters go on to it.

3. Click the Alarm Clock. It is now the active application.

   If you want to switch to the Finder, click the desktop outside an open window. Besides clicking an application to activate it, there is another way that you saw in Chapter 3, "Menus"—by using the Applications menu on the far right of the menu bar, shown here:

The Applications menu lists all of the applications that have been started including the Finder. The active application has a check mark beside it. You can switch to another application by choosing it from the menu.

4. Select the Applications menu and choose the Calculator. It again becomes the active application.

You can tell which is the active application by a number of indicators:

- The check mark in the Applications menu indicates the active application.

- The icon for the active application replaces the Finder icon as the symbol for the Applications menu.

- The menu for the active application is in the menu bar.

- If the applications overlap, the active application is on top.

- The active application is highlighted on the screen. Its title bar has lines in it, its title is dark, and its scroll bars are turned on, as you can see in Figure 5-7.

5

Figure 5-7. *Three applications with the active one highlighted on top*

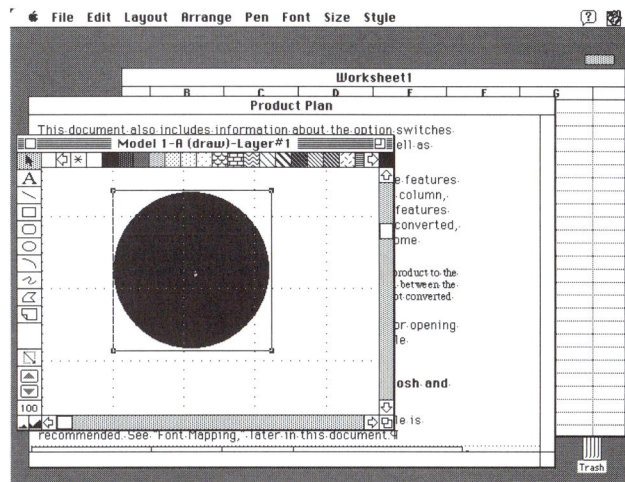

Running in the Background Versus in the Foreground

When you start multiple applications, all are said to be *running*, and in a sense they are. The active application is running in the *foreground* while the other applications are running in the *background*. When many computers run several applications, the foreground is doing something while the background is waiting—that is, not doing anything that requires any of the computer's resources except memory.

System 7, though, allows you to do background processing. With the Calculator in the foreground, note that the Alarm Clock is still running in the background. There are many things that you can do in the background. The following are just a few examples.

- Start a lengthy copy process with the Finder and while it is working switch to another application you have previously started.

When you leave the Finder, the mouse pointer will be a wristwatch icon that tells you to wait. Ignore this and use the wristwatch as a pointer to select the Applications menu and choose the application you want to use.

- Recalculate your spreadsheet. If it is a long process you can switch to another application you have already started.

- Sort a large file. While you are waiting for it to complete you can switch to another running application.

All of these processes as well as others will run in the background. The key, then, to switching to another application while these tasks complete is to have previously started a second application and have it waiting for you. Then all you need to do is to click the second application or switch to it in the Applications menu.

When something is running in the background, your foreground work may be a little slower or you may notice a pause in your work that wouldn't otherwise occur. This is due to the work being done in the background. The more powerful your Macintosh is the less you'll notice this. If your background work needs attention or completes its task, you will either get an alert message or a diamond will appear beside the background program in the Applications menu.

Printing in the Background

System 7 has built into it a special facility for printing to a PostScript printer in the background. Without this facility or a third-party program with similar features, you can't print in the background.

To print in the background you need to turn on background printing in the Chooser window, as shown here:

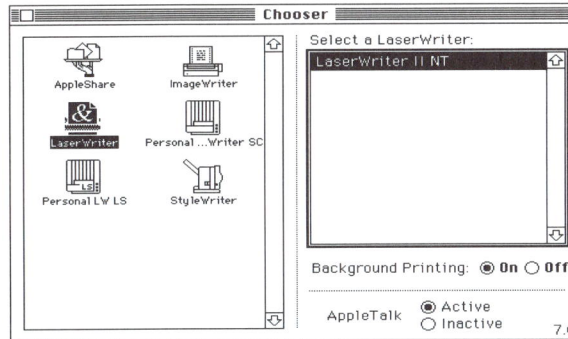

With background printing turned on, when you start printing to a PostScript printer, your printing is stored on disk and then the PrintMonitor extension is automatically started as another application. The PrintMonitor prints the information you stored on disk; you can switch to another application while the printing is in progress in the background. If you want to cancel your printing or see what its status is, choose PrintMonitor from the Applications menu. The PrintMonitor window opens, as you can see here:

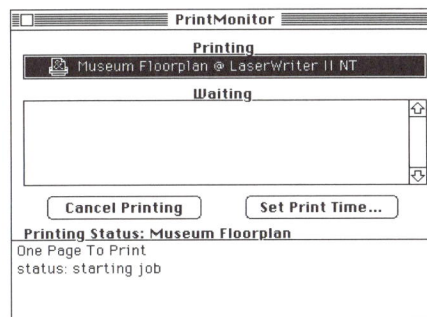

From the PrintMonitor window you can cancel what is currently being printed and set a time to print other files waiting to be printed. To set a time to print, select one of the files in the waiting list using the scroll bar if necessary, and then click the Set Print Time command button. The Set Print Time dialog box opens, with a time and date and a radio button to Postpone Indefinitely. Changing the time and date is similar to setting the Alarm Clock (see "The Alarm Clock" in Chapter 3, "Menus"). Click the element (hour, minute, day, and so on) you want to change and then click the up or down arrows. If you are not sure when you want to print a job, click the Postpone Indefinitely button. The PrintMonitor is discussed more fully in Chapter 7, "Fonts, Printers, and Printing."

Hiding Background Applications

In Chapter 3, "Menus," you saw that the Applications menu had an option for hiding the active application and another for hiding all other applications (Hide Others). The Hide Others option will hide background applications without interrupting background processing. This has two benefits: it cleans up your screen so the screen is less confusing and it speeds some background processing because there is no longer an image to redraw. The negative side to hiding the background applications is that you can't click them to bring them to the foreground—you must use the Applications menu.

Using the Finder with the Keyboard

Almost all of the discussion of the Finder so far has used the mouse to identify what the Finder will work with. System 7 has also provided a set of keyboard shortcuts that allows you to use the keyboard to perform many of the mouse functions. The shortcuts can only be used when the Finder is the active application. These shortcuts, which are listed in Table 5-1, are also listed under the Finder Shortcuts option of the Balloon Help menu.

Use these shortcut keys with the menu shortcut keys to provide extensive keyboard capability.

Table 5-1. *Finder Shortcut Keys*

Task	Shortcut	Comments
Open an icon	⌘-down arrow	Same as double-clicking the icon
Select an icon by name	Begin typing the name	You should need only a few characters
Select the next icon alphabetically	tab	
Select the previous icon alphabetically	shift-tab	
Select an icon to the right or left	right arrow or left arrow	Icon view only
Select an icon above or below	up arrow or down arrow	
Select the desktop	⌘-shift-up arrow	
Open the window that contains the current window	⌘-up arrow	
Open a folder in list view	⌘-right arrow	Expands the hierarchical list
Close a folder in list view	⌘-left arrow	Contracts the hierarchical list
Open all folders in list view	⌘-option-right arrow	Expands the hierarchical list
Close all folders in list view	⌘-option-left arrow	Contracts the hierarchical list
Take a snapshot of the screen	⌘-shift-3	Creates a TeachText graphic image of the screen

5

6

Customizing with Control Panels

Chapter 1, "Meet the Macintosh," said that you can make your Macintosh an extension of you—you can set it up to reflect your personality and operate the way you do. This is very important because the more your computer operates like you, the easier it is for you to use, and the more you can accomplish with it.

Control panels are the facility within the Macintosh that allows you to customize it. *Control panels* are dialog boxes that allow you to set how things look and how they act. For example, you can set the speed of a mouse click and the color of your screen.

There are 15 standard control panels that are automatically installed on all Macintosh computers with System 7. System 7 also comes with three special-purpose control panels that you only install if you need them. In addition, many third-party software and hardware producers supply control panels with their products.

This chapter will cover in depth each of the 15 standard control panels and will look briefly at the three special-purpose control panels. By learning generally how to work with control panels you will also be able to use third-party control panels.

Locating the Control Panels

There are two ways to get to the control panels: by opening the Control Panels folder from within the System folder, as shown in Figure 6-1, and by choosing the Control Panels option in the Apple Menu as shown here:

The Control Panels option is on the Apple menu because an alias of the Control Panel folder is placed in the Apple Menu Items folder during System

Figure 6-1.   *The Control Panels folder opens from the System folder*

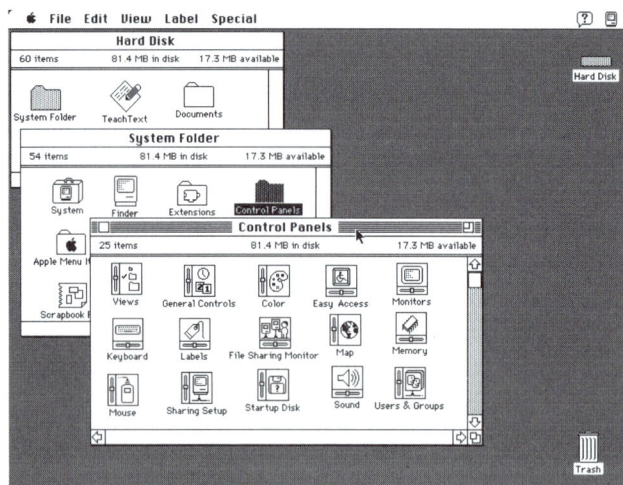

7 installation. This setup of the Control Panels folder, its standard contents, and the alias in the Apple menu are all built for you when you install System 7, without your having to take any extra steps.

As you install application software that has control panels, the control panels are automatically placed in the Control Panels folder, as discussed in Chapter 5, "System 7 and the Finder." Again, you do not have to do anything. As a general rule, you should not manually place files or folders in the Control Panels folder. Let the System do it for you.

Standard Control Panels

The 15 standard control panels are General Controls, Color, Easy Access, File Sharing Monitor, Keyboard, Labels, Map, Memory, Monitors, Mouse, Sharing Setup, Sound, Startup Disk, Users & Groups, and Views. Each of these control panels is discussed in the following sections of this chapter.

In all control panels, you open the control panel, change the settings as discussed in the following paragraphs, and then close the control panel. The changes take effect immediately (in a few cases you must restart your computer) and remain in effect until you change them again.

6

Start now by opening the Control Panels folder through the Apple menu.

1. Select the Apple menu and choose the Control Panels options. The Control Panel folder will open, as you saw in Figure 6-1.

The order of the icons in your folder is probably different than that shown in Figure 6-1. That does not matter.

The General Controls Control Panel

General Controls

The General Controls control panel is where you set the color and pattern of your desktop, the rate the insertion point blinks, the number of times a menu option blinks when it is selected, and the current time and date, as shown in Figure 6-2.

Figure 6-2.   *The General Controls control panel*

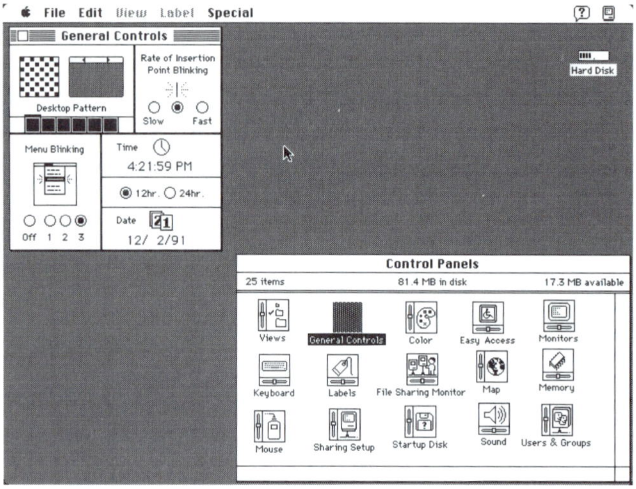

Desktop Color and Pattern

In the upper-left corner of the General Controls control panel are the controls for setting the color and pattern of the desktop. There are three sets of controls.

At the top of the small desktop are two arrows, as shown here:

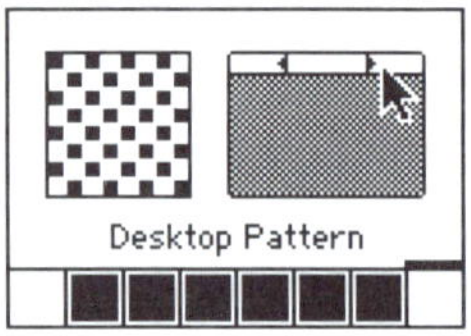

Clicking either of the arrows scrolls you through a series of ready-made patterns. As you scroll through the patterns, they appear on the small desktop. Use these arrows to select the pattern closest to what you want. If you want to see the pattern on the full desktop, click the small desktop.

To the left of the small desktop is a grid in which you can create the pattern you want, as shown here:

By first selecting a color at the bottom of this corner of the control panel and then clicking squares in the grid, you can create the pattern you want by having certain squares one color and other squares another color.

If you don't see the color you want at the bottom of this corner of the dialog box, double-click the color closest to what you want. A Color wheel dialog box will open, as shown here:

To use the color wheel, drag the small circle around the color wheel to the color you want. You can also change the brightness using the vertical scroll bar on the right. Move up within the scroll bar to increase brightness, and down to make it less bright.

When you have the color and pattern you want, click the small desktop to transfer it to the large desktop.

Menu and Insertion Point Blinking

In the upper-right corner of the General Controls control panel you can set the speed at which an insertion point blinks by clicking one of the three radio buttons, as shown here:

```
┌─────────────────────┐
│  Rate of Insertion  │
│   Point Blinking    │
│                     │
│        ⊱|⊰          │
│                     │
│    ○    ◉    ○       │
│   Slow  ▲  Fast      │
└─────────────────────┘
```

In the lower-left corner of the General Controls control panel you can set the number of times a menu option will blink when it is chosen or you can turn this off. The default is three times.

Date and Time

The system date and time are used to put the date and time stamp on files. They are also used in other ways, including producing the current date and time in the alarm clock. Setting the date and time is very similar to setting the alarm clock as you did in Chapter 3, "Menus." You click the date or time element, for example the minutes or the month, and then click the up or down arrow or type a new value to change the element. This illustration shows the minutes being decreased:

```
┌──────────────────────┐
│  Time   🕐            │
│      7:43:40 PM ⬍     │
├──────────────────────┤
│  ◉ 12hr. ○ 24hr.     │
├──────────────────────┤
│  Date   21           │
│       12/ 2/91       │
└──────────────────────┘
```

You can also change whether the clock displays military (24-hour) time, or normal 12-hour time with A.M. or P.M. by clicking the appropriate radio button.

The Color Control Panel

The Color control panel allows you to change both the color given to highlighted text (for example when you edit a folder name), and the color given to a window border.

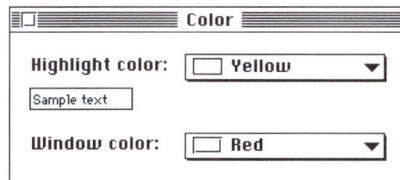

Both of the controls in this control panel are pop-up menus that allow you to choose the color you want. The pop-up menu for the highlight color is shown here:

To change to a new color for either the highlight or the window border, open the menu and drag to the color you want, or choose Other and use the Color wheel to select any color you want.

The Easy Access Control Panel

The Easy Access control panel, shown in Figure 6-3, provides control for three facilities that aid people who have difficulty using the keyboard and/or the mouse. These three facilities are Mouse Keys, Slow Keys, and Sticky Keys.

Figure 6-3.   *The Easy Access control panel*

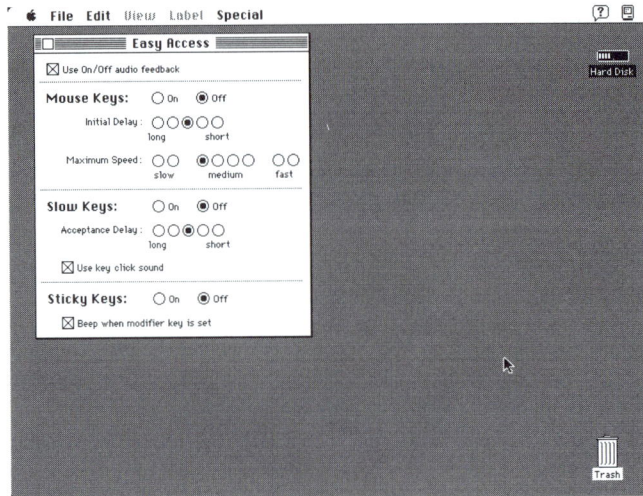

Mouse Keys

With Mouse Keys you replace the mouse with the numeric keypad on the keyboard. This lets you move the pointer, click, double-click, and drag as you can with a mouse, except more precisely. You'll see exactly how to use the numeric keys shortly.

You can turn on Mouse Keys either with the On/Off radio buttons in the Easy Access control panel or with ⌘-shift-clear. Optionally, you will hear a whistle going up the scale when you turn on any of the three Easy Access facilities and a whistle going down when you turn them off. This whistle can be turned on and off by the Use On/Off audio feedback check box at the top of the Easy Access control panel.

Try the Mouse Keys now with these instructions:

1. Double-click the Easy Access icon to open the control panel and then click the Mouse Keys On radio button. You should hear a whistle going up. If you didn't, make sure that the Use On/Off audio feedback check box is checked. If it isn't, click it and then turn the Mouse Keys off and then on again to hear the sound.

2. Use the Mouse Keys, shown in Figure 6-4, to move the mouse pointer around. Use the ⑥ on the numeric keypad to move the pointer to the right. Use the ② to move down, use the ⑦ to move diagonally up and to the left, and use the ③ to move diagonally down and to the right.

   As you move the pointer around, notice how quickly it accelerates and how fast it ultimately moves. You can adjust both of these speeds with the radio buttons below the Mouse Keys On/Off buttons.

3. Use the Mouse Keys to move the pointer to the Short radio button opposite Initial Delay.

   When the pointer is in the Short button, press and release the ⑤ key. This is the same thing as clicking the mouse button. Again, use the numeric keypad to move the pointer around the screen to get a feel for what changing the Initial Delay does for the movement of the pointer.

4. Select the Long Initial Delay button, try it, and then select the delay that is right for you. Similarly, try out the various settings for the Maximum Speed and then pick the one that is right for you.

6

Figure 6-4.   *Mouse Keys*

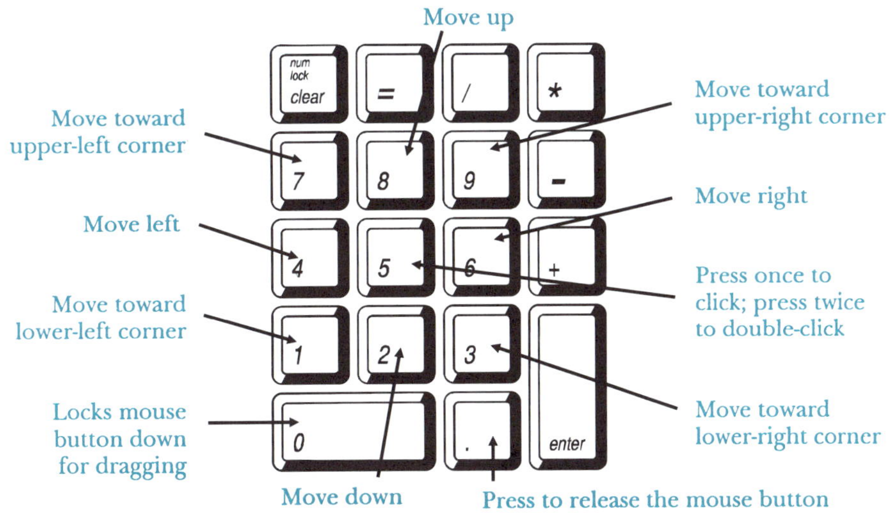

5. Use the Mouse Keys to move the pointer to the Easy Access title bar, anywhere except in the close box. Press and release the ⓪ (zero) key. This locks the mouse button for dragging. Again use the Mouse Keys and notice that you are dragging the entire control panel around the screen.

   When you have moved the control panel to where you want it, press either ⑤ or the decimal point key to release the mouse button and stop dragging.

6. When you're finished using the Mouse Keys, turn them off by either clicking the Off radio button or pressing (clear).

Mouse Keys can be very handy and are particularly useful for exact placement of the pointer or something it is dragging.

Slow Keys

Slow Keys tells the computer to pause between when you first begin pressing a key and its acceptance of the keystroke. You must hold a key down for a period of time for the keystroke to register. This allows you to recover from a mistakenly pressed key. You can adjust the length of the pause to Long, Short, or to one of three pause lengths in between. Also you can turn on or off a double-click sound. If the Use Key Click Sound option is on, you hear a sound when you first press a key and then again a moment or so later when the keystroke is accepted. If you don't hear the second sound, you can release the key and your original keypress won't be accepted by the computer.

You turn on Slow Keys either by clicking the On button in the control panel or by pressing and holding the (return) key for about 8 seconds (you will hear a sound after holding the (return) key for 4 seconds).

1. Turn on Slow Keys now and try it with various delays and both with and without the Use Key Click Sound option. When you are done, turn Slow Keys off.

The key click sound can be very helpful in determining how long you need to hold a key down.

Sticky Keys

Sticky Keys allows you to operate the keyboard single-handedly by letting you press keys one after the other that are normally pressed together. For example, to turn on Mouse Keys, you saw in a preceding section that you needed to press ⌘ shift clear all at once. In other words, you need to press and hold ⌘, while pressing and holding shift, and simultaneously pressing clear. With Sticky Keys you can press these keys one after the other without holding any down continually.

The keys that are held while you press another key are called *modifier keys*. There are four of these keys: the ⌘ key, the option key, the shift key, and the control key.

You turn on Sticky Keys either by clicking the On button in the control panel or by pressing a Shift key five times without moving the mouse. When you turn on Sticky Keys you will notice an icon on the far-right side of the title bar that looks like this:

When you press a modifier key, if the check box is checked, you will hear a sound, and the icon on the far right of the title bar will change to this:

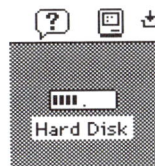

If you want to press and lock down a modifier key so it can be used several times, press that key twice in succession, and the icon on the right will change to this:

The icon will stay like that only until you press another key, but the key will remain locked down until you press the same modifier key again.

1. Experiment with Sticky Keys now by turning it on and then pressing several multikey commands like (⌘)-(G) for Find and (⌘)-(shift)-(clear) for Mouse Keys. Then press a modifier key twice and notice how it stays locked down until you press the same key again.

2. When you are done experimenting, turn Sticky Keys off by clicking Off in the control panel, by pressing a (shift) key five times, or by pressing any two modifier keys at the same time.

The File Sharing Monitor Control Panel

File Sharing Monitor

You can attach your Macintosh to other Macintoshes or other computers and share files and programs with other Macintosh users. The File Sharing Monitor control panel, shown in Figure 6-5, tells you which folders and disks on your computer have been identified as shared and therefore accessible to others and also tells you of any other users connected to your computer.

You identify which folders and disks can be shared by using the Sharing option from the File menu. The process of setting up and using file sharing and allowing users to connect to your system is discussed in Chapter 10, "Communications."

The File Sharing Monitor control panel has one control, a Disconnect button. You can select a user from the list of connected users and then click Disconnect. A dialog box will open asking you how many minutes you want to give the user before disconnecting. Type a number, 0 or greater, and then click OK. The user will be disconnected after the number of minutes you entered, once you click OK.

Figure 6-5. *The File Sharing Monitor control panel*

The Keyboard Control Panel

The Keyboard control panel allows you to adjust the rate at which a key will repeat if it is held down and to adjust the length of the delay before a held-down key begins repeating. Also, if you have an international keyboard you can change its layout with this control panel. Your keyboard may only have one layout option, as shown in this example:

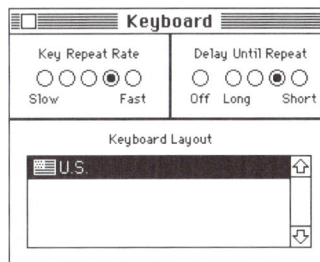

Adjusting How Keys Repeat

A standard feature of all Macintosh keyboards is that most (but not all) keys repeat when they are held down. This is a beneficial feature most of the time. If you have a heavy touch, though, you may find that keys repeat even when you don't want them to. Also you may find that keys repeat so fast that you are getting more characters than you want. Both of these problems can be corrected in the Keyboard control panel. Follow these steps to see how:

1. Start TeachText and try typing normally to see if any keys repeat when they shouldn't.

2. If you do have some repeated keys when you don't want them, open the Keyboard control panel and then under Delay Until Repeat, click one radio button to the left of the current button to lengthen the delay before repeating. Try typing again and see if that cured the problem. Repeat this step if you still have a problem.

3. Try holding a key down and see if you can determine how many characters you get before releasing the key. If you get more characters than you wanted, which is usually the case, then you may want to adjust the repeat rate.

   If you normally only hold a key down for such things as underlining, you probably don't care if you can determine how many times the characters repeat; chances are you want it to be as fast as possible. Otherwise you may want to adjust the Key Repeat Rate to where you can determine how many characters you are getting.

Changing Keyboard Layout

If you have an International keyboard and the software extensions for it, you can change the layout of your keyboard from among several national standards such as British, French, and German. If you have these options, the alternative layouts will be listed under Keyboard Layout in the Keyboard control panel. To use a different layout, click its name.

The Labels Control Panel

In Chapter 3, "Menus," you saw how the Label menu allowed you to attach a label and a color to an icon. This allowed you to group your folders and files into areas that made sense to you. System 7 comes with an initial set of labels and colors, but you can change these with the Labels control panel, shown here:

```
≣▢≣≣  Labels  ≣≣≣
  ▉   Essential
  ▉   Hot
  ▉   In Progress
  ▉   Cool
  ▉   Personal
  ▉   Project 1
  ▉   Project 2
```

To change a label, open the Labels control panel, highlight the label, and retype or edit it to get the label you want. To change a color, double-click the color in the control panel and the Color wheel dialog box will open, as you saw in "Desktop Color and Pattern," earlier in this chapter. Drag the small circle around the color wheel and adjust the brightness to get the color you want.

6

The Map Control Panel

The Map control panel is not really essential, but it is fun to play with. Type in a city in the text box and then select Find. If the city you typed is a major city, it will be found and its location and coordinates will be displayed, as shown here:

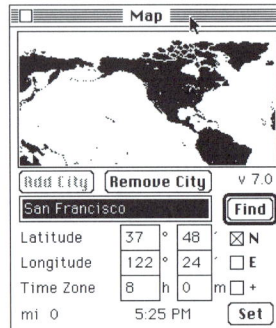

Then click Set to establish this city as the starting point and enter another city. Click Find and the second city will be found, its location and coordinates displayed, as well as the mileage and zone difference between the two cities.

The Memory Control Panel

The Memory control panel allows you to set up to four memory features. These are the amount of RAM to be set aside for disk caching, whether to use virtual memory, 32-bit addressing, or a RAM disk, as you can see in Figure 6-6. Not all Macintosh computers can use virtual memory, 32-bit addressing, and/or a RAM disk; for example, RAM disks are only on Power Books and Quadras. If your computer cannot handle these, your Memory control panel will not show them.

Disk Cache

Disk cache uses memory to hold additional information from your disk. If you are doing a lot of reading from the disk, the cache will significantly speed up what you are doing. Memory, though, that is allocated to disk cache cannot be used for loading programs, so you must decide which is more important to you—disk cache or having more programs resident.

To change the amount of disk cache, click the up or down arrow to get the amount you want. To have the disk cache take effect you must restart your computer.

Figure 6-6. *The Memory control panel*

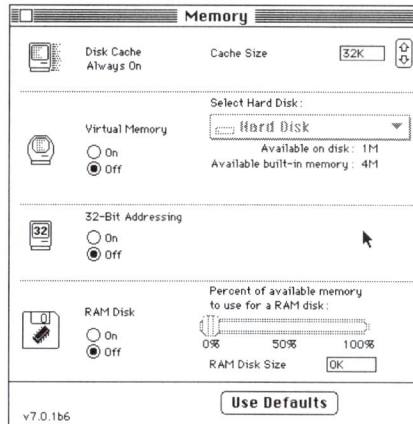

Virtual Memory

Virtual memory allows you to set aside some of your disk space and temporarily place some of your memory contents there to free up memory. This allows you to run programs as if you have more memory than you physically have. Most programs run fine with virtual memory except that they run much slower. Because of the slowness, virtual memory is only used in unusual circumstances such as when you must have two large programs in memory at the same time.

Virtual memory takes up disk space, so you must also consider that. Use the radio buttons to turn the Virtual Memory option on or off.

32-Bit Addressing

With *32-bit addressing* you can address memory beyond 8MB. If your Macintosh can use memory beyond 8MB, 32-bit addressing is a much better alternative than virtual memory. Use the radio buttons to turn the 32-Bit Addressing option on or off.

RAM Disk

RAM disk allows you to use some memory as a temporary disk drive and use it like a disk. If you turn on the RAM Disk option, a Floppy Disk icon appears on your screen with the name RAM Disk and a memory chip in the middle of the floppy, as shown here:

You can drag files and folders to and from this icon, using it as a very fast disk—until you shut down your computer. RAM disk, like all memory, is erased when you turn off the power. You'll be reminded of this if you use the Shut Down option on the Special menu.

RAM disk requires that you drag files or other items on and off it just as you would with a floppy drive. Disk cache, on the other hand, is automatically used by the system.

To return everything in the Memory control panel to its original or default state, click the Use Defaults command button at the bottom of the control panel.

The Monitors Control Panel

The Monitors control panel allows you to determine if you want to display colors or grays and if you want 2, 4, 16, 256, or more of colors or shades of gray. You do this by clicking one of the two radio buttons and one of the numbers of colors, as shown here:

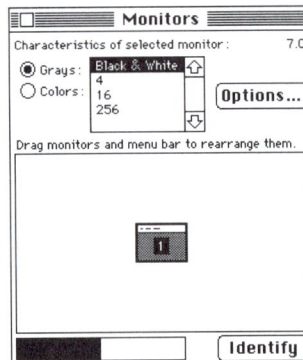

If you are using more than one monitor you can determine their relative position—which monitor displays what part of the screen—by dragging them around the lower part of the control panel. Also, you can determine which monitor has the menu by dragging the little menu to the monitor you want to have it.

The Identify command button puts each monitor's number in the center of its screen and the Options command button gives you information about the type of video card being used.

The Mouse Control Panel

The Mouse control panel allows you to determine the movement of the mouse pointer on the screen and the speed of double-clicking by manipulating these options:

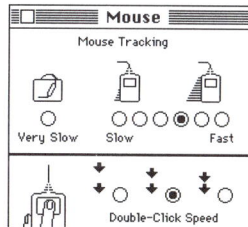

Movement of the Mouse Pointer

You may have noticed that the mouse pointer moves further the faster you move the mouse. As a result, the pointer moves further than the mouse by as much as twice as much. The purpose of the Mouse Tracking control on the Mouse control panel is to adjust the relationship between the movement of the mouse and the movement of the pointer.

In the Mouse Tracking settings, Fast means that the pointer will move more than twice as far as the mouse, depending on the speed of the mouse movement. Slow means that the mouse and the pointer will move about the same distance and the points between slow and fast give you gradations between 1:1 and over 2:1. Very Slow means that the pointer moves at a constant speed independent of how fast you move the mouse so the pointer will not move as far as the mouse has moved if the mouse is moving very fast.

To pick a setting that is right for you, click one after the other and try them out. Note that Very Slow is good for drawing and using a digitizing tablet, but it is not as good for the normal click and drag work of a mouse. Therefore, you may want to use Very Slow just for a drawing session and then switch to a higher speed when you finish drawing.

Speed of Double-Clicking

Double-clicking is sometimes difficult to master. To ease that, a control has been added that allows you to change the speed of double-clicking so it's comfortable for you but still recognized as a double-click by your Macintosh.

1. Click each of the three radio buttons representing the three speeds and watch the mouse button pictured in the control panel. It will blink twice at the rate for the button clicked. For a legal double-click, you must click twice between the first and second blink.

2. Try out double-clicking for each of the rates and select the one that feels best for you.

The Sharing Setup Control Panel

Sharing Setup

The Sharing Setup control panel allows you to identify the owner of the system on which the control panel is displayed as well as the password and computer name for that system. Also, through this control panel you can turn on (Start) or turn off (Stop) both file sharing and program linking, as you can see in Figure 6-7. Chapter 10, "Communications," will discuss these features in depth.

The Sound Control Panel

Sound

The Sound control panel, shown in Figure 6-8, lets you select the sound that will be used as the alert sound, set the volume of that sound, or record

Figure 6-7. The Sharing Setup control panel

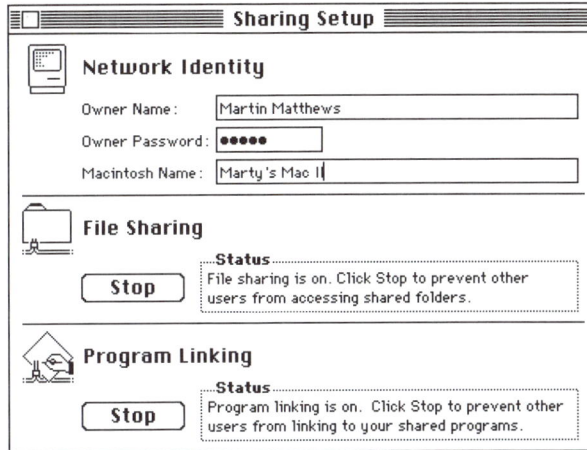

a new sound. The Alert Sounds list box contains a list of sounds you can use as the alert sound. Your list may be different than what is shown in Figure 6-8. Clicking a sound name in the list box will allow you to hear the sound and select the one to be used.

The slide control on the left controls the volume with 7 being the loudest and 0 being no sound at all. Drag the control to the setting you want. When you release the mouse button after dragging, you will hear the alert sound at the volume you have selected.

If your Macintosh has sound input capability, your Sound control panel has some additional controls that allow you to record sounds to be added to your list of sounds. At the bottom of the control panel is one or more icons representing the sound input device or devices that are available. Click the icon you want to use, and then click the Add command button. This will open the Record dialog box with controls similar to a tape recorder, as you can see here:

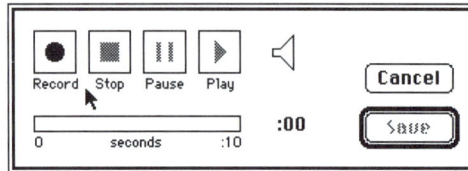

Get ready to produce the sound and then click Record. You have ten seconds to produce it. Click Stop when you are finished and click Play to hear the sound. You can rerecord as many times as you want. When you are happy with the sound, click Save. Type a name for the sound and click OK in the final dialog box that is presented.

The Startup Disk Control Panel

Startup Disk

The Startup Disk control panel allows you to specify which disk is to be searched for a System folder when you start up the computer. If you have only one hard disk, as shown here, you don't need to specify anything:

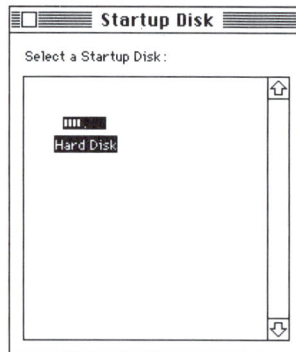

If you have several, though, specifying the one you want searched first will save you time. The icons for each of your hard disks will appear in the control panel. Click the drive you want to use as the startup disk and then close the

Figure 6-8. The Sound control panel

control panel. The next time you start the computer, the disk you chose will be used.

The Users & Groups Control Panel

Users & Groups

The Users & Groups control panel allows you to establish the individuals or groups you are willing to give access to your computer. The "control panel" is really just a window that contains a set of icons for the users and groups that have been allowed access, as shown here:

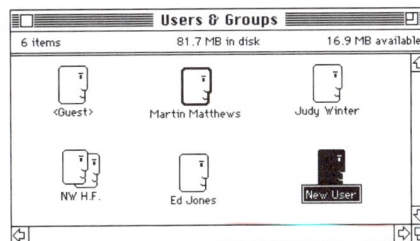

To add a new user or group, select the File menu and choose New User or New Group. A new icon will be created and added to the window. Then double-click the icon and a dialog box will open, like this:

In this dialog box you can set the new user's password and privileges. This process is discussed further in Chapter 10, "Communications."

The Views Control Panel

The Views control panel allows you to specify how the Finder displays folders and files. As you can see in Figure 6-9, the control panel lets you set the font and the font size that are used for icon names and the text in list view. Both the font name and font size are pop-up menus that, when opened, allow you to choose a different font name and size.

You can also specify whether icons should lie in a straight or staggered line and whether you want icons forced onto a grid alignment or left where you place them. Finally, you can determine the size of the icon to be used in list view and the information to be shown in that view.

Figure 6-9. *The Views control panel*

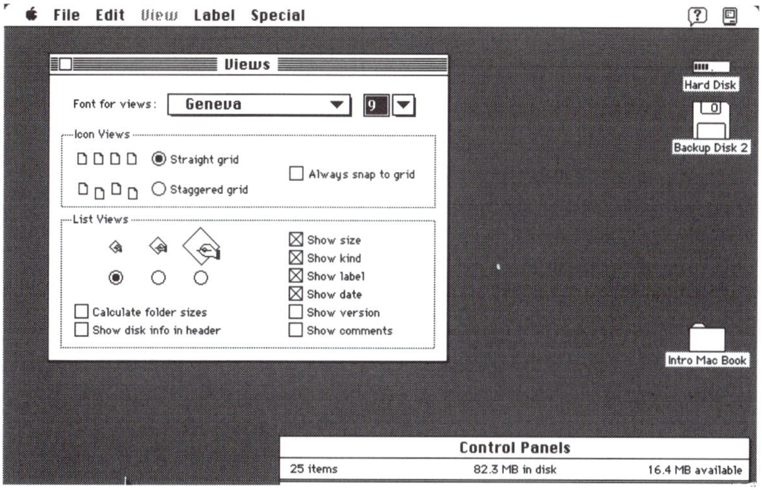

Special-Purpose Control Panels

There are three special-purpose control panels packaged with System 7. The first is Brightness—this allows you to adjust the brightness on a Classic or Classic II computer. The icon for the Brightness control panel is shown here:

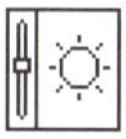

Brightness

The second special-purpose control panel is CloseView. The icon for CloseView looks like this:

CloseView

The CloseView control panel allows you to magnify the screen so it is easier to read. To use it, you must drag the icon from the install disk to your

Control Panel folder on your hard disk and then restart your computer. Then open the control panel to get the screen shown here:

The CloseView control panel has switches to turn CloseView on and off and to turn magnification and keyboard shortcuts on and off. You can also invert the screen, changing it from black on white to white on black, and you can increase and decrease the magnification power from two times (2x) to four times (4x).

The third special-purpose control panel is the Portable control panel used with the PowerBook portable computers. The Portable icon looks like this:

Portable

The Portable control panel allows you to set the amount of time the PowerBook will keep operating ("stay awake") if you are not using it. This helps you conserve battery power. There are two controls for this—one to shut down the System, and the other to shut down the hard disk. (If you are doing tasks that do not often use the hard disk, you should set the controls so the hard disk shuts down earlier than the System.) In either case, when shut down occurs, the memory is maintained so "sleeping" is different than turning off the computer. The other controls allow you to prevent sleeping when the computer is plugged in (when the computer sleeps, it takes a moment or two to wake up and begin operating—like most of us) and to set several modem parameters, such as the baud rate.

7

Fonts, Printers, and Printing

Since its introduction, the Macintosh has been known for its ability to display and print different fonts and styles within a document. One of the foundations of this ability is its unique way of handling fonts. The Macintosh environment offers an enormous variety of fonts with which you can format your documents. You can choose between different font families, such as Times and Helvetica, as well as different font technologies, such as PostScript and TrueType. This chapter provides information on the basics of Macintosh typography to help you make choices that meet your document, equipment, and budgetary needs.

The chapter also discusses printers and printing, with an emphasis on how you control the printing process from the Macintosh screen. You choose a printer with the Chooser desk accessory that comes with your system software. To do this, you must have installed in your system the printer driver (the extension) that corresponds to your printer. *Printer drivers* are programs that allow your Macintosh and your printer to communicate with each other. (You'll learn more about them in the "Printer Drivers" section of this chapter.) Printer connections may be direct or part of a network. This chapter discusses two Macintosh dialog boxes used for printing: the Page Setup and Print dialog boxes. These give you many printing options, some of which are explained in this chapter. Finally, the chapter discusses background printing, a Macintosh feature that allows you to continue with other work while your documents are being printed.

Fonts

A *font* is a specific design of type such as Palatino or Times in a specific size (measured in points), and style (such as italic or bold). For example, 12-point Palatino bold is one font. All the characters in different sizes and styles that make up one design of type such as Palatino are a *font family* or *typeface*. In the computer environment, as opposed to traditional typography, the terms font and typeface are often used to refer both to a specific font and to a whole font family.

Fonts are in disk files; you purchase them, use those that come with your system software, or use special software to create them. Fonts are accessed by the Macintosh from font files located in the System folder, as explained in the "Using Fonts on the Macintosh" section, which appears later in this chapter. You change the font applied to text from within an application as part of your document formatting. Figure 7-1 shows a sample of different fonts.

Fonts can enhance the visual interest and readability of your documents. To make the best use of fonts, however, you need to know some basic typographic design principles as well as the relevant computer techniques.

Depending on how you use your Macintosh, you may be satisfied with the fonts that come with your system software, or you may want to build a font library. If you primarily use the Macintosh to do accounting for your business, for example, the fonts that come with your system may be fine for your needs. If you produce newsletters or other publications, however, you will probably want to use additional fonts.

Font Design Basics

With the wide array of fonts available for your Macintosh, it is easy to go overboard. Unless you are an experienced graphic designer, it is best not to mix many fonts within one document. A lot of fonts on a page can distract

Figure 7-1. *A sampling of Macintosh fonts*

Caslon

Eras Light

Brush Script

(Carta)

Courier

Garamond Italic **Helvetica Bold**

your readers and look unattractive as well. Most documents will use just one or two font families; in a report, for example, you might use one typeface for the main text and another for heads and subheads.

You should also limit your use of all uppercase letters, since they are not as easy to read as upper- and lowercase letters, as shown here:

ALL CAPS ARE HARDER TO READ
THAN UPPER- AND LOWERCASE.

All caps are harder to read
than upper- and lowercase.

All-cap letters are best reserved for headlines or other short selections of text.

Try to match the font to the tone and purpose of the document. For example, you would not want to use Brush Script (shown in Figure 7-1) for the heads in a financial report, but it might be just the thing for a party invitation. Some fonts, such as Times and Helvetica, which came with the first LaserWriter printer, have been overused. If you want to avoid a "computer" look within your documents, you may want to choose a less familiar font. If you are printing spreadsheets for the office financial records, however, the size and the clarity of the font will be more important considerations.

In addition to deciding how many different fonts to use in a given document, you must also choose between sans serif and serif fonts, proportional and monospaced fonts, and different font sizes, styles, and weights.

Serif and Sans Serif Fonts

Serif fonts have serifs or small strokes at the end of the lines that compose each letter; the letters in *sans serif* fonts lack these serifs. In Figure 7-1, Caslon and Garamond are examples of serif fonts and Eras Light and Helvetica are sans serif. Serif fonts are thought to be easier to read, so a good general rule is to use them for large blocks of text, and save sans serif fonts for shorter elements, such as headlines or logos. The serif font New Baskerville is used for the body text of this book.

Proportional and Monospaced Fonts

With *proportional* fonts, as the term suggests, the characters have widths proportional to the widths of the individual letters. This means that a *g* will take up more space, for example, than an *i*, as seen in the word *Light* in the Eras Light font shown in Figure 7-1.

With *monospaced* fonts, such as Courier, also shown in Figure 7-1, each character within a font has the same width. The *i* in *Courier* is given as much space as the *C*. Monospaced fonts are traditionally used on typewriters, and have had limited use in the Macintosh environment.

Font Size

Font size is measured in *points*, which is a measure derived from traditional typography. One point equals 1/72 of an inch. Figure 7-2 shows some different sizes of the Times typeface.

You will notice that a selection of text in one font, such as 12-point Avant Garde, may take up more room on the page than text in a font of the same size in another family, such as 12-point Palatino, as shown here:

Some fonts are wider than others, so the
same text may take up more or less ◄——————— AvantGarde
space.

Some fonts are wider than others, so the
same text may take up more or less ◄——————— Palatino
space.

That is because font size is determined only by the *height* of the characters.
Some fonts are wider than others or have letters that are more compressed
or expanded in width; the amount of room taken up by each letter varies from
font to font.

When choosing a font size, make sure that the characters are large enough
to read easily and that there is enough space between each line of text. The
space between lines is called *leading* or *line spacing*. You adjust this from within
the application. The exact size of font you need and the amount of line spacing
will depend on the characteristics of the font family, the layout of your
document, and the font-handling capabilities of your application.

Figure 7-2. *Different sizes of the Times typeface*

10-point Times

12-point Times

18-point Times

24-point Times

36-point Times

7

Font Style

You can also vary fonts by *style*, such as bold, italic, underline, and shadow. Figure 7-3 shows Palatino with different styles applied. Do not overdo the use of different styles: too much bold or italic is hard on the eyes. Save their use for contrast or emphasis.

Some fonts for the Macintosh come in just roman, or normal text. When you want an additional style such as bold or italic, you apply that style by using menu options or keyboard combinations provided by an application. Other fonts come with a roman version, but also have versions for different styles such as bold, italic, semibold, and so on. Some font families also come in different *weights*; an example of this is Gill Sans, which not only comes as plain Gill Sans and Gill Sans Bold, but also includes Gill Sans Light, Gill Sans Ultra Bold, and Gill Sans Extra Bold. Figure 7-4 shows the different weights of Gill Sans. Some typefaces also include condensed versions, such as Helvetica Compressed, Helvetica Extra Compressed, and Helvetica Ultra Compressed.

Figure 7-3.   *Palatino with different styles applied*

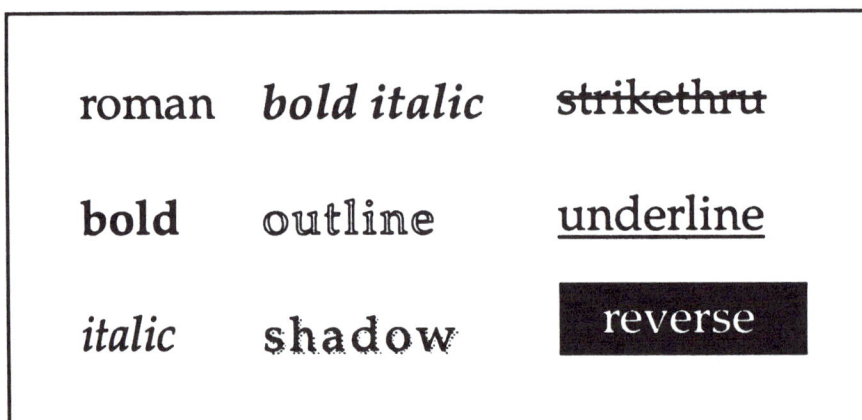

roman   ***bold italic***   ~~strikethru~~

bold   outline   <u>underline</u>

italic   shadow   reverse

Figure 7-4. *Different weights of the same font family*

Gill Sans Light

Gill Sans

Gill Sans Bold

Gill Sans Extra Bold

Gill Sans UltraBold

Special Character Fonts

There are whole fonts that produce symbols or other graphic elements instead of letters and numbers. One example is the font Carta, shown in Figure 7-1, which offers many symbols used in producing maps. Zapf Dingbats and Symbol (which comes with System 7) are two other examples of these kinds of fonts. You apply these fonts just like any other font. To see what symbol corresponds to what key, use the Key Caps desk accessory, as described in Chapter 3, "Menus."

In most fonts, you can also access special characters by pressing certain keys. For example, you get a • (bullet) by pressing (option)-(8)*; you can type the accent marks used in many languages by pressing* (option) *with a letter, like e, followed by the letter alone to be accented—e in this case.*

Customizing Type

With various Macintosh applications, you can also produce special effects with type, such as rotating text, running it around a circle, or creating a three-dimensional appearance. Figure 7-5 shows an example of two effects

7

you can easily produce with type in the Aldus FreeHand drawing application. If this interests you, you can even use an application such as Fontographer to customize or create your own fonts.

Using Fonts on the Macintosh

How fonts are actually used on the computer and with the printer can be confusing, especially since font technology is always changing. Basically, there are two kinds of font files for the Macintosh: bitmapped font files and outline font files. *Bitmapped font* files are used to display text on the screen and *outline font* files are used by the printer for printing. The various fonts used on the Macintosh either work together or coexist quite comfortably, so you can use bitmapped fonts and outline fonts together within one Macintosh system or network.

Figure 7-5.   *Two special effects easily achieved*

Bitmapped Fonts

Bitmapped fonts, which were the first type of fonts available for the Macintosh, are created pixel by pixel (dot per dot) and come in different fixed point sizes. They are used most often to display text on the Macintosh screen, and so are often referred to as *screen fonts*. Note that bitmapped fonts can also be used for printing on printers such as ImageWriters, which have the same resolution (72 dots per inch) as the Macintosh screen. Although you can print with bitmapped fonts on other printers, it is best to use outline fonts for those purposes. Bitmapped fonts, in a variety of sizes, come packaged in files whose icons look like suitcases, as shown here:

Monaco

Outline Fonts

Outline fonts, also called *printer fonts*, are constructed mathematically using the outline of the shapes of characters. They can be *scaled* to almost any size and you can use them with any printer resolution.

The two technologies that use outline fonts with a Macintosh are Post-Script and TrueType. *PostScript fonts* are based on the PostScript page-description language created by Adobe Systems and are designed for use with printers that contain the PostScript language. *TrueType* is a new outline font technology from Apple that was introduced with System 7. It works alongside QuickDraw, the part of the System software that displays text and graphics on the screen. The next sections give you more information about PostScript and TrueType fonts.

7

PostScript Fonts

An enormous variety of PostScript fonts is available commercially from third-party vendors such as Adobe, Linotype, and Bitstream, as well as from users groups and information services. (See Chapter 10, "Communications," to learn more about information services.) In addition to PostScript printers, these fonts can be used with non-PostScript printers that have the proper system extension.

Each PostScript font comes with two types of files: as noted earlier, your system uses bitmapped font files to display text on screen, and your printer uses outline font files to print. Shown here are the bitmapped font file (in the suitcase) and the outline font files for the PostScript typeface Cochin:

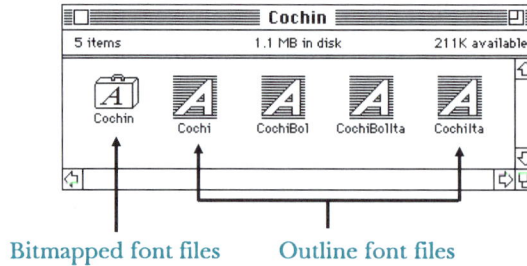

Bitmapped font files   Outline font files

(For more details, see the section "Installing and Using PostScript Fonts" later in this chapter.)

Because PostScript fonts use the fixed-size bitmapped fonts for screen display, they will often look jagged on your monitor. When you use a type size for which you don't have the fixed-size file installed in your system, the Macintosh must scale the closest installed size of the bitmapped font, resulting in a jagged display. You can get a smoother and more accurate screen display of PostScript fonts by using the Adobe Type Manager (ATM) with your System. ATM improves the appearance of your on screen text by using installed outline font software to generate smoother on screen characters for that font. ATM also allows non-PostScript printers to print PostScript fonts. The icon for this utility is shown here:

~ATM™

These show how the screen displays the Stone Serif font first without and then with ATM:

Stone Serif without
ATM.

Stone Serif with ATM.

ATM is accessed from the Control Panels desk accessory under the Apple menu. It comes free with some Macintosh applications, or can be purchased as a separate package. Although you can use ATM on a Macintosh that has TrueType as well as PostScript fonts, ATM has no effect on the TrueType fonts.

TrueType Fonts

While PostScript fonts can be either bitmapped or outline, TrueType fonts come as outline fonts only. They do not have separate screen and printer fonts; each file comes in just one size that is scaled as needed for both printer and screen use. A TrueType font file icon is shown here:

Chicago

TrueType outline fonts are designed to look good both on screen and in print, and with all types of printers. Shown here is on screen text formatted in the TrueType version of the Times font:

This is Times with TrueType.

To compare TrueType's ability to scale for the screen, the bitmapped screen font Times without the use of Adobe Type Manager is shown here:

Bitmapped Times without ATM

System 7 currently comes with the following TrueType fonts: Chicago, Courier, Helvetica, Symbol, and Times. These are shown in Figure 7-6.

7

Figure 7-6.   *System 7 comes with five TrueType fonts*

Chicago

Courier

Helvetica

Σψμβολ (Symbol)

Times

If you want to use other TrueType fonts, you need to purchase them commercially or produce them from other, existing fonts using a utility designed for that purpose, for example Fontographer from Altsys Corporation. You cannot use TrueType fonts with any system prior to version 6.0.7.

System 7 still comes with some bitmapped, fixed-size fonts, such as Geneva. For its screen display, the Macintosh first will always try to use the bitmapped font in the correct size. If that's not available, it then will use a TrueType font as its second choice, then an ATM font, and as a final alternative, will scale a bitmapped font to the correct size.

TrueType Versus PostScript

Since both TrueType and PostScript fonts can exist without conflict in the same System, you do not have to choose between them, but can use both. But why use one rather than the other?

Using the TrueType fonts that come with your system software is simple and inexpensive. You do not have to install or purchase fonts and you can be assured they will look good both on screen and with your printer. They are also a good choice to use with a non-PostScript printer.

However, as discussed earlier in the "TrueType Fonts" section, only a few TrueType fonts currently come with the Macintosh. If you want additional TrueType fonts, you have to buy them or go to the trouble of creating them.

PostScript offers you a much wider variety of high-quality fonts from which to choose. So, if your budget allows, you will probably want to build a PostScript font library. You may already have PostScript fonts, either on disk, or as outline fonts stored in your printer.

If you use ATM, the screen display of PostScript fonts will be as smooth as with TrueType fonts. Also, you do not need to use any particular version of the system software to use PostScript fonts. (For other PostScript printing issues, see the section on "Printers," later in this chapter.) In short, TrueType has not replaced PostScript.

You may have in your System both a TrueType and a PostScript version of the same font, such as Times. If this happens, the Macintosh will use the TrueType version for both screen display and printing.

If you intend to use a font that did not come with your System, you will need to install the font. The installation procedures for both TrueType and PostScript fonts have been greatly simplified with the introduction of System 7, as described in the next sections.

Installing and Using TrueType Fonts

TrueType fonts are all stored in the System file. You can double-click the System file to view them.

Quit all applications before you open your System file to view fonts and before you perform other actions to install or remove fonts.

If you completed your System 7 installation, the fonts that came with the System should already be installed. If you are adding TrueType fonts, just drag the files to the closed System folder. The Macintosh will place them correctly in the System file, after asking if you want them placed there.

You can double-click a TrueType font file to see a sample of that font. Do this with the following steps:

1. Quit any open applications and return to the Finder.

2. Open your System folder and then open your System file.

3. If your System file is not in icon view, select the View menu and choose By Icon so you can easily identify the TrueType files. (TrueType files have three A's and no size in the name.)

4. Double-click a TrueType font, such as the one shown here:

Chicago

You will see a sample of that font, as shown in Figure 7-7.

If you want to remove a TrueType font, just quit any open applications, open the System file, and drag the font file out of the System file and into another location.

Installing and Using PostScript Fonts

PostScript fonts come on a floppy disk (or on a CD-ROM, which will be covered in Chapter 8, "Applications and Transferring Data") with two types of files, one being a suitcase containing bitmapped screen fonts. You can double-click a suitcase icon to see its contents. As noted earlier, you have two types of PostScript fonts: bitmapped and outline. The bitmapped fonts come in different sizes, as shown in Figure 7-8. Remember to quit all open applications before you perform any font installation procedures.

With System 7, the bitmapped fonts go in the System file itself. Before System 7, you had to use the more unwieldy Font/DA Mover to add these screen fonts to the System, but now you can just drag them directly to the System folder. You can either drag the whole suitcase icon into the System folder (this will install all of the fixed-size font files inside the suitcase file), or you can double-click the suitcase icon to open it, and just drag the specific font sizes you want to the System folder.

You can preview a font by double-clicking a bitmapped font file, as shown in Figure 7-9. If you are using ATM, you only need to install one size for each different font. You need these screen fonts to be able to preview text on screen and for the printer to identify what font you want to use.

The second type of PostScript font files is the outline fonts, or printer fonts, which go in the Extensions folder of the System folder. Although you

Figure 7-7. *Previewing a TrueType font*

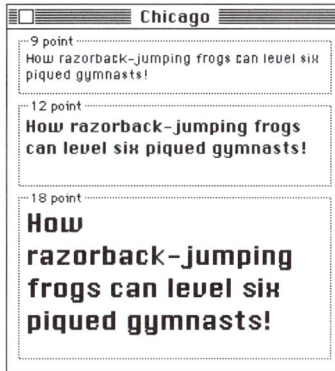

can place the bitmapped font files directly into the System file and the outline font files directly into the Extensions folder, it is much simpler and better to

Figure 7-8. *Bitmapped font files in a variety of sizes*

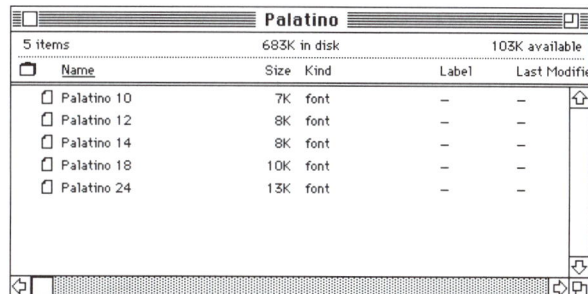

Figure 7-9.   *Previewing a PostScript font*

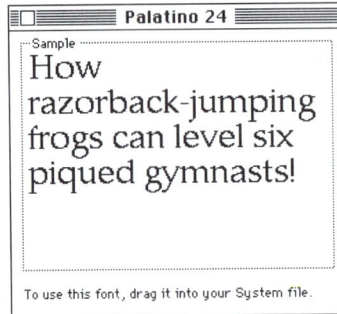

simply drag both types of files to the System folder. You will get a message, shown next, asking if you want to place each item in its correct folder:

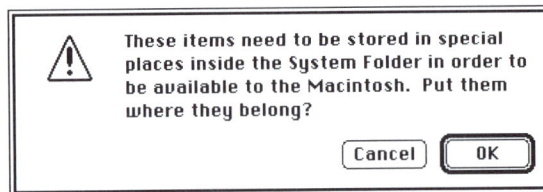

Click OK and the Macintosh will put the files where they belong.

To remove PostScript fonts, open the System file and drag the bitmapped font files to another location. Open the Extensions folder and drag the outline fonts to another location.

Printing with PostScript Fonts   Both the outline and the bitmapped fonts must be installed before you can print properly. You could just install the screen font, however, if you are working on the computer without printing. Also, you do not need to have the outline font in your Extensions folder if it is otherwise available to your printer. For example, with some printers, you can connect a hard disk directly to the printer to store outline fonts.

Also, PostScript printers contain some resident outline fonts, which means you do not need those PostScript outline fonts in your System. All PostScript printers come with at least Times, Helvetica, Courier, and Symbol installed. See your printer's manual to find out about any other resident PostScript fonts.

Outline fonts that you do need get *downloaded,* or sent, to your printer during the printing process. This happens automatically when the fonts are in your System. These automatically downloaded fonts are erased from your printer's memory after each printing job so they do not continue to take up a portion of your printer's memory.

PostScript fonts frequently come with each style or weight of a font family as a separate font file, such as Garamond Light, Garamond Bold, and Garamond Bold Italic. They will appear on your font menu as separate fonts. Because of their customized design, it is best to use them as they come; that is, apply the font Garamond Bold to your text rather than using Garamond Light and then adding bold formatting.

Resources for Fonts   Service bureaus often maintain large PostScript font libraries, so you can apply and print the font at the service bureau when you do not want to purchase a particular font. Remember, however, that if you do not have the bitmapped screen font on your own Macintosh, you will not be able to preview that font on your Macintosh screen. Since line and page breaks change depending on the font, you will need to spend some formatting and proofing time at the service bureau.

Managing Your Fonts

A system with a lot of fonts will require a lot of disk storage space as well as memory (RAM). One way to keep disk usage under control is to use the Suitcase II utility from Fifth Generation Systems. In addition to other features, it allows you to load fonts into your system as you need them. Or you could keep only the most frequently used fonts in your System folder and store the others on floppies to use as needed.

You can use different Macintosh utilities to create, organize, and preview fonts. One example of such a utility is Adobe Type Reunion, which groups each PostScript font family into one main menu item with a submenu listing the different styles. This does not save memory, but it does save you time and effort when you are applying styles from your font menu. For example,

7

instead of Berkeley Medium, Berkeley Black, Berkeley Black Italic, and Berkeley Book Italic listed as separate items on your font menu, there will be one menu option, "Berkeley," with the other Berkeley fonts accessed through a submenu, as shown in Figure 7-10.

Printers

Printers for the Macintosh use different technologies and also differ in terms of speed, resolution, and cost. See the discussion of printers in Chapter 1, "Meet the Macintosh," for more information about ink-jet, dot matrix, and laser printers, as well as imagesetters. High-resolution imagesetters (which produce typeset quality text and graphics) can print to film for a photographic negative as well as directly to photographic paper. Color laser printers and imagesetters are also available.

When deciding on a printer, you will find a wide variety made both by Apple and by third-party vendors. If you are buying a laser printer, you will need to decide between a PostScript and a non-PostScript printer. PostScript

Figure 7-10.   *The Font menu using Adobe Type Reunion*

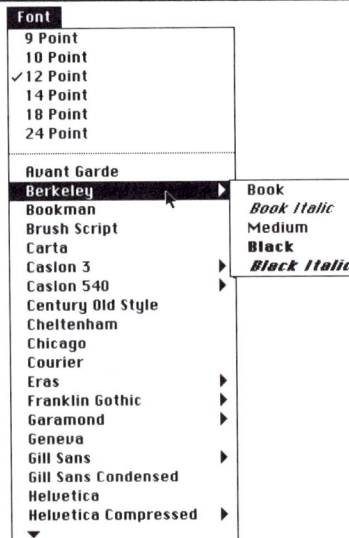

printers are generally more expensive because Adobe Systems receives a royalty for the use of the language inside the printer. A PostScript printer is necessary when your work involves applications based on that language, such as the PostScript drawing applications Adobe Illustrator or Aldus FreeHand. You will not get the same results when you print these complex illustrations on non-PostScript printers.

If you do not have a PostScript printer, you can use your printer to proof your graphics or other files and then go to a service bureau and print your final output on a PostScript printer. (See the discussion later in this chapter for more on doing this.) If you have an ImageWriter, StyleWriter, LaserWriter IISC, Personal LaserWriter LS, Hewlett-Packard DeskWriter, or one of many other non-PostScript printers, you can use Adobe Type Manager when you print files that contain PostScript fonts.

Exactly which printer you should get depends on the kind of work you do; whether one computer or several will be connected to the printer; and what your other needs are in areas such as cost, speed, printer memory, and resolution.

Attaching a Printer

Printers for the Macintosh are connected to the computer either through the Macintosh serial ports (the modem or printer port), the AppleTalk port, or the SCSI port, depending on the specific type of printer. The printer's manual will provide the specifics of what port to use and other connection information. Refer to Chapter 10, "Communications," for more information on using a printer with an AppleTalk network.

Printer Drivers

To print, your System folder must contain the printer driver that is appropriate for your printer. Printer drivers are part of the system software. System 7 comes with Apple printer drivers that work for a variety of Apple and non-Apple printers. The icons for some of these Apple printer drivers in the Chooser window are shown in Figure 7-11. Some third-party printers come with their own printer drivers.

7

Figure 7-11.   *Printer drivers displayed in the Chooser window*

When you install System 7 using Easy Install, printer drivers are automatically installed in the Extensions folder. If you need to add an Apple or third-party printer driver for any reason, just drag the printer driver icon into the System folder. You will get a message asking if you want the file placed in the Extensions folder, as shown here:

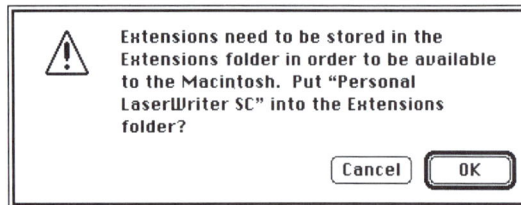

Click OK. Alternatively, you can install the printer driver by using the Installer utility that comes with the System 7 printing disk. When you install a LaserWriter printer driver, you should also install the PrintMonitor application (described later in this chapter).

Networks with Both Systems 6 and 7

If you are working on a network that has Macintosh computers running both System 6 and System 7, you can still print to the same printer. However, you will need to make sure that all the computers have the updated System 7 printer driver.

The Chooser

The Chooser, which is automatically installed with System 7, is a desk accessory that comes with your system software. It allows you to specify the printer to which you want to print, as well as other output devices such as AppleTalk file servers. You can also use the Chooser to adjust some print settings.

To change any Chooser settings, you first need to open the Chooser by selecting the Apple menu and choosing Chooser. The Chooser window appears, as shown in Figure 7-11.

On the left of the Chooser box, you select the type of device to which you want to send your output. If your Macintosh is on a network linked to other networks, you also choose the zone from the left side of the Chooser window.

After you have selected a printer type (or other kind of output device) from the left side of the Chooser, you then make a choice from the right side. For some printers, such as the ImageWriter and the StyleWriter, the right side of the Chooser window offers a choice of the printer port or modem port. Click the icon that represents the port where your printer is connected.

For printers that can be networked together, the right side will present a list of the available printers of the type you selected on the left even if you only have one of those devices, as shown in Figure 7-12.

Choose the name of the specific printer you want to use. For example, there may be five LaserWriter printers connected on a network; you could choose to print to any of them. You can tell the difference between them because a user can give a name to a printer with Apple's Namer utility. Maybe you usually print to the printer named Arizona because it is closest to your desk. You may want to use another printer on a particular day because someone else is printing a huge report on Arizona. You can switch to the

7

Figure 7-12.   *Choosing an available printer*

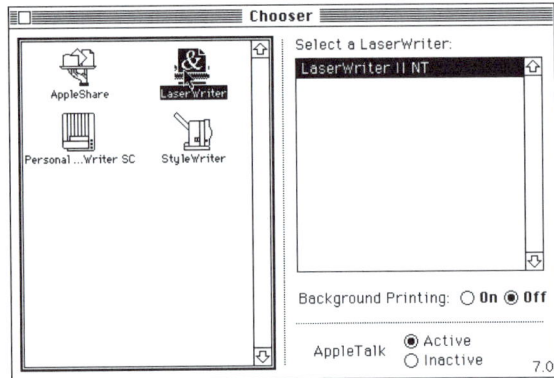

printer named Alaska by opening the Chooser, clicking the LaserWriter icon, and then clicking "Alaska" in the list of LaserWriter names on the right.

When you are done making your selections, click the close box of the Chooser to close the window. Your Macintosh will continue to output your documents to the printer you specified with the Chooser until you select another device in the Chooser window.

Note that you also turn background printing on and off from the Chooser. (See the discussion on this feature later in this chapter.)

LaserWriter Font Utility

You can use the LaserWriter Font Utility (shown next) that comes with System 7 to perform several printer-related functions.

LaserWriter Font Utility

For example, you can prevent printing of the annoying sample page each time you turn on a LaserWriter by following these steps:

1. Make sure you have the LaserWriter Font Utility on your hard disk or on a floppy disk on your desktop.

2. Start the LaserWriter Font Utility program by double-clicking its icon.

3. Select the Utilities menu and choose Start Page Options.

4. Click Off to turn off the sample page, as shown in Figure 7-13.

5. If you want to start the sample page again, open the utility, choose Start Page Options, and click On.

With the LaserWriter Font Utility, you can also manually download fonts and PostScript files and restart a LaserWriter printer.

Printing

You can print your files while you are working in an application, for example, Microsoft Word; you can also print them from the Finder. In addition to printing your documents, you can print the contents of an active Macintosh window as well as what appears on the screen at any given moment.

Figure 7-13. *Turning off the LaserWriter start page*

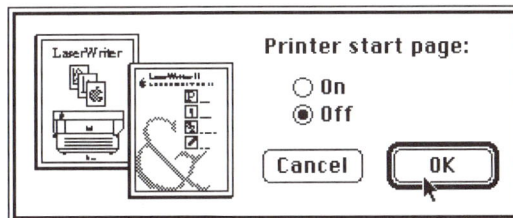

Printing Window Contents and Screen Shots

You can print the contents of specific windows from the Finder by following these steps:

1. Make sure the window you want printed is active.

2. Select the File menu and choose Print Window, as shown in Figure 7-14.

3. Select options from the dialog box that appears and click OK. The contents of the window will be printed in whatever is the active view; for example, a group of icons or a list of files organized by date.

Printing a window can be a helpful tool for keeping track of which files you have in which folders and on which disks.

If no windows are open, the Print Window command will change to read "Print Desktop". You can then choose that option to print the contents of the desktop.

You can also take and print a *screen shot* (also called a *screen dump*) of what is on the current Macintosh screen. Just press the key combination ⌘-shift-3 and the Macintosh will create a PICT file showing what was on the screen at the time you pressed the keys. You can create this kind of file from the Finder

Figure 7-14.   *The File menu's Print Window option*

or from within an application. You can open and print the file in TeachText or in other applications that support this file format. There are also third-party utilities, such as Capture from Mainstay, that provide tools to take screen shots. Screen shots are especially useful when you are providing training to others on how to use the Macintosh. Most of the figures in this book are screen shots created with Capture.

Printing Your Files

When you are working in an application, you usually print the active file by selecting the File menu and then choosing the Print option. The Print dialog box appears; in it you select printing options and then click OK to print. (The Print dialog box and its options are discussed later in this chapter in the section on "The Print Dialog Box.")

Some applications have more than one printing option in the File menu. For example, MacPaint offers two printing options, Print Selection and Print, so you could print the whole document or just a selected portion. When you're in HyperCard, the File menu offers four printing options, as shown in Figure 7-15.

While you are printing, a message box is displayed on the screen to let you know printing is ongoing. Depending on the application, the message box may contain a Cancel button, allowing you to stop the printing of the document at any time. If there is no Cancel button, you can usually press ⌘-(period) to cancel the printing operation, as suggested in the message box from Microsoft Word shown here:

7

```
Printing "My Memo"

To cancel, hold down the ⌘ key and type a
period (.).
```

You can print the files from the Finder by following these steps:

1. Select the file or files you want to print by clicking their icons. (If you want to print more than one file, they all need to be the same kind of file—all from the same application.)

Figure 7-15.   *HyperCard print options*

```
 File
 New Stack...
 Open Stack...        ⌘O
 Close Stack          ⌘W
 Save a Copy...

 Compact Stack
 Protect Stack...
 Delete Stack...

 Page Setup...
 Print Field...
 Print Card           ⌘P
 Print Stack...
 Print Report...

 Quit HyperCard       ⌘Q
```

2. Select the File menu and choose Print.

3. Make the appropriate choices in the Print dialog box and click OK. See Figure 7-16 for an example of this dialog box.

4. The application will open and the document(s) will print.

You still need the application that created the documents on your disk to print from the Finder.

If you are working on a network, see Chapter 10, "Communications," for information on working with printers and print servers.

Printing Problems

If you have trouble printing, there is often a simple solution. First check to make sure that the cables connecting the Macintosh to the printer are

Figure 7-16.   *The Print dialog box*

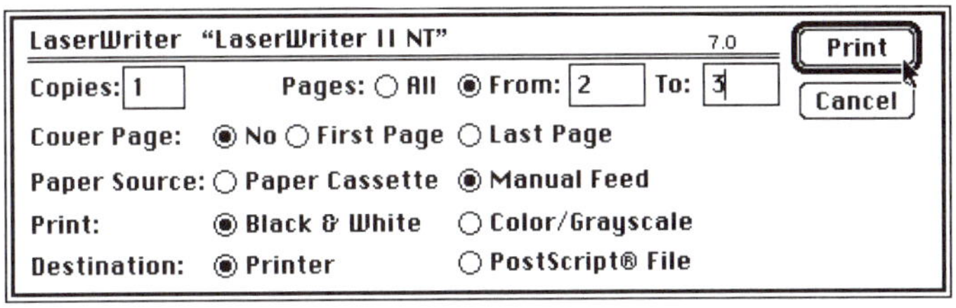

```
┌─────────────────────────────────────────────────────────────┐
│ LaserWriter  "LaserWriter II NT"              7.0   ┌ Print ┐ │
│ Copies: 1          Pages: ○ All  ◉ From: 2  To: 3  └───────┘ │
│                                                    ┌ Cancel ┐│
│ Cover Page:   ◉ No ○ First Page ○ Last Page        └───────┘ │
│ Paper Source: ○ Paper Cassette ◉ Manual Feed                 │
│ Print:        ◉ Black & White  ○ Color/Grayscale             │
│ Destination:  ◉ Printer        ○ PostScript® File            │
└─────────────────────────────────────────────────────────────┘
```

attached correctly. Then check the Chooser to see if the appropriate printer is selected. If there is no icon for the type of printer you are using, then you probably do not have the correct printer driver installed. If the icon is there, but your particular printer does not show up in the list on the right of the Chooser window, the printer might not be on or warmed up or the cables may be disconnected. If nothing else works, try turning the printer on and off. Doing this will, however, cancel any print jobs that might be waiting in line to be printed.

Depending on the application and the problem, messages may be displayed on the screen when there are specific problems, as shown in this printing message in PageMaker:

> Printer "LaserWriter II NT" needs attention: out of paper.

You will find that some documents, especially those that contain many downloadable fonts or complex graphics, will take a long time to print. You may sometimes need to print long graphics-intensive documents a few pages at a time instead of all at once.

The Page Setup Dialog Box

In most applications, the File menu contains the Page Setup option. The Page Setup dialog box contains choices that let you choose how a document is printed on the page (for example, you can choose the *orientation*, which means whether the page is printed normally or sideways, you choose the size of the paper you'll print on, and so on). The choices vary depending on the type of printer, since different printers handle printing differently. These options may also vary depending on the application. For example, the Microsoft Word 4.0 Page Setup dialog box (shown in Figures 7-17 and 7-18 for different printers) contains the Document button that takes you to a Document dialog box where you can set page margins and other document settings. The Macintosh knows which dialog box to display based on the printer you have selected in the Chooser.

If you want to change the default settings for these options, select the File menu and choose Page Setup. The Page Setup dialog box appears. Figure 7-17 shows a Page Setup dialog box for the LaserWriter.

From this dialog box, you specify the paper size by selecting one of the sizes next to the radio buttons or using the pop-up menu of other paper sizes. You can also reduce or enlarge how the image on the screen will be printed on paper; the default is for the image to be printed at 100 percent.

With the Orientation settings, you can select vertical (portrait) or horizontal (landscape) paper position. Vertical is the norm—most letters are printed in

Figure 7-17.   *The LaserWriter Page Setup dialog box*

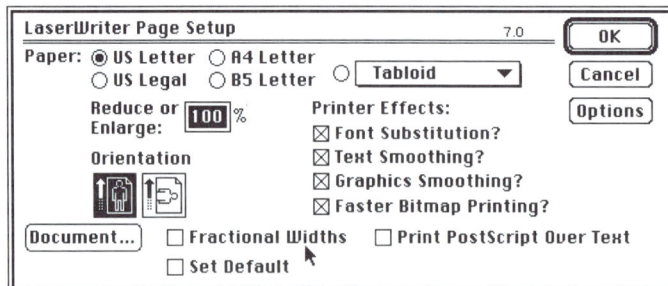

Figure 7-18. *The ImageWriter Page Setup dialog box*

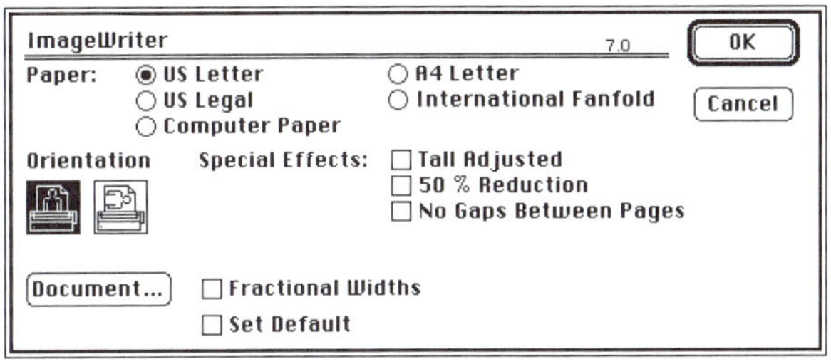

vertical orientation, for example, so vertical is therefore the default; you can print the image sideways on the page with the horizontal option. Several options under Printer Effects, such as text and graphics smoothing, enhance printing on a LaserWriter. The Options button displays more printing options for that printer.

When you first install a new printer driver or switch to a different type of printer in the Chooser, you need to open the Page Setup dialog box and confirm or change the settings. These settings will remain in effect until you change them.

7

The Print Dialog Box

Like the Page Setup dialog box, the Print dialog box differs based on the type of printer as well as on the application you are using. Compare the Microsoft Word Print dialog box shown in Figure 7-19 to the Aldus PageMaker Print dialog box shown in Figure 7-20.

You can move around a Print dialog box, just as in other Macintosh dialog boxes, by pressing the (tab) key.

The options shown in Figure 7-19 are common to what is listed here; you will see these in the Print dialog box for laser printers using the LaserWriter printer driver.

Figure 7-19.   *The Microsoft Word LaserWriter Print dialog box*

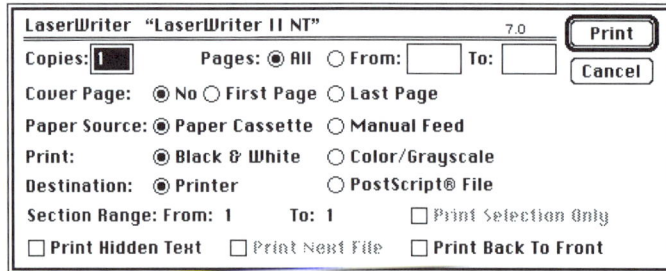

```
LaserWriter   "LaserWriter II NT"                    7.0    ┌──────────┐
┌────────────────────────────────────────────────────      │  Print   │
Copies:█         Pages: ⦿ All  ○ From:      To:            └──────────┘
Couer Page:    ⦿ No ○ First Page ○ Last Page              ┌──────────┐
Paper Source: ⦿ Paper Cassette ○ Manual Feed               │  Cancel  │
Print:        ⦿ Black & White    ○ Color/Grayscale         └──────────┘
Destination:  ⦿ Printer          ○ PostScript® File
Section Range: From: 1     To: 1        ☐ Print Selection Only
☐ Print Hidden Text    ☐ Print Next File    ☐ Print Back To Front
```

- In the first text box, you type the number of copies of each page that you want to print, with the default being 1.

- In the Pages area, you can specify that all pages of a document be printed or only a range of pages. If you want to print pages 3 through 6, you would type **3** in the From text box and **6** in the To text box. If you want to print only page 3, enter **3** in both the From and the To text boxes.

Figure 7-20.   *The Aldus PageMaker LaserWriter Print dialog box*

```
Print to:  LaserWriter II NT                         ┌──────────────┐
                                                     │    Print     │
Copies:  █    ☐ Collate  ☐ Reverse order             └──────────────┘
                                                     ┌──────────────┐
Page range: ⦿ All  ○ From 1   to 1                   │    Cancel    │
                                                     └──────────────┘
Paper source: ⦿ Paper tray ○ Manual feed             ┌──────────────┐
                                                     │  Options...  │
Scaling: 100 %  ☐ Thumbnails, 16 per page            └──────────────┘
                                                     ┌──────────────┐
Book: ○ Print this pub only ○ Print entire book      │ PostScript...│
                                                     └──────────────┘

Printer: LaserWriter II NT              Paper: Letter

Size:        8.5 H 11.0   inches    Tray:  ⦿ Select
Print area:  8.0 H 10.8   inches
```

- Sometimes you may wish to feed paper manually into your printer; in that case, select Manual Feed.
- You can select black-and-white or color/grayscale printing, depending on the type of document you are printing.

In some applications, as in the Microsoft Word and PageMaker dialog boxes, you can reverse the order of how the pages are printed so the last page will be printed first.

Figure 7-21 shows a Microsoft Word Print dialog box that is displayed if you have chosen the StyleWriter in the Chooser. Notice that some of the options differ, even from within the same application.

Proofing and Printing a Document on Different Printers

You may sometimes use a Macintosh connected to one printer to create your document and then use a different printer to produce your final document. For example, you may use a Macintosh connected to an ImageWriter at home to write a report, but plan to print the final report on a laser printer at a service bureau, at school, or at work. Different types of printers, such as the ImageWriter and LaserWriter, print the same file differently, in terms of the line and page breaks. This means that if you carefully format the

7

Figure 7-21.   *The StyleWriter Print dialog box*

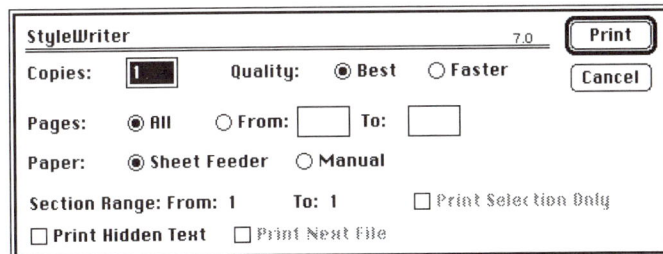

document based on the ImageWriter settings and then print it on a laser printer, you may be unpleasantly surprised with ugly line and page breaks.

One way to avoid this problem when you are working on your own Macintosh is to select the printer that you will use for your final output in the Chooser. As long as you have the appropriate printer driver installed, it does not matter that you are not actually connected to that printer. If you do this, your document will have the same line and page breaks on the screen that it will have when printed on that final printer. Of course, you must then print on the printer you selected in the Chooser. For example, if in the Chooser you select to print to a LaserWriter when the Macintosh is actually connected to an ImageWriter, you will not be able to print to the ImageWriter unless you change the Chooser settings.

You will not have this problem if you are moving between a PostScript laser printer and an imagesetter. Except for the difference of resolution (which can affect the appearance of such graphic elements as lines and patterns), the imagesetter will print your file exactly as it is printed on the laser printer.

Background Printing

If you use the Macintosh's Background Printing feature, a document is sent to the printer while you do other work. The Macintosh sends the information in amounts that the printer can handle; while the printer processes that information, you can be working in another application instead of waiting for the printing message box to disappear from the screen.

You can use the Background Printing feature with LaserWriter printers and with other printers that use the LaserWriter printer driver. This is a feature that you may or may not want to use. Even though you can continue working, the performance of your application is often slowed while background printing takes place. Also, you may just want to print your document at that moment and have it in front of you before you go on to other work.

To use background printing, you need the PrintMonitor file shown here in your System folder:

PrintMonitor

The PrintMonitor file will already be installed if you used the System 7 Easy Install. If it is not in the Extensions folder, just drag the icon from the system software Printing Tools disk to the System folder. The Macintosh will place it in the Extensions folder.

You turn background printing on and off in the Chooser, as shown in Figure 7-22. Once on, it will remain on until you turn it off and vice versa.

The PrintMonitor Application

You control how background printing works with the PrintMonitor application, which opens when you begin to print using the Background

Figure 7-22. *Background printing selected in Chooser*

Printing feature. If you want to change certain settings or to view the PrintMonitor window, select PrintMonitor from the System 7 Application menu while you are printing a document, or double-click the PrintMonitor icon when you are not printing. The PrintMonitor window appears, as shown in Figure 7-23. It shows the name of the document currently being printed as well as any documents waiting to be printed.

You can click Cancel Printing to stop the current printing job. If you want to cancel a printing job that is in the Waiting list, just click the name of that document, then click Remove From List, which is what the Cancel Printing button changes into.

You can click the Set Print Time button to choose a time when you want the document to be printed. You can also select the PrintMonitor File menu and choose Preferences to set options for manual feed jobs, for the handling of printing errors that may be encountered, and for display of the PrintMonitor window, as shown in Figure 7-24.

Figure 7-23.   *The PrintMonitor window*

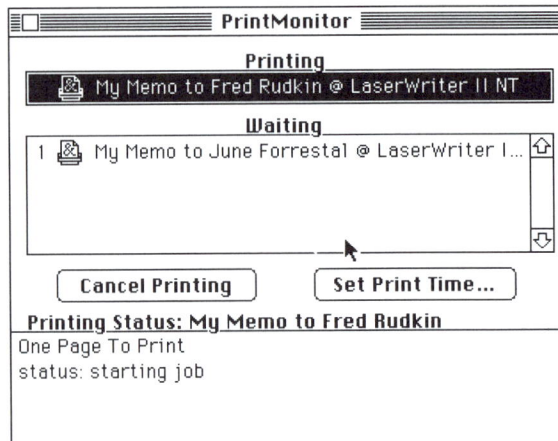

Figure 7-24.   *The PrintMonitor Preferences dialog box*

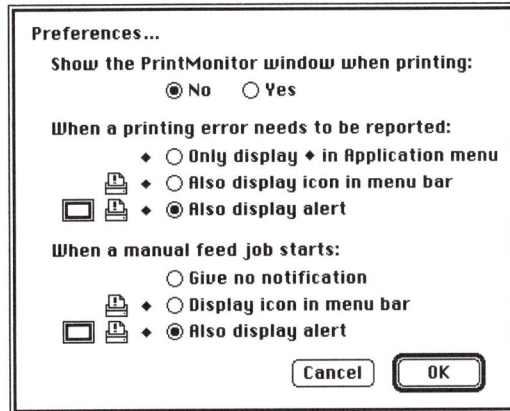

In this chapter, you have learned how to select and use fonts on the Macintosh. In addition, you've gotten an overview of printers and the printing process, including the Chooser, the Page Setup and Print dialog boxes, and background printing. The next chapter covers the different types of applications available for the Macintosh and some of the ways you'll work in Macintosh applications.

7

8

Applications and Transferring Data

It is hard to believe that there was ever a time when there was a shortage of Macintosh applications, given the number of applications from which you can choose today. The programs available allow you to perform a wide range of activities, such as managing large projects, designing a house, preparing your income taxes, backing up your hard disk, or even learning photography. Applications are designed for different levels of user skills and needs, for a wide range of budgets, and to work with varied hardware systems.

Because applications designed for the Macintosh share the same visual user interface, you perform many of the same tasks in the same way in various applications. That makes it easier to learn new applications as well as to share information between applications. This chapter describes some of the categories of software available to you and then discusses some of the menu options that are found in most applications. A brief tutorial gives you a chance to practice using some of the commonly used menu options, text entry, and editing techniques. Finally, you'll learn how to transfer information between Macintosh applications.

Application Basics

Application software instructs the computer to perform specific tasks, such as drawing, page layout, or word processing. System software, on the other hand, controls the basic operations of the hardware, such as what you see when you turn on your computer. System software provides the foundation you need to be able to work with any application. (See Chapter 1, "Meet the Macintosh," for more information about the differences between system software and application software.)

Like system software, applications come on one or more floppy disks along with printed reference manuals. Applications that take up a lot of storage space sometimes come on *CD-ROMs* instead of on floppy disks. (CD-ROM stands for Compact Disk Read Only Memory; these are plastic disks that can each store up to 550 megabytes of information. You can't change their contents—that's why they're called "read only"—and you need a CD-ROM drive connected to your computer to use them.) In addition to the actual program file, the application disks may also include additional files, such as tutorial files, templates, or sample files, or other files such as the dictionaries used with a spelling checker.

Not all applications work with all Macintosh computers. Certain applications require a certain model, such as a Macintosh II, while others are designed for color monitors. You should make sure you have sufficient RAM to run your applications, since some require more working memory than others. How many applications you can have open at the same time also depends on how much RAM you have installed. You may want to add more RAM, especially if you like to have two applications that use a lot of memory open at the same time during your work sessions. Otherwise, if you try to open an additional application, you may get a message that there is insufficient memory to open that application. To proceed, you would need to quit one of the open applications.

Types of Applications

A variety of applications for the Macintosh are available from commercial vendors. You can also obtain many applications from user groups and information services. (See Chapter 10, "Communications," for more information about using information services.) Some of the more common categories of applications are described here, with specific products given as examples.

Frequently some overlap exists between types of applications, so an application in one category may contain features thought of as belonging to another software type. For example, spreadsheet applications may also contain database management tools and many word processing applications have some page layout capabilities. So depending on what you need to accomplish, one package may meet diverse software requirements.

Word Processing

Word processing applications let you enter, edit, and format text to produce all sorts of documents from letters and memos to reports, manuals, and books. Spelling checkers included with word processing applications look for misspelled words, giving you some electronic assistance in the proofreading of your documents. Print merge features allow you to print individualized letters to those on your mailing list. Graphics created in other applications can be integrated into documents in many word processing applications. Some of the popular word processing applications for the Macintosh are Microsoft Word, WordPerfect, and MacWrite II. An example of a typical word processing document is shown in Figure 8-1.

Page Layout

With page layout applications, you can combine text and graphic elements on the screen to produce newsletters, flyers, ads, catalogs, business cards, magazines, menus, and many other publications. These desktop publishing applications have helped to change the print industry and are one of the reasons the Macintosh has become so popular. In page layout applications such as Aldus PageMaker, FrameMaker, and Quark XPress, the cutting and

8

Figure 8-1.   *A word processing document*

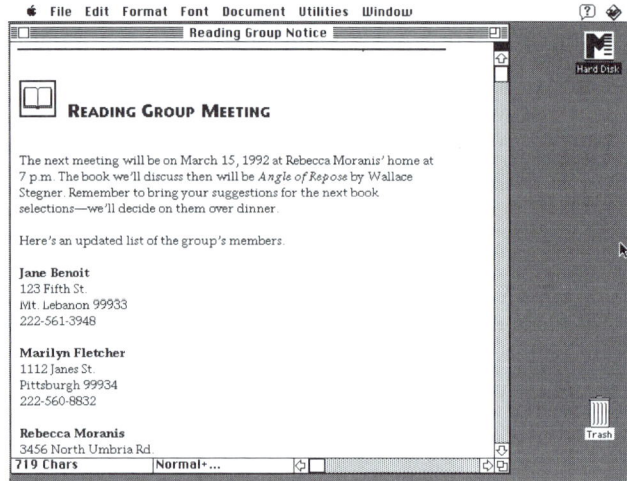

pasting of text and graphic elements are done on the screen instead of by hand. Frequently you import text and graphics created in other programs, although most of these applications also include some word processing and drawing tools.

Spreadsheets and Financial Management

Spreadsheet applications organize data in on-screen rows and columns. Figure 8-2 shows an example of a worksheet file that includes a bar chart. These applications provide the means to analyze, project, compute, chart, and organize financial and other numerical information. You can use spreadsheet applications such as Microsoft Excel and Lotus 1-2-3 for the Macintosh for a range of activities from adding and then updating a single column of figures to performing complex financial projections to creating charts for a report. Business financial management software packages for the Macintosh offer comprehensive accounting tools, while applications designed for personal finances allow you to perform such tasks as charting trends in the stock market, managing your personal budget, preparing your tax forms, and even writing your will.

Databases

You use databases, such as 4th Dimension and FileMaker Pro, to organize and access information such as customer lists, personnel records, inventories, and so on. With databases, you can enter, find, update, sort, analyze, and report information. Database files can be linked so that if data in one file changes, another is automatically updated. Database applications vary in complexity; some are designed for the beginning user while others are more appropriate for computer consultants who produce customized databases for highly specialized purposes.

Figure 8-2. **A spreadsheet document**

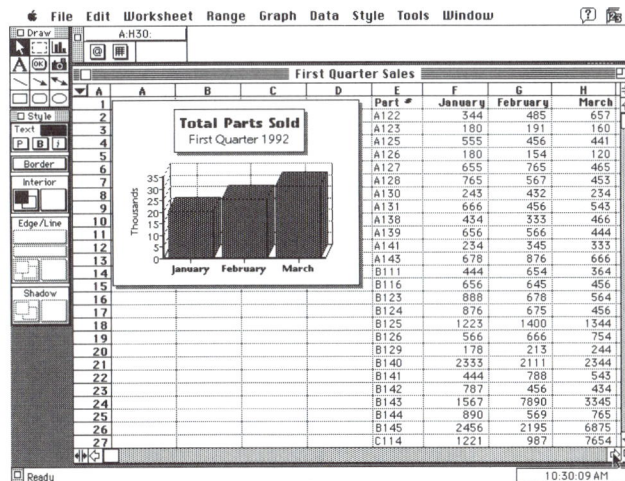

Integrated Programs

Integrated programs, such as ClarisWorks and Microsoft Works, combine different types of applications into one package. For example, both ClarisWorks and Microsoft Works include word processing, graphics, database, spreadsheet, and communications tools in their packages. In any of the integrated programs, you simply switch back and forth between the different types of applications. Integrated programs provide the basic features for each of the applications included and so can be an especially good choice for beginners.

Utilities

Utilities are mini-applications that customize or help you work with your computer. They are like add-ons to your operating system. Some utilities are desk accessories; they're accessible from the Apple menu at any time. Other utilities are inits, so called because they are loaded when you start up (or restart) your computer. You will probably find some utilities that are indispensable; some that are helpful but not absolutely necessary; and others that you have little use for.

Screen savers, such as Berkeley Systems' After Dark and Pyro! from Fifth Generation Systems, are inits that automatically display moving images when the screen has been idle for a certain period of time. This prevents screen burn in, a permanent ghost image on the screen, which means that damage has been done to your monitor.

Virus detectors, such as Symantec's SAM, are also inits that check disks for computer viruses and repair infected disks. Figure 8-3 shows SAM's Virus Clinic window after it has scanned all of the contents of a hard disk and a floppy disk.

Other products, such as Norton Utilities for the Macintosh, are designed for protecting and recovering data on your hard disk. Still other utilities provide tools for making backups, compressing files, organizing the contents of your hard disk, and performing myriad other tasks. These are just a few examples of the large number of available utilities. Be careful, however, not to go overboard in using them. Running a multitude of utilities can sometimes mean they conflict with each other, causing problems for your System.

Figure 8-3. *A virus detector utility dialog box*

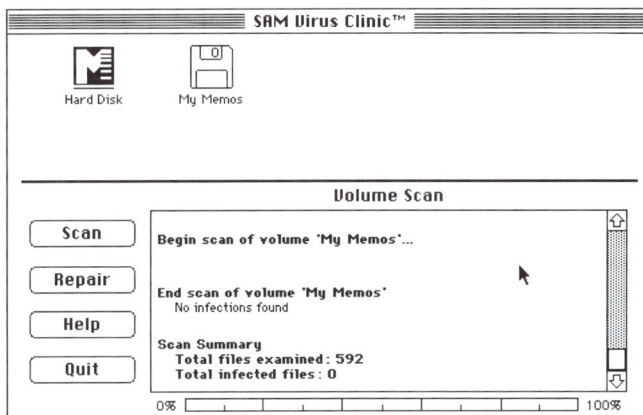

Graphics and Design

The general category of graphics and design contains many different types of applications. You can create and modify artwork with painting applications such as Studio 8 and MacPaint, or drawing applications such as MacDraw and Canvas. Figure 8-4 shows an illustration created in a painting program.

In painting applications, bitmapped images are created dot by dot (or more exactly, pixel by pixel) with tools that resemble traditional artists' tools such as brushes and erasers. With drawing programs, you work with basic shapes and lines to create images called *object-oriented graphics* because you manipulate the drawn object, not the elements (lines and curves) that create it. Some painting and many drawing applications support the use of color.

A wide range of graphics applications exist, ranging from programs specifically for printing professionals to those for beginning graphics users. Sometimes you may want to work with photographs or other existing two-dimensional artwork. You can transform such artwork into Macintosh files with the use of a *scanner*, a piece of hardware that connects to a Macintosh.

Figure 8-4.   *An illustration created in a painting program*

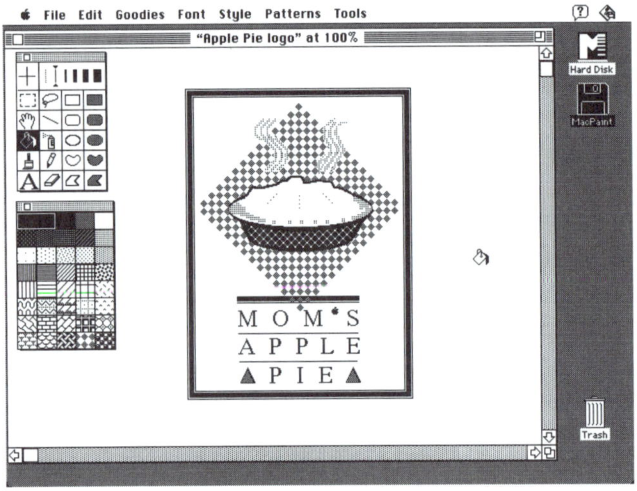

You put artwork or photos into the scanner much as you would into a photocopying machine, and the scanner translates the image into a graphics file your Macintosh and graphics applications can use. You can then modify that artwork on screen or simply paste it as is into your documents. (You don't have to own a scanner to use one; scanning is a service offered by many service bureaus.)

With image processing applications, you can enhance black-and-white and color photographs that have been scanned into your Macintosh. These applications, such as Digital Darkroom and Adobe Photoshop, have tools to perform image editing tasks such as color-correcting or changing contrast and brightness. There's more: You can take advantage of clip-art disk libraries when you want illustrations but do not have the time or skills to create your own. You can simply copy these illustrations or modify them to suit your needs.

Color pre-press applications are employed to prepare color artwork for printing. Architects, engineers, and others use computer-aided design (CAD) applications for two- and three-dimensional drafting. Three-dimensional modeling and rendering applications are frequently used to create images that will be used in animated sequences.

Presentations

With applications such as Aldus Persuasion and Microsoft PowerPoint, you can create black-and-white or color on-screen presentations that your audience can view on a computer or via overhead projections (for the latter, you simply copy your computer screens onto transparencies). You can also use special equipment or send your onscreen presentation file to a service bureau to create 35-mm slides.

Multimedia

Multimedia applications offer a way to combine text, images, animation, sound, and video; some or all of these elements can be combined in a multimedia presentation. This category encompasses different types of applications, including animation, sound, and video applications, as well as interactive media applications.

MacroMind Director and FilmMaker are two examples of animation applications in which the user can create color or black-and-white presentations with animated sequences and other graphics, sounds, text, and special effects.

HyperCard, which comes with your Macintosh, is another multimedia tool used to create interactive presentations. (See Chapter 9, "HyperCard," for a full description of HyperCard and examples of some of its many uses.) Often used for educational purposes, interactive multimedia presentations allow users to view information in a set sequence and to research a topic to their own level of understanding and to a degree that suits their own time and interest level.

Special hardware, such as sound recorders and videodisc players, are often used as part of the creation or display of multimedia presentations. Software is used to create presentations as well as to provide the interface between the Macintosh and other equipment. For example, a HyperCard

8

stack running on the Macintosh can give a user access to video clips on a laserdisc player attached to the computer.

Multimedia on the Macintosh has recently been enhanced by the intro-duction of QuickTime, extensions to the system software that add new multimedia-related capabilities. With QuickTime, you can synchronize the different elements of multimedia, such as sound and animation. QuickTime offers a new movie file format. QuickTime movies can be cut and pasted between applications using the Clipboard and Scrapbook just as with a graphics file. (This was briefly mentioned in Chapter 3, "Menus.")

Summing Up Applications

These are just some of the many kinds of applications available for your Macintosh. In addition, project management programs help you organize work projects, and data analysis packages give assistance with heavy-duty statistical work. Education applications provide training in all sorts of subjects, and games designed for the Macintosh can give you a welcome break from your work—and give children a head-start in using computers. There are also music applications, network and communications software (see Chapter 10, "Communications,"), and so on.

Using an Application

After you've purchased your software, you'll need to install it before you can begin working. This may be as simple as copying the files to the hard disk, but many of the larger applications come with their own installer applications.

Installing an Application

To install a new application, follow the instructions in the accompanying manual and in any Read Me document that appears on the first program or installation disk. The manual will also tell you how much room you need free on your hard disk in order to store the application.

Remember to send in the application registration form so you will hear about program updates. Also, make sure to follow the manufacturer's copyright protection instructions.

Each application has a unique icon so you can recognize it on screen. Documents created in an application also have a distinct icon, as shown in Figure 8-5.

Using the Get Info Option

You can obtain on-screen information about an application when you're in the Finder by selecting the application's icon and then selecting the File menu and choosing Get Info. A Get Info dialog box appears; Figure 8-6 shows a Get Info dialog box for PageMaker 4.0. (See Chapter 3, "Menus," for more information about the use of this menu option.)

Figure 8-5. *Application and document icons*

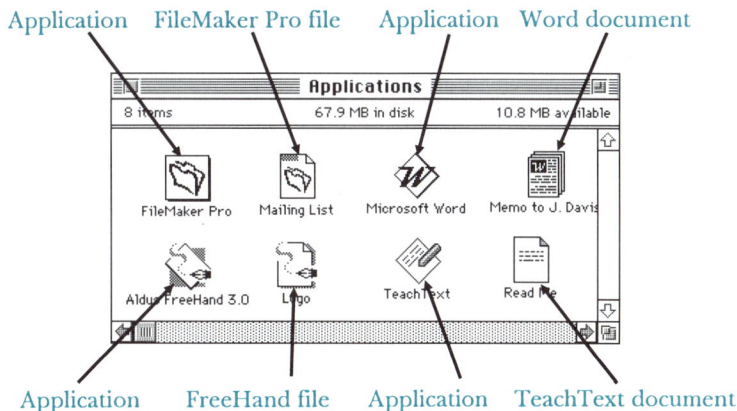

Figure 8-6.   *The Get Info dialog box for Aldus PageMaker 4.0*

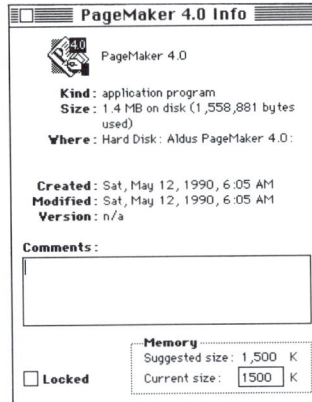

You can now see what version of the application you have, how much
storage space it requires, and when it was created and modified. You can also
lock or unlock the file so, when locked, someone cannot accidentally delete
it. The Get Info dialog box also tells you how much memory should be set
aside to run the application. You can increase the amount of memory
allocated for that application by changing the figure in the Current Size box.
You may sometimes need to do this if, for example, you are working on a
very large, complex document.

Opening an Application

Once you have installed an application and are ready to begin working,
you first have to open the application. There are several ways to open an
application:

- You can double-click the application's icon; this is probably the
  method you will use most frequently.

- You can click on the application's icon once to select it and then
  select the Open option from the File menu.

- You can double-click the icon for a document that has been created with the application (or click once and then select Open from the File menu). Opening that document also starts the application.

- With System 7, dragging a document icon on top of the application icon starts the application and opens that document.

- You can put an application in the Startup Items folder in the System folder so that it will open when you start your computer. (See Chapter 5, "System 7 and the Finder," for more information on this technique.)

- You can make an alias of the application and place it in the Apple Menu Items folder; then you can choose the application and open it just like a desk accessory.

Opening TeachText

You can learn more about applications by opening the TeachText application. Follow these steps:

1. Return to the Finder if you are working in some other application and locate the TeachText application, as shown here:

TeachText

2. Double-click the TeachText icon. A new, untitled window appears with the insertion point blinking at the upper-left corner of the window, as shown in Figure 8-7. Note that there are three menus, Apple, File, and Edit, and that the window resembles other Macintosh windows. (See Chapter 2, "Using the Macintosh," for details about working with windows.)

3. Browse through the Apple, File, and Edit menus to see the options that are available.

These three menus—Apple, File, and Edit—appear in almost all Macintosh applications. As described in Chapter 3, "Menus," the Apple menu options are the same regardless of the application in which you are working. Exactly which items appear in this menu depends on what desk accessories you have

8

Figure 8-7.   *The TeachText document window*

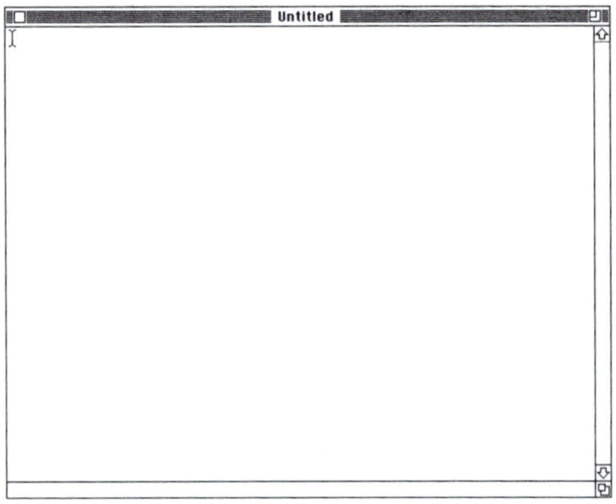

installed. However, the first item on the Apple menu, About *xx*, reflects the name of the active application. Here it is About TeachText.

The File and Edit Menus

The File menu and the Edit menu contain similar options in different applications.

The File Menu
The File menu contains options relating to an entire file, with these options commonly appearing in Macintosh applications: New, Open, Close, Save, Save As, Page Setup, Print, and Quit. Additional options are included in the File menu depending on the application. The TeachText File menu is shown in Figure 8-8. The New option allows you to create a new file in that application. You use the Open option to open an existing file. The Close option closes the currently active file, but the application remains active.

The Save option allows you to store a document on disk. The first time you save a document, you see a dialog box in which you name your file, choose its location, and often select a file format. When you have saved a document

Figure 8-8. *The File menu in TeachText*

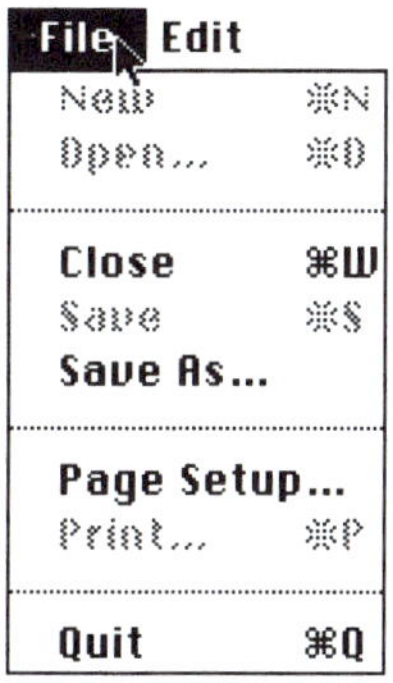

once, for all subsequent uses of the Save command the application saves the changes to the file without displaying a dialog box.

You use the Save As option to display the Save dialog box when you want to save the file with a different name, to a different location on the current disk or on another disk, or in another format. You can use Save As when you want to create a backup copy of your file onto another disk from within the application. Remember that using the Save command after you have made changes to a named document replaces the copy of the file on disk with the copy of the changed file. If you do not want this to happen, use Save As to create a new file and avoid overwriting the original file.

Page Setup, as described in Chapter 7, "Fonts, Printers, and Printing," provides options relating to the document setup for printing. Print allows you to choose printing options and to print the document. With Quit, you actually leave the application and close any open documents. Other File menu options appear depending on the application. For example, some programs have Import and Export options to work with files in formats different than the current application format, a Print Preview option to allow you to see what the document will look like when printed, or a Revert option that lets you return to a previously saved version of a document.

8

The Edit Menu

Edit menu options differ depending on the application, but most applications will contain the Undo, Cut, Copy, and Paste options, as illustrated in the Edit menu from TeachText shown in Figure 8-9.

Undo lets you reverse the last action you took in the application. For example, if you moved a graphic and then changed your mind, you could immediately choose Undo to reverse the move. The Undo menu option usually changes to reflect the nature of the last action that can be undone, such as Undo Move or Undo Typing. In some applications, you can set the number of actions that can be undone with this command.

The Cut, Copy, and Paste options all use the Macintosh Clipboard, a temporary holding place in the computer's memory for text or graphics, as described in "The Edit Menu" in Chapter 3, "Menus." When you use the Cut or Copy option, the selected text or graphics is placed on the Clipboard. You can then paste the Clipboard's contents into the current document, into another document, or even into a document in another application. The contents of the Clipboard remain the same until you use the Cut or Copy option again or until you turn off or restart your computer. Because of this, you can easily paste the same selection into several different locations.

Figure 8-9.   *The Edit menu in TeachText*

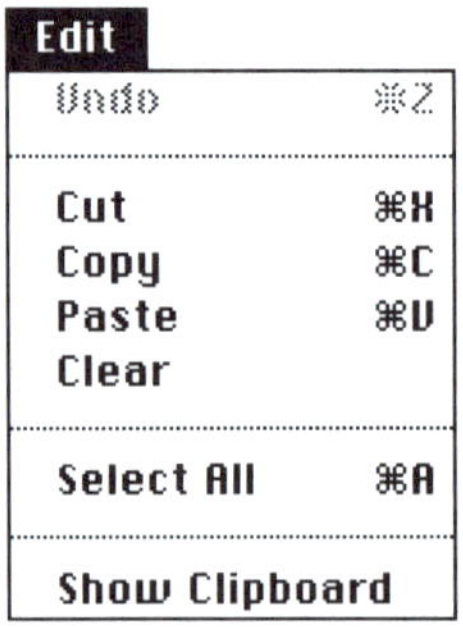

The Cut option deletes selected text or graphics and places them on the Clipboard, replacing the Clipboard's previous contents. The Copy option leaves the selected graphics or text in place, but puts a copy onto the Clipboard, allowing you to paste into another location. The Paste option places the contents of the Clipboard into the location you selected. You will practice using these options later in this chapter.

The options on the Edit menu in other applications will vary depending on what kind of work is done in that program. For example, in Aldus FreeHand, a drawing application, the Edit menu options are Undo, Redo, Cut, Copy, Paste, Clear, Cut Contents, Paste Inside, Select All, Duplicate, Clone, Move, and Transform Again.

Due to its limited capabilities, the TeachText application does not have any menus in addition to Apple, File, and Edit, but most applications do. Again, the menus and the options contained in them are related to the specific tasks you can perform in that application.

Entering and Editing Text

In addition to many Macintosh applications having similar menu options, some tasks are performed the same way in different applications. For example, you enter, edit, and format text using many of the same basic techniques in most Macintosh applications.

You enter text from the keyboard, or depending on the program, you paste or import it from other documents or applications. You can change text with the mouse, the keyboard, and menu options. Before you can format, cut, copy, or move text, you must first select it.

Note that some of the ways you work with text also apply to working with graphics. For example, when you want to move, resize, or otherwise alter a graphic element, you must first select it.

There are some standard Macintosh techniques for selecting text, many of which have been explained in earlier chapters. For example, to select a character, word, or any other sections of text, you can simply drag through that text to highlight and therefore select it. You can double-click a single word to select it. Another shortcut, called shift-clicking, is described in the next section. Other text selection techniques exist within specific applications.

8

Working with Text in TeachText

By creating a document with TeachText, you can see how to work with text in a Macintosh application and also experiment with some of the File and Edit menu options.

Entering Text

Here you'll enter text, make some corrections, and save your file for the first time. Follow these steps:

1. If it is not already open, open the TeachText application by double-clicking its icon.

2. Type the following two sentences of text, making sure to make the typing mistake shown:

   The annual office porty is set for Friday, December 5. Let's celebrate the holidays and our best year ever.

   Your document should look like that shown here:

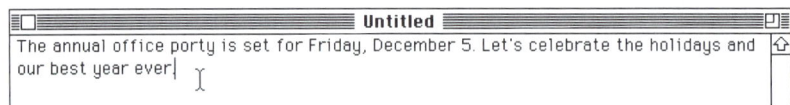

   ```
   ┌──────────────────────── Untitled ────────────────────────┐
   │ The annual office porty is set for Friday, December 5. Let's celebrate the holidays and │
   │ our best year ever|                                        │
   │                                                            │
   └────────────────────────────────────────────────────────────┘
   ```

3. Select the File menu and choose Save. The Save dialog box opens.
   Type a name, such as **Office Party**, designate where you want it saved (you can save it in the Document folder created in the exercise in Chapter 4, "Files, Folders, and Disks,"), and click Save, as shown in Figure 8-10. You have just created a new file and saved it on your hard disk.

4. Now correct the typo (or typos) that you made. In the example shown, move the insertion point and click once when it is just to the right of the "o" in "porty." Press (delete) and then type **a**. You have corrected the typo. If you made any other typos, you can use the same technique to correct them now.

5. You discover that December 5 is really a Thursday. To replace a whole word, first double-click "Friday" as shown here:

```
┌─────────────────────────────── OFFICE PARTY ───────────────────────────────┐
│ The annual office party is set for ▓Friday▓, December 5. Let's celebrate the holidays and │▲│
│ our best year ever.                                                         │ │
│                     I                                                       │ │
```

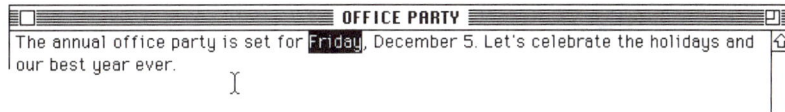

The word is selected. Now type **Thursday**. The text is changed.

6. Select the File menu and choose Save. You've saved the changes to your document.

In these steps, you have created a new document and have entered text. You have also made and saved corrections to your document.

Working with the Clipboard

Now you'll make further changes to your document using the Edit menu's Cut, Copy, and Paste options. You will also use shortcuts to delete and select text, then you will type additional text, make an additional copy of your file, and quit the application. Follow these steps:

1. You decide that you want to change the order of the document's two sentences. Select the first sentence by dragging across it.

Figure 8-10.   *The Save dialog box*

8

2. Select the Edit menu and choose Cut. The sentence is deleted from the document and is placed on the Clipboard. Note that you must always select text or graphics first before you can cut it.

3. Select the Edit menu and choose Show Clipboard. The Clipboard opens and you can see the sentence you just cut, as shown here:

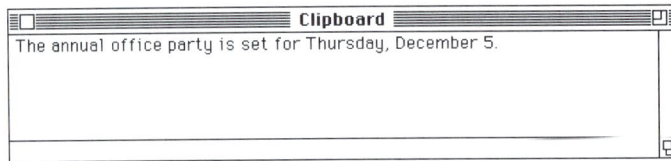

```
┌──────────────────────────── Clipboard ────────────────────────────┐
│ The annual office party is set for Thursday, December 5.            │
│                                                                     │
│                                                                     │
│                                                                     │
└─────────────────────────────────────────────────────────────────────┘
```

4. Close the Clipboard by clicking its close box. Even though you can no longer see the Clipboard, it is still functioning as the temporary holding place for the text you cut.

5. Click immediately after the first sentence to move the insertion point there, and press the (spacebar) once. Then select the Edit menu and choose Paste. The cut sentence appears where you placed the insertion point.

6. Now select both sentences. Select the Edit menu and choose Select All. This selects (highlights) all of the document's text. (Note that this menu option is available in some, but not all, Macintosh applications.)

7. Select the Edit menu and choose Copy. The sentences are copied to the Clipboard, replacing its previous contents. The original set of sentences remains in the document.

8. Click to place the insertion point at the end of the document and then press (return). This marks where you want to paste the copy of the two sentences.

9. Select the Edit menu and choose Paste. The two sentences appear a second time in your document below the first set, as shown in Figure 8-11.

10. Select the second set of sentences using the following text selection shortcut: Position the insertion point before the second "Let's" and click once. Then, holding down the (shift) key, click once at the end

Figure 8-11. *The copied sentences are pasted into the document*

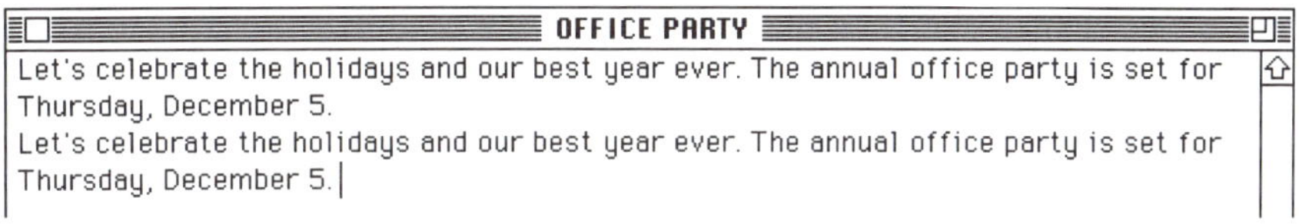

```
▤▢▥▥▥▥▥▥▥▥▥▥▥▥▥▥ OFFICE PARTY ▥▥▥▥▥▥▥▥▥▥▥▥▥▥▢▥
Let's celebrate the holidays and our best year ever. The annual office party is set for   ⇧
Thursday, December 5.
Let's celebrate the holidays and our best year ever. The annual office party is set for
Thursday, December 5.|
```

of the second sentence, after the "5." This selects all of the text in between the two clicks. Now press ⌈delete⌋. The two sentences are deleted.

When you delete text using the ⌈delete⌋ key, it is not copied to the Clipboard. You can retrieve it using the Undo command if you use it before you do anything else. But if you think you might want the text back, it's safest to use the Cut command to delete text.

11. Position the insertion point at the end of the second sentence and click once. Press the ⌈spacebar⌋ once and then add a sentence of your choice to the announcement. You can use the text shown in Figure 8-12 if you want.

    You can insert text anywhere you want by clicking once to place the insertion point where you want the text to begin and then typing.

12. Select the File menu and choose Save. You have saved the changes to your document.

13. To make a backup copy of your file, select the File menu and choose Save As. Type a new name for the file, such as **Party Backup**, designate where you want it saved (such as in the Other Stuff folder created in Chapter 4), and click Save. The title bar changes to reflect the name of the new file. Any changes you made to the file from now on would be made to this new file and not to the Office Party document.

8

Figure 8-12.   *Text is added by positioning the insertion point and typing*

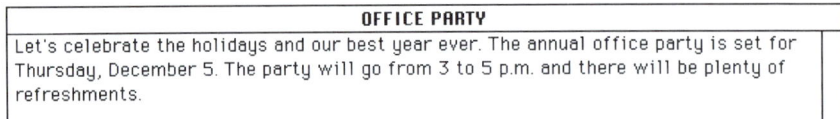

OFFICE PARTY
Let's celebrate the holidays and our best year ever. The annual office party is set for Thursday, December 5. The party will go from 3 to 5 p.m. and there will be plenty of refreshments.

14. Now you're done working with both your document and the application. Select the File menu and choose Quit. The document window closes and you're returned to the Finder.

In these steps, you have edited text in a variety of ways, saved a copy of your document from within an application, and quit an application.

Transferring Data Between Macintosh Applications

The Macintosh operating system offers several different ways to transfer data between different applications. The Clipboard, as described in the previous section of this chapter, and in "The Edit Menu" in Chapter 3, "Menus," is one way to do this. Another is via the Scrapbook desk accessory, also described in Chapter 3. System 7 added two new powerful capabilities: the Publish and Subscribe feature and AppleEvents, also called IAC (Inter-Application Communication).

Using the Clipboard to Transfer Data

In an exercise earlier in this chapter, you cut and copied text to the Clipboard and then pasted those contents to another location within the same TeachText document. You can also use the Clipboard to paste a selection of text, graphics, or sound from one application to another. To do this, you use the same techniques you used to cut, copy, and paste within an application.

When you need to copy or cut and then paste a lot of material between applications, you can open both applications (provided you have sufficient memory to do so) and organize the windows so they are side by side. Then you can easily switch back and forth between windows to transfer the data using the Cut or Copy option and the Paste option, clicking each window as needed to activate it.

Transferring items this way via the Clipboard is sometimes more efficient than using an application's Import or Export options. If you have just created and saved an illustration in a painting program, creating a graphics file, for example, and want that graphic in a page layout program, you quit the painting program and use the the page layout program option to import graphics files. It may be faster, however, before leaving the paint program, to simply select the graphic and copy it to the Clipboard with the Edit menu's Copy option, then open your page layout document and use the Paste option to place the graphic in the document.

Since the contents of the Clipboard remain until you replace them with another item or shut down or restart your computer, you can paste the same contents in multiple locations. For example, you might copy a pie chart created in a spreadsheet application to the Clipboard, as shown in Figure 8-13.

You then paste that chart into a presentation application to be part of an on-screen slide show, and paste it again into a report you are preparing in a word processing application, as shown in Figure 8-14.

It is easy to view the current contents of the Clipboard: From the desktop, select the Edit menu and choose Show Clipboard.

There are two drawbacks to using the Clipboard for transferring data: the Clipboard can only hold one item at a time, and it is only a temporary holding place.

Pasting Selections with the Scrapbook

The Scrapbook desk accessory offers functions similar to the Clipboard, but can store multiple selections at a time. These remain in the Scrapbook when you turn off your computer. The Scrapbook can store selections of text, graphics, sounds, and QuickTime movies that you can then paste into your

8

Figure 8-13.   *A chart copied to the Clipboard*

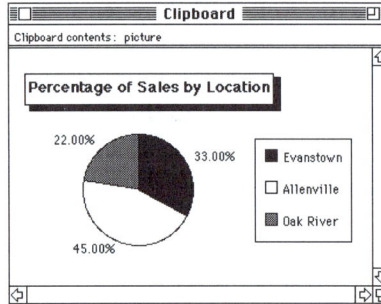

documents. (See "The Scrapbook" in Chapter 3, "Menus," for more information about this desk accessory.)

Figure 8-14.   *The chart pasted into a word processing document*

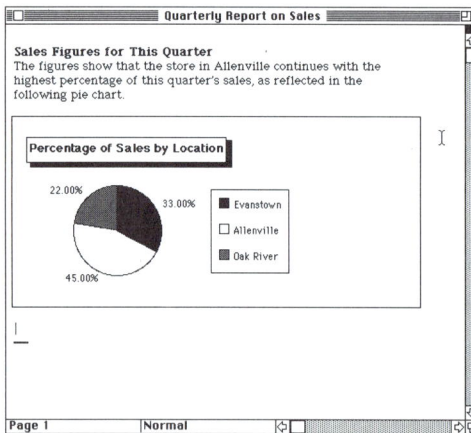

The Scrapbook can also be used to transfer material within the same document or application, although the Clipboard is often sufficient for those purposes.

You can see the contents of your Scrapbook file by selecting the Apple menu and then choosing Scrapbook or by double-clicking the Scrapbook icon in the Apple Menu Items folder. You can look at the items in the Scrapbook by clicking the arrows at the bottom of the Scrapbook window. Figure 8-15 shows a graphic that comes with the Scrapbook in System 7.

To copy an item to the Scrapbook, select the text or other material, and then select the File menu and choose either the Cut or Copy option. Open the Scrapbook by selecting the Apple menu and then choosing Scrapbook. Select the Edit menu and choose Paste. The item is pasted into the Scrapbook.

To paste an item in the Scrapbook into a file in another application, just open the file where you want the item to go. Open the Scrapbook by selecting the Apple menu and choosing Scrapbook. Use the scroll bar to locate the item you want to paste, such as the graphic shown in Figure 8-16. Then select the Edit menu and choose Copy.

Unlike most other times you copy and paste, you do not select a Scrapbook item before copying it; the computer knows to copy the portion of the Scrapbook that is displayed on screen.

The Scrapbook item remains but a copy is placed on the Clipboard. Click the cursor where you want the item to go in the document, then select the Edit menu and choose Paste. The selection is pasted into the document, as shown in Figure 8-16. Close the Scrapbook window.

The Publish and Subscribe Feature

The Publish and Subscribe feature is a good method to use when you want to copy and paste text or graphics from one application to another that you expect to update later. The copies are linked to the original so that when you update the original, the copies will automatically reflect the changes.

This feature, new with System 7, uses a magazine metaphor. You select material in the original document to publish. This causes an edition file to be created. Other documents can then subscribe to this material. Changes made

Figure 8-15.   *A graphic that comes with the System 7 Scrapbook*

to the publisher, the original file, are automatically reflected in the edition file, and in all the subscriber files.

Figure 8-16.   *A Scrapbook graphic pasted into a word processing document*

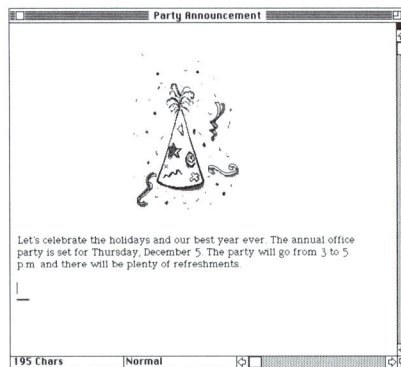

Not all programs currently have this capability. You can check to see if an application supports Publish and Subscribe by looking to see if there are Edit menu options that refer to Publishers and Subscribers.

Perhaps you have financial information that is part of a spreadsheet and you want this information to appear in two other documents: in a report in a word processing application, and in a newsletter in a page layout application. You could copy and paste this information into each of those applications using the Clipboard. However, you expect that the figures will change before you complete the final drafts of the report and the newsletter. You could use Publish and Subscribe to link the files, so the newsletter and the report figures will be automatically updated when you change the spreadsheet.

In this example, the spreadsheet data is the publisher. You select the appropriate portion of the spreadsheet and then select the Edit menu and the Create Publisher option. You give the edition file a name, such as 1st Qtr. Projections, and determine where you want it located on your disk, as shown in Figure 8-17. You then click Publish.

The edition file is created, as shown here:

1st Qtr. Projections

You then open the document in which you want to paste that material, in this case, a word processing document. You select the Edit menu and choose Subscribe To. You click to select 1ST QTR. PROJECTIONS from a list of edition files (as shown in Figure 8-18), and click Subscribe.

The item appears where you want it. This material will stay in your document until you delete it, cancel it as a subscriber, or cancel the publisher to which it relates. If you cancel its subscriber status or cancel the publisher, the material will remain in your document, but it will not be updated.

You can choose whether updates to the publisher are reflected in the edition file and in the subscribers either manually or automatically. You cannot change the edition file itself, although you can open it and examine it. You must make the changes to the publisher itself in the original document. There is no limit to the number of files that can subscribe to a given file.

You can use this feature on just one Macintosh or over a Macintosh network when you want to send out the same information and updates of that information to many people.

Figure 8-17.   *The Publish dialog box*

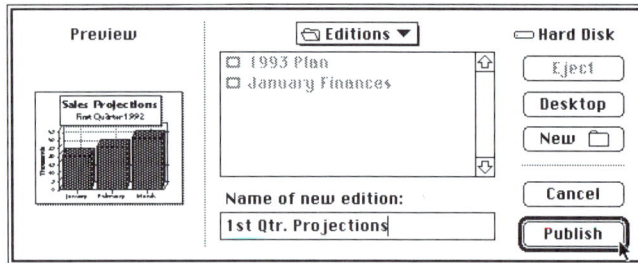

AppleEvents

Another new capability implemented with System 7 is AppleEvents, also called Inter-Application Communication (IAC). With this program linking feature, applications actually communicate directly with each other without

Figure 8-18.   *The Subscribe dialog box*

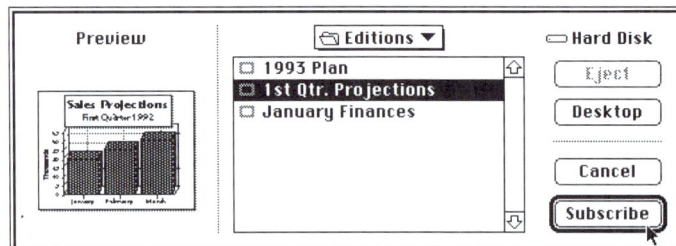

the user taking the actions. This automated program linking can be done either on the same computer or over a network. A database program, for example, could instruct a word processing application to check the spelling and format a document. This is different from Publish and Subscribe in which only the data is linked. Here the applications actually communicate with each other to work with data. If you use AppleEvents over a network, you grant permission to network users to be linked to your shared programs. AppleEvents is only available with applications that have been developed to support it.

In this chapter, you have learned about some of the different types of software packages as well as the similar ways in which Macintosh applications allow you to perform frequently used operations, such as entering and editing text. You've also seen different methods you can use to transfer information both within and between Macintosh applications.

In the next chapter, you'll become familiar with the major features and functions of HyperCard.

8

9

HyperCard

The full power of HyperCard is not immediately apparent. You can use HyperCard just as it comes packaged with your Macintosh to maintain a file of names and addresses and an appointment diary. However, if you want to extend its power you can do so in several ways. The first way is to acquire HyperCard applications written by others. The second is to write your own. This chapter takes you step by step through using the Addresses and Appointment utilities in HyperCard, and explains the other HyperCard files that come with your Macintosh.

HyperCard is a filing program (or *database*), which means it lets you store information. The information you store can be *structured*—that is, split into defined chunks, such as names, addresses, and zip codes. The stored information can also be *free-form*, like the information you keep in a diary or notebook of ideas.

HyperCard also lets you mix other types of data with the text you store, such as graphics that you create or acquire, and sounds (which it lets you record). Finally, it includes a powerful programming language that lets you do almost anything you want to do, such as creating multimedia presentations, customizing utilities for storing your information, or writing computer games.

HyperCard's basic unit of information is called a *card*. Think of a card as being similar to a card in a Rolodex, or a recipe card. Cards are organized into *stacks*, which are simply separate files on disk. HyperCard's cards are like paper cards in that you can store information on each one. But HyperCard brings the power of a computer to its stacks, letting you sort them automatically or search through them for a particular piece of information in much less time than it would take you to search through a paper stack of cards. Extensions to HyperCard let it do a lot more: with extensions, HyperCard can reach into a mainframe computer to search for information there, or it can control an unusual device (such as a LaserDisc player) connected to your Macintosh.

At the core of HyperCard is its programming language, HyperTalk. HyperTalk is the basis for the easy-to-understand commands that you use to move through stacks.

Why Is HyperCard on Your Macintosh?

One of the main reasons that HyperCard is on your Macintosh is that Bill Atkinson wanted it that way. Atkinson was one of the first Macintosh programmers. He wrote the programming code known as QuickDraw that the Macintosh uses to draw the screen. He then wrote the first graphics program for the Macintosh, MacPaint. Along the way, he came up with the idea for HyperCard and convinced John Sculley, president of Apple Computer, to support his efforts. Atkinson would ask for no royalties for his product if Sculley would include HyperCard with every Macintosh. Thus, HyperCard was born, and has been shipped on every Macintosh since. (Until late 1990, Apple was the source of HyperCard. At that time, Apple transferred ownership of HyperCard to Claris, its software subsidiary.)

Since its birth in 1987, HyperCard has steadily evolved; each release has increased its power while maintaining its original concepts. The HyperCard version shipping with all Macintoshes as of Spring, 1992, is version 2.1.

The version that shipped with your Macintosh is not the full version of HyperCard, although it can do everything that the full version can do. Its documentation is limited, as is the number of utilities that come with it. You can purchase the full version, marketed by Claris for $195 (list price) from software dealers. You will see later in this chapter how to enable some of the features of HyperCard that are hidden in the version packaged with your Macintosh.

What You Can Do with HyperCard

As it comes out of the box, HyperCard includes several stacks that you can use right away for such tasks as keeping a name and address book and maintaining a to do list. But that's not all. Besides the bundled HyperCard stacks, there are literally hundreds, if not thousands, of other stacks written by others that you can use. You can acquire these stacks from a number of sources. Some are commercial; these are available at your local computer store. Others are *shareware* or public domain; you can get these from a Macintosh user group (check your local telephone book) or download them from an online service.

Additionally, HyperCard has been called a "software erector set," meaning that you can use it to create your own interesting applications. These can range from the simple to the complex. For instance, teachers can create interactive tutorials for their students, children can learn about programming, and sales representatives can maintain files on client contacts.

Creating your own stacks is beyond the scope of this book, and so is not discussed here. If you'd like to create your own HyperCard applications, it is recommended that you purchase the Development Kit from Claris or purchase a book about HyperCard.

Using HyperCard

9

To get you started with HyperCard, this section explores the HyperCard stacks included with recently shipped Macintosh computers. These are Appointments With Audio, Addresses With Audio, Audio Help, and Home. Most Macintosh computers come with these stacks and the HyperCard application bundled together on one or two floppy disks. If you have not done so already, copy these floppy disks to a single folder on your hard disk. (Your Macintosh may include other HyperCard stacks as well; after reading this chapter you are encouraged to explore those other stacks.)

HyperCard Components

HyperCard consists of three main parts: the HyperCard application, the Home stack, and other stacks. Although the Home stack doesn't look any different from the other stacks, it contains information and settings that HyperCard needs to function properly.

There is another option on the HyperCard disks, HyperCard Fonts, that needs to be installed in the System folder. Do this by dragging the HyperCard Fonts file onto the System folder. The fonts will automatically be added to those in the System file.

Starting HyperCard

You start HyperCard just as you start any other Macintosh program: by double-clicking its icon. When HyperCard has finished loading into memory, you'll see the Home stack. It should look something like the screen shown in Figure 9-1.

Before going further, let's look at the entities you'll be working with on cards in HyperCard: graphics, fields, and buttons. *Buttons* are areas on the screen that trigger actions when you click them. *Fields* are areas into which you can type text. *Graphics* can be used to make everything look nice, as well as convey information in and of themselves. Besides the elements that appear on cards, HyperCard (like every other Macintosh program) has its own menus. These menus can change as you move from stack to stack, just as the other elements of HyperCard (buttons, fields, and graphics) change.

There are four buttons on the Home card shown in Figure 9-1, although only one is obviously a button. The obvious one is labeled More. If you click this, the screen will change, and the More button will change to Previous. Remember that HyperCard documents are like stacks of cards; this button

Figure 9-1. The HyperCard Home card

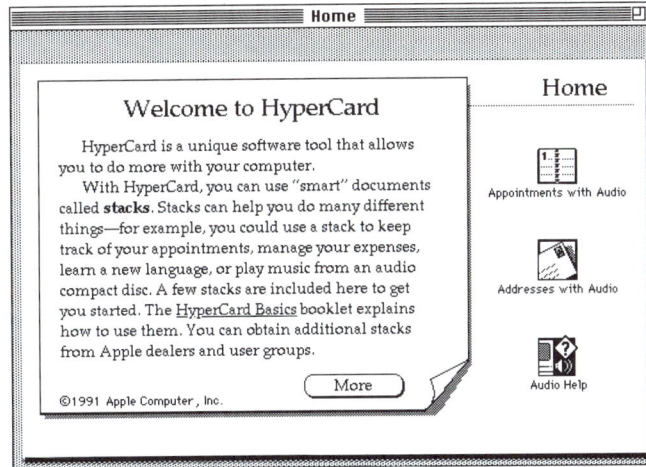

has merely flipped the first card off the screen to show you the second card. Click the Previous button to return to your starting place.

The three less-obvious buttons are located on the right side of the window, labeled with the names of the stacks: Appointments With Audio, Addresses With Audio, and Audio Help. These don't really look like standard Macintosh buttons (the kind you see in dialog boxes, such as the Page Setup dialog box in most programs). Instead, HyperCard buttons often resemble icons on the Macintosh desktop. There's a crucial difference, though: icons on the desktop represent things (disks, folders, and files) that you select and then open. HyperCard buttons don't need to be selected; instead you just click them to trigger them.

Click the Addresses With Audio button. After a moment you'll be taken to the Addresses With Audio stack, as shown in Figure 9-2.

9

Using the Addresses With Audio Stack

One of the most common uses for computers is storing names and addresses. The Addresses With Audio stack resembles a card file in which you can store the names and addresses you use regularly. This stack, though, can do several things that a paper-based card file can't do: it can search through the cards looking for a name (or city or zip code) that you specify. You can sort it in any of several ways with a simple command. It can dial the phone for you automatically. And using the Audio palette and the microphone provided with many Macintoshes, you can even record your own audio notes and attach them to the cards for later playback. You'll see how to do this later in this chapter.

The Addresses With Audio stack includes ten fields into which you can type the name, company name, address, and phone numbers of the person whose information you want to record. Figure 9-2 shows the card for A. Royce Walthrop, so his name is in the first field.

Move the mouse pointer over the name A. Royce Walthrop. You'll see that the pointer changes from a small pointing hand to a text cursor (just as it does when you point to text in a word processor). When you click within the field, a text insertion point appears at the place you clicked so you can easily type or edit text. You can also use standard Macintosh techniques for selecting text, if you want to change it (that is, point to a place in the text,

Figure 9-2.   *The Addresses With Audio dialog box*

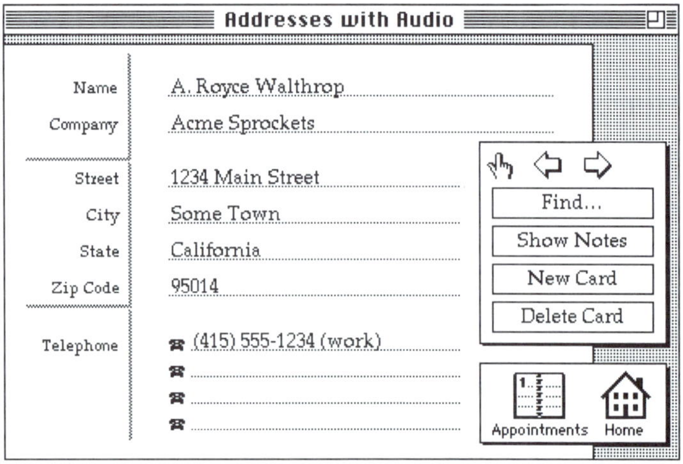

hold down the mouse button, and drag to select more of the text). This will be discussed more later in this chapter.

The Addresses With Audio stack has four obvious buttons: Find, Show Notes, New Card, and Delete Card. These allow you to find a particular piece of text in the stack you are currently viewing, show the notes attached to the current card, add a new card, or delete the current card. There are two less-obvious buttons in Figure 9-2: Appointments and Home. These take you to two other stacks.

The two arrows are also buttons; you use the arrows to look at the other cards in this stack. The arrow pointing to the right takes you to the next card, and the arrow pointing to the left takes you to the previous card. When you reach the last card in the stack (the bottom card) the right arrow takes you back to the first card. The same happens when you are at the first card: the left arrow takes you to the last card (as though your card stack were a circular-type Rolodex).

Finally, each of the telephone icons at the bottom of the screen is also a button, and will produce actual touch tone sounds to dial the phone number when you click them.

Entering Information

To see the stack in action, follow these steps:

1. Click the New Card button. The old card will be replaced by a new one with empty fields for name, company name, and so on.

2. Point on the Name field. When the mouse pointer changes from the hand to the text pointer, click once. Type your name.

3. Press the (tab) key to move to the next field, the Company name. (Pressing (tab) always takes you from one field to another. To go back to the previous field, press the (tab) key while holding down the (shift) key.)

4. Type the name of your company.

5. Repeat steps 1 through 4 until you've entered all the pertinent information on the card. If you make mistakes as you type, use the (backspace) key to correct your errors, or select the text with the mouse and retype it.

9

6. You can also add notes about any of the people in your card file. To do so, click the Show Notes button. (Note that when clicked, the Show Notes button becomes the Hide Notes button.) If you do this with the A. Royce Walthrop card, you'll see that the person who created this card file recorded Royce's birthday and some other notes. Of course, you can add notes to any of your cards. Click the Hide Notes button to hide them.

7. To create a new card for a new name, click the New Card button again. A new card is created, and the current one is saved automatically.

8. Repeat steps 1 through 7 to add as many cards as you like. The more information you put into your computer, the more information you'll have at your fingertips, and the more the power of the computer (and more specifically, the power of HyperCard) becomes apparent and useful to you.

When you're done, use the left and right arrow buttons to move through the stack. You'll see that the new card or cards you created appear right after the one that was on the screen when you clicked the New Card button.

Make use of this Address book. HyperCard's address book is not as powerful as some that you can purchase for the Macintosh, but it does have one big benefit: it's free. There's nearly no limit to the number of cards you can add to the stack. And should you decide, later, to use a different address program, you can transfer the information you've entered into this stack into the new program.

HyperCard's Menus

One of the unique features of HyperCard is its reliance on buttons on the screen to perform most of its functions. However, as do all Macintosh programs, HyperCard includes its own menus, as shown here:

**   File Edit Go Font Style Utilities**

You'll notice as you work with HyperCard that the menus and options on them will change. HyperTalk, the HyperCard scripting language, is responsible for these menu changes (just as it is responsible for the actions taken when you click buttons). Let's look at the individual menus in the following sections. Later in this chapter you'll see how you can change the contents of the menus by changing HyperCard's User Level.

The File Menu

The File menu is typical of Macintosh applications; as in other Macintosh programs, the File menu is where you open or close a stack, print the stack or a card, and quit HyperCard. Note that the File menu has no Save option on it—just a Save a Copy option. HyperCard is constantly saving your changes to disk so you can worry less about losing your work.

The Print Report option on the File menu is very useful. It lets you print a compact list of names and addresses, instead of just pictures of the cards. Use it to create a paper address book that you can use when you're away from your computer.

The Edit Menu

The Edit menu contains commands that work basically the same way other Macintosh commands do: they let you undo your last action, and cut, copy, and paste text. You can use the New Card and Delete Card options to perform those functions instead of using the buttons on the card. The New Card command is handy because it includes a keyboard equivalent, (⌘)-(N), that lets you make a new card without removing your hands from the keyboard. (There's also a shortcut for the Delete Card option, although it isn't explained on the menu: it's (⌘)-(delete).)

Because the Addresses With Audio stack works with Macintosh computers that have the ability to record sound, the Edit menu also contains audio commands to add and delete Audio Memos, as well as Audio Help. You'll learn more about sound later in this chapter.

The Go Menu

Use the options in the Go Menu to navigate through the cards in the stack. The Back option takes you to the last card you saw before the current card. The Home option takes you to the Home stack. And Help takes you to the Help card for Addresses With Audio.

9

The Recent option lets you jump around through the cards you've seen recently. It will show you miniature representations of as many as 48 cards; clicking one of these cards takes you directly to it.

The First, Next, Previous, and Last options simply let you jump quickly to those cards in the current stack.

The Find option in the Go menu is not as useful as the Find button on the card. It merely brings up HyperCard's Message Box and lets you type in the text you want to find.

The Message Box is a special HyperCard "command line" into which you can enter commands in HyperTalk's programming language. Later in this chapter you'll use this command line to unlock the doors to some of HyperCard's hidden power.

As with the Edit menu, one of the benefits of using these menu options instead of buttons on the card is that they have keyboard shortcuts, letting you navigate through a stack without removing your hands from the keyboard.

The Font and Style Menus

The last two standard menus are Font and Style. If you select some text on a card (such as in the Name field), you can change that selection's font, size, and style. These commands work the same way they do in any word processing program.

The Utilities Menu

The Utilities menu is unique to this stack, and is available whenever this stack is opened. Because you are using an address book when you open it, this menu contains the commands to sort by Name, Company, City, State, and Zip. There are additional commands to print addresses, mark cards, and import text. The last option on the menu takes you to a special Help card in the stack that explains each of its functions in detail.

Besides the cards for entering names and addresses, the stack includes some special-purpose cards, and many of these cards include their own help. For instance, you access the card shown in Figure 9-3 by selecting Mark Cards from the Utilities menu, and then clicking the light bulb next to the words "Using Marked Cards." You return to the stack by selecting Return To Addresses in the lower-right corner.

Figure 9-3.   *The explanation for marking cards*

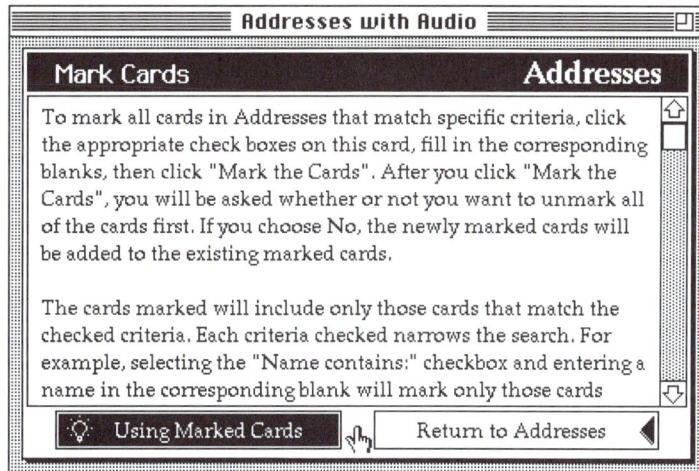

If you've typed a number of names and addresses, now's the time to take a look at the Appointments With Audio stack. To get to that stack, click the button labeled Appointments.

Using the Appointments With Audio Stack

The Appointments With Audio stack is shown in Figure 9-4. A common use for computers is to maintain a to do list. That's what the Appointments With Audio Stack does: it lets you keep a record of things you have to do at a certain time. It can also serve as an electronic diary.

Even though the Appointments With Audio stack is separate from the Addresses stack, the two are linked by the buttons in the lower-right corner of the screen. Clicking the appropriate button will take you right from the Appointments stack to the Addresses stack, and from the Addresses stack back to the Appointments stack. Depending on how much memory has been allocated for HyperCard, you may see the Addresses stack on top of the Appointments stack when you do this, as shown in Figure 9-5. If you don't

9

Figure 9-4.   *The Appointments screen*

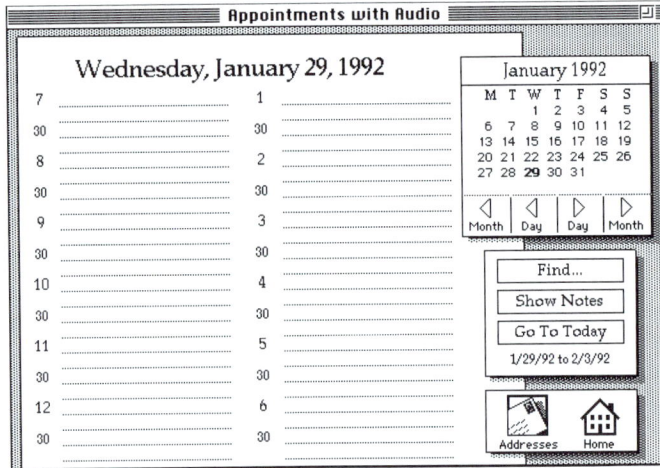

Figure 9-5.   *The Addresses screen on top of the Appointments screen*

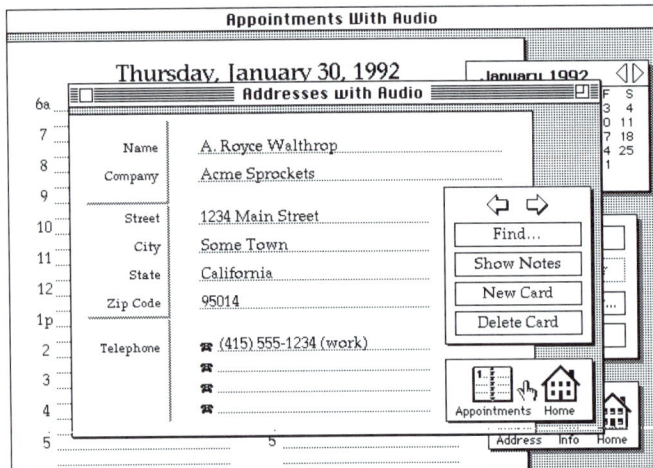

have enough memory, you'll be taken to just the Addresses stack. Either way, you can jump between the stacks by simply clicking the right button. You'll see more about linking the two stacks in "Linking the Appointments and Addresses Stacks" later in this chapter.

To increase the amount of memory that HyperCard asks for when it starts up, you need to quit HyperCard, find the HyperCard application on your hard disk, (it should be in the folder called HyperCard), select HyperCard, and then select Get Info from the File menu. You will see the HyperCard Info dialog box shown in Figure 9-6; in the lower-right corner is a box where you can increase the size. 1200KB is a good size, but you can set this to any number, assuming you have enough memory available. The amount of memory in your computer can be checked by selecting the About This Macintosh option from the Apple menu. The minimum size that will work effectively is 875KB.

Entering Appointments

Looking at the Appointments stack in Figure 9-4, you'll see some of the same buttons you used in the Addresses stack, such as Find and Show Notes, along with a calendar in the upper-right corner. Along the top are the same

Figure 9-6. *The Get Info dialog box for HyperCard*

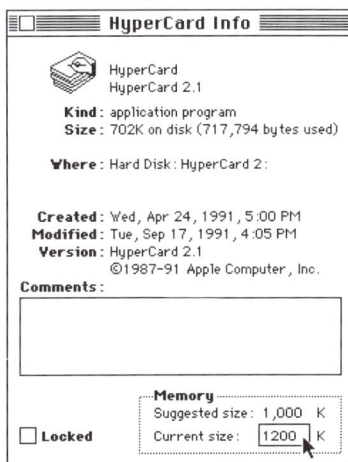

menus, but if you open the Utilities menu, you'll see it has changed to reflect the tasks that can be done in the Appointments stack, such as Go to a Day.

Just as you used fields to enter names and addresses into the Addresses stack, so you use fields to enter appointments. And just as the Addresses stack used separate cards for every name you stored, so does the Appointments stack use a separate card for each day.

Hidden Notes   You can type text next to the time the activity will start. One nice feature of this stack is the hidden note attached to each hour's time. Click an hour, and a pop-up note appears, as shown in Figure 9-7. Each of these notes can contain about 16 full pages of text, so you don't need to worry about running out of room. HyperCard creates a note for you automatically whenever you type more information on a line than will fit. A pop-up note window will automatically appear to contain what you have written.

Now, say that you want to write a note to yourself about an appointment a week from now. To get to this card, click the calendar on the day of the week your appointment is scheduled, and a message similar to the one shown here pops up:

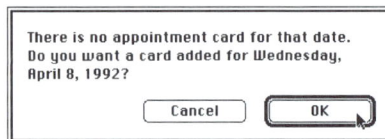

This dialog box asks if you want a card added to the stack. If you click OK, HyperCard will automatically create that card for you. Now you can add information for any day you choose, yet have cards only for the days you need. You can create a month's worth of cards by clicking the button labeled Month.

Every so often, delete cards when a date is past. HyperCard doesn't forget any days for which you have added cards. If you don't delete cards, your stack will get big fast and will take up a lot of disk space.

Linking the Appointments and Addresses Stacks

Here's how you can link the Appointments and the Addresses stacks to make finding addresses easy:

1. Open the Appointments With Audio stack, if you're not already there. You can do this with the Open option on HyperCard's File

menu, or if you are in the Addresses stack, by clicking on the Appointments button in the lower-right corner of the card.

2. Click the line labeled 10 and type **Royce Walthrop** to indicate you have an appointment with him at 10:00.

3. Select Royce's name by pointing at the beginning of his name, holding the mouse button down, and dragging until the entire name is selected.

4. Without deselecting the name (that is, without clicking anywhere else on the card), click the Find button to the right of the card. In a few moments the Addresses stack will open (if it's not already open in a different window), and you'll be taken directly to the A. Royce Walthrop card.

Using Audio

Some Macintosh models come with a microphone that you can attach to the back of the computer. These models include the Classic II, Macintosh LC,

Figure 9-7.   *A pop-up note*

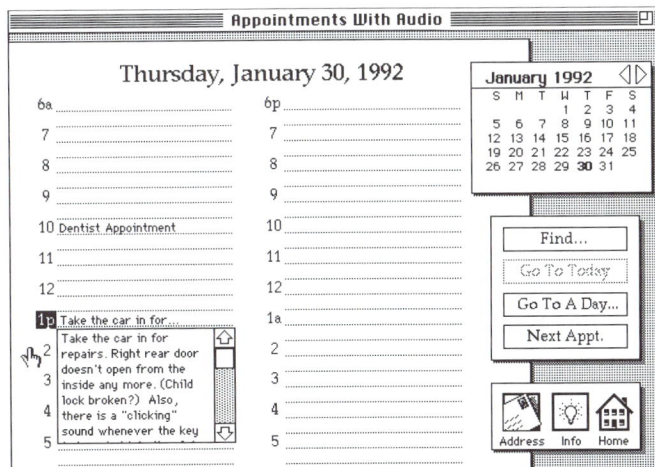

Macintosh IIsi, PowerBook 140, PowerBook 170, and Quadra series. Both the Addresses With Audio and Appointments With Audio stacks include palettes that let you add audible notes to the cards, just as you can add text notes. To add audible notes to the cards, follow these steps:

1. Choose the Add Audio Memo option from the Edit menu. This brings up the Audio palette, shown here:

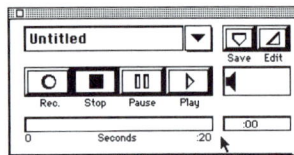

   This palette allows you to control what is entered into your note, and also allows you to do some simple editing of your words. This control palette was designed to look like a cassette recorder, with Rec. (record), Stop, Pause, and Play buttons. To the right of the Play button is the sound level indicator and above that are buttons that allow you to save or edit the sound.

2. Make sure your microphone is plugged into the correct port (the one with a microphone symbol).

3. Talk into the microphone to check the sound level. You don't have to hold the microphone very close to get a strong reading on the level indicator.

4. Click the Rec. button to start recording, and say the following phrase: "Hello, my name is (your name). I live in (your city)" and then click the Stop button.

5. Click the Play button to hear how you sound.

6. Save what you've created so far by typing a name, such as **My name** in the box where the word Untitled is, then click the Save button.

   Once you've saved the sound, HyperCard creates a button that plays it back, and gives it the icon of a small speaker. At the bottom of the screen is a message box telling you how to move the button. Since the new button is probably hidden by the Audio palette, you need to move that palette.

7. Drag the Audio palette aside, then hold down the (option) key and
    drag the speaker icon until it's placed where you want it, as shown
    in Figure 9-8.

Editing Audio

You can play your sound simply by clicking the Play button. But you aren't
limited to just playing back the sound once you've recorded it. You can use
standard Macintosh techniques to edit the recorded sound. To do so, simply
click the Audio palette's Edit button.

In the middle of the palette, as shown in Figure 9-9, is a waveform, or
graphic representation of your voice and the sentence you just spoke. The
thicker areas of the waveform are your voice and the thin areas are the periods
of silence.

Just below this is a smaller section showing a miniaturized view of the
entire sound. The white box around a portion of it represents the portion of
the sound that is in the upper box. You can view different portions of the
sound by sliding the box around with the mouse pointer.

Figure 9-8.   *Moving the new sound*

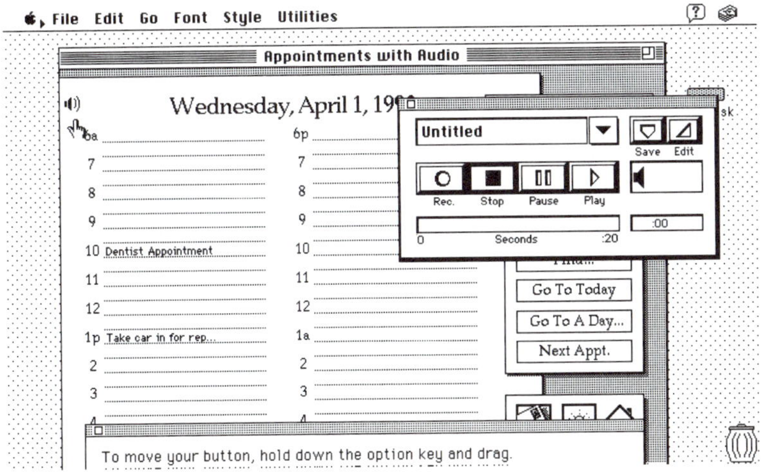

Figure 9-9.   *The expanded Audio palette*

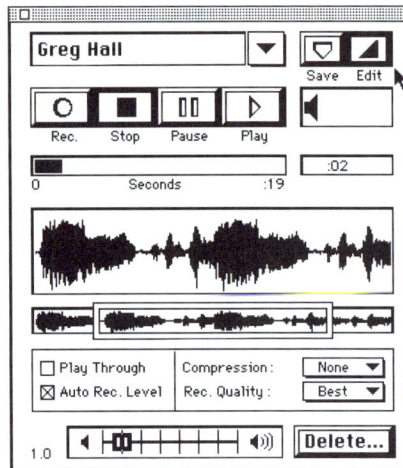

You can also change the amount of detail visible in the upper box by resizing the white box in the area below. To do so, point to the right edge of the white box, and drag it toward the center making the box smaller. You'll see that more detail becomes visible in the larger box.

The rest of the buttons allow you to change the *audio level*, or volume, the *compression* (which controls how the sound is stored and its fidelity), and the quality of the sound. Just remember that sound can take up large chunks of memory, and the more you record, the larger this stack will become. (You can access a lot more detailed information about compression and other points about using sound with HyperCard by selecting Audio Help from the Edit menu.)

The final audio option to experiment with is pasting: you'll copy a section of your sound and paste it somewhere else in the sound. Look at your waveform, and select the first big chunk. This should be the beginning of the sentence "My name is...."

1. Point on the beginning of the sound, hold down the mouse button, and drag to the right to select the first big chunk of the sound, which should represent the first sentence.

2. Press the Play button at the top of the palette to listen to just the section you selected, as shown in Figure 9-10. You should hear "My name is (your name)."

3. If necessary, adjust the size of your white box in the lower display of the waveform to allow you to grab the entire sentence.

4. Notice that the Edit menu now has an option called Cut Sound. Select this option to cut the section of sound that you have selected.

5. Click at the end of the waveform.

6. Use the Paste Sound option on the Edit menu to paste to the end of the sound the portion you cut from the beginning of the sound.

7. Click the Play button. If everything has worked out, you should hear "Hello, I live in (your city). My name is (your name)."

Figure 9-10.   *An audio "sentence" selected*

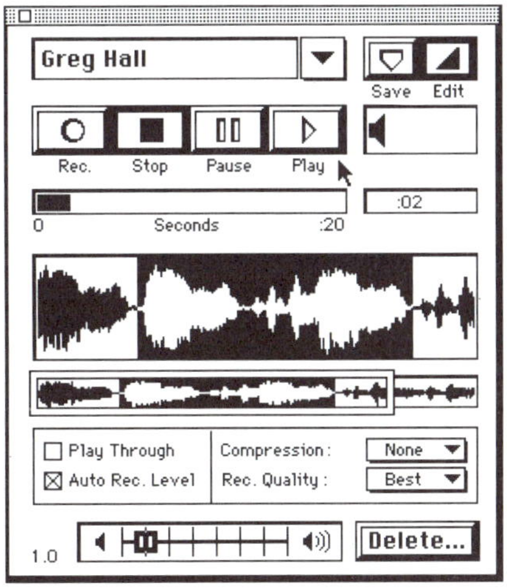

9

Now that you've seen that you can work with sound as easily as with written words, let's look at what you can do when you combine all these things together to make your own personalized stack.

Unlocking HyperCard's Power

As mentioned at the beginning of this chapter, there are several ways of using HyperCard: by using the stacks that come with your Macintosh, by purchasing other stacks, or by creating your own.

Creating your own stacks requires programming in HyperTalk, HyperCard's programming language. If the thought of programming scares you, don't worry. You won't be expected to learn programming in this chapter. Instead, you'll see how you can unlock the doors to HyperCard programming, or *scripting* as it's called, and you'll learn some of the basic concepts of HyperCard.

As you saw earlier in the chapter, the basic unit in HyperCard is the card. Collections of cards are called stacks, which are separate files on your hard disk. There is a special stack called Home, which controls much of HyperCard's behavior, and which always opens when you double-click HyperCard's icon.

In HyperCard, contrary to the old saying, you can always go Home. You can always go to the Home stack by choosing the Home option from the Go menu or using its keyboard equivalent, ⌘-Ⓗ. Additionally, most stacks have a Home button (generally with the icon of a small house, as you saw in the Addresses and Appointments stacks) that do the same thing.

Press ⌘-Ⓗ now to go to the Home stack, which is shown in Figure 9-1.

HyperCard's User Levels

HyperCard's Home stack contains a special card called Preferences that lets you control some of the ways that HyperCard operates. To go to the Preferences card, select the Prev option from the Go menu (the card that the Go Home command takes you to is the first card in the Home stack; going

Figure 9-11. *The Preferences card*

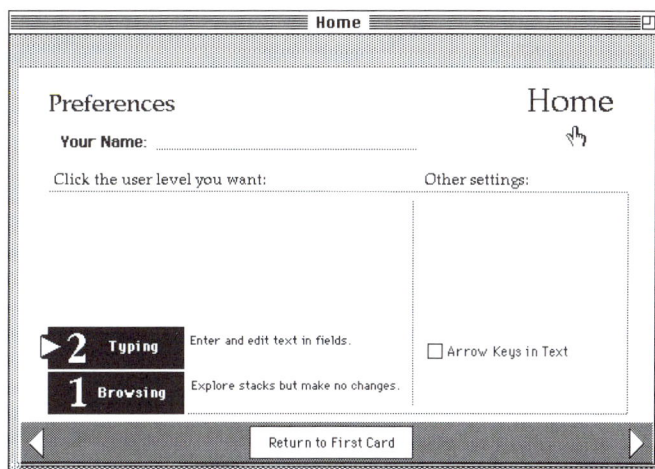

to the previous card takes you to the last card in the stack, which is the Preferences card). The Preferences card is shown in Figure 9-11.

Originally, Apple shipped a full version of HyperCard with all Macintoshes. In late 1990, they changed this policy, and now the Macintosh ships with a minimal version without much documentation. This minimal version cloaks your ability to customize the environment and create your own stacks—you can do these things with the minimal version but you have to find out about them from another source because the minimal version never displays instructions on accessing this power.

HyperCard also gives you a mechanism for controlling how much power you have over the program in its User Levels. In the card shown in Figure 9-11, only two of these User Levels are visible: Typing and Browsing. However, HyperCard actually has five User Levels. Here's how to make them visible to you:

1. Open the Message box by choosing Message from the Go menu or typing its equivalent, ⌘-Ⓜ. A small window will open at the bottom of the screen (the same window that gave you instructions on placing a button in the Appointments With Audio stack).

2. Type the word **magic** into the message box and press (return). You'll see three new User Levels appear on the screen, directly above the two that were visible previously. All five User Levels are shown in Figure 9-12.

So what are these User Levels? The text to the left of each of the buttons that enables them gives short explanations of what each allows you to do, but this section gives you more detail.

Browsing is the most basic level. Each subsequent User Level gives you powers over HyperCard that were missing in the lower levels. And each higher User Level unveils new options on the various menus (or presents new menus). Watch the menu bar as you click the higher levels, and examine the contents of the menus.

Figure 9-12.   *The five User Levels*

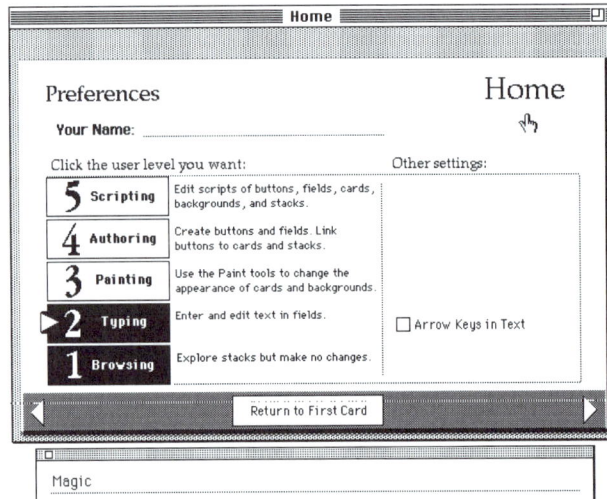

Level 1: Browsing

Browsing is the first HyperCard User Level. When your User Level is set to browsing, you can only read information from the screen—you cannot change information in any stack. This makes stacks such as Appointments and Addresses useless, since you can't enter any information into them.

Level 2: Typing

Typing is the lowest User Level at which you can do more than just read what's on screen. At this level, you can use the Appointments and Addresses stacks, since it allows you to type text into HyperCard fields.

Level 3: Painting

Painting exposes a new menu called Tools, which includes a number of tools for modifying the graphics in a stack. You can now draw pictures on your cards.

Level 4: Authoring

When you're in the Authoring User Level, you finally have some real power in that you can customize HyperCard to suit your needs. The Authoring level lets you add your own fields and buttons to cards. HyperCard can assist you in specifying what buttons do (such as linking one card to another), but you need the next higher level to get to the real power of the program.

Level 5: Scripting

In the Scripting User Level, HyperCard's full capabilities are open to you. You can now change the programming, or scripts, that control how HyperCard operates. When working at this level, you need to have some knowledge of HyperTalk (HyperCard's programming language), and it's recommended that you approach scripting gingerly until you're sure you understand the consequences of your actions. (A detailed discussion of HyperTalk is beyond the scope of this book.)

Each new User Level includes all the power that the previous level had. Thus, at the Painting level you also have the powers of the Typing level.

9

Summary

It's important that you remember that in this short chapter you've only gotten a taste of what HyperCard can do for you. It is not just an address book program or an appointment diary. By acquiring stacks from others, you can tap into its powers and expand what it can do for you. If you want to take the time to learn HyperTalk programming, then HyperCard can be nearly anything you choose it to be.

10

Communications

It's one thing to store your own information in your computer. But the usefulness of your Macintosh is compounded when you use it to share information with others. This chapter introduces you to network communications, by which you can easily share your Macintosh files with other Macintoshes in your office, as long as they are connected to one another. You'll also learn something about communicating via modem with distant computers, and about sharing files with IBM PC users.

Network Communications

For much of the history of personal computers, the only way to move information from one machine to another was by copying a file to a floppy disk, removing the disk from the drive, and taking it to another machine. This was jokingly called "sneaker net" because it wears out shoes quickly, and because it's a low-tech way to communicate, rather like going to visit someone on the next floor when a telephone call would suffice.

One of the major features of the Macintosh since its introduction has been its built-in support for networking. *Networking* involves connecting two or more machines together using special cables and software. Once the cabling and software has been installed correctly, files can be transferred between the computers, and mail can be sent, without a lot of work and without leaving your computer. Even today, the Macintosh leads the computer world in the ease of use of its networking software and hardware.

As you probably guessed, there are two elements to the network: the hardware and the software.

Networking Hardware

At its most basic level, every Macintosh includes the hardware necessary for it to be on a network. You only need to connect a small box (called the LocalTalk connector, generally priced at about $50) to the back of the machine, and connect the network cabling. Apple's basic level of hardware is called LocalTalk. This hardware implements a low-speed (for a network) level of communications between machines. You can use Apple LocalTalk hardware, or use some alternatives.

The leading alternative is called PhoneNet, and is available from Farallon Computing (though compatible boxes are available from other vendors). PhoneNet has the advantage of allowing you to use standard telephone cables for connecting the machines. In some installations, you can even use existing telephone wires to connect Macintoshes.

Beyond LocalTalk, there are other alternatives available. A more high-speed network is Ethernet. Ethernet is quicker, but also much more expensive to install. IBM's Token Ring network is yet another mechanism for connecting machines.

Chances are, if you share a printer with others, you are already connected to a network. Many of the printers that are used with the Macintosh, such as Apple's LaserWriters, use a network to allow them to connect with more than one computer. This is typically done with LocalTalk cabling, though printers such as the LaserWriter IIg can also use Ethernet.

Networking Software

Hardware is part of the picture, but it's software that really drives the network. Networking software allows you to share information on your Macintosh with others, and to use information from other users. Fortunately, the basic software that lets you do both is part of the basic Macintosh system software. In this chapter, you'll first see how to share your Macintosh with others, and then you'll see how to use a file server to access information shared by other users.

Sharing with Others

The first step is to turn AppleTalk on by selecting the Chooser from the Apple menu, and then clicking the AppleTalk Active button in the lower-right corner of the window as shown in Figure 10-1. A dialog box like this one will appear to remind you to make sure you are physically connected to the network:

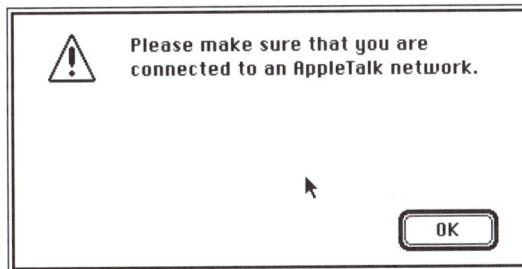

AppleTalk was designed to allow individual users to connect and disconnect from a network with the same ease that they plug or unplug a lamp from an electrical socket, so making the appropriate hardware connection and clicking this button is all you need to do to register your presence on the network.

You may already have AppleTalk turned on because AppleTalk is necessary to use many of the printers that are available for the Macintosh.

10

Figure 10-1.   *The Chooser desk accessory*

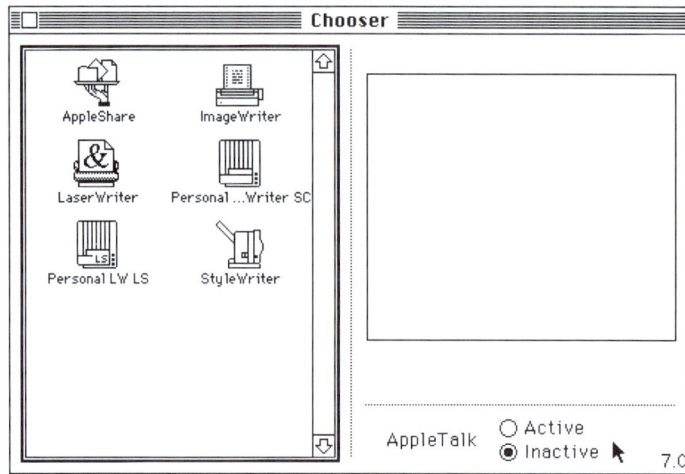

Figure 10-2.   *The Sharing Setup control panel*

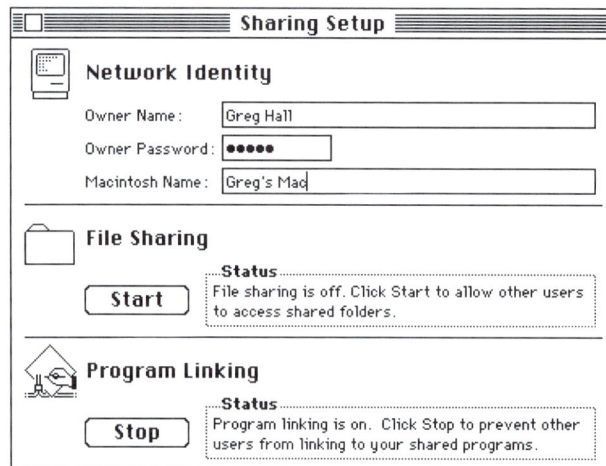

The second step in turning on file sharing is to select the Sharing Setup icon from the Control Panels folder. This opens the control panel shown in Figure 10-2. Note that it has three areas that can be filled in, and two buttons that can be activated.

The Network Identity section is where you identify yourself. The Owner's Name is you. Type in your name, or a name that you will remember. This is used to create an automatic user, (yourself) so you can access your own Macintosh from anywhere on the network.

Next is a text box for Owner Password. A password safeguards your files by making certain that only you log on as yourself. Of course, the usefulness of any password is only good so long as you keep it secret. Use a password that will not be immediately evident to others (don't use your middle name, your spouse's name, or something else easily guessed), and at the same time won't be hard for you to remember.

Finally, in the Macintosh Name text box you can identify how others will see your Macintosh. This name can be humorous, like a CB handle, or an alter ego, but if you are connecting to a large network, it is advisable to keep it simple, for example "Greg's Mac," so others know exactly which Macintosh they are connecting to. Don't use something like "Macintosh LC" when there may be several computers of that type on the network.

Once you have filled in these boxes, you are ready to start file sharing. Click the Start button in the File Sharing section. The status box changes to tell you that file sharing is starting up as shown in Figure 10-3. It will take a few moments for Sharing to start completely. Once it's running, you can turn off file sharing at any time by clicking the Stop button.

File sharing costs you an additional 256K of RAM, which might leave your memory pretty cramped in a 2MB system. Thus you might not want to keep file sharing on at all times.

The bottom section of the Sharing Setup control panel is called Program Linking. You can turn on program linking here, but there are very few programs that can currently make use of this feature. In the future, you may be able to buy applications that "talk" to each other, without a user's intervention. For example, a graphics program on your system might need to render a large and complicated drawing, and could ask other Macintoshes on the network if they are busy. To the ones that are not busy, your system

10

Figure 10-3.   *Starting up file sharing*

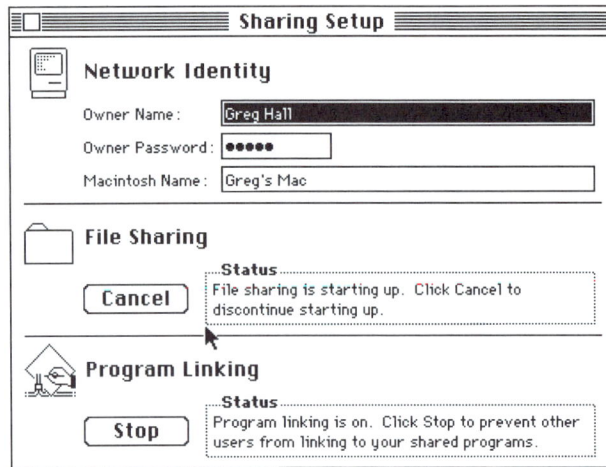

sends portions of the drawing for them to render. This feature will allow processing power not in use to be accessible for others to use. In the meantime, don't worry about whether Program Linking is turned on or off; it takes a lot more than turning it on here to let others link to programs on your Macintosh, and there's no memory or performance penalty in turning it on.

Allowing Others to Connect

Now that file sharing is turned on, you need to specify who can access files on your Macintosh. Select the Users & Groups icon from the control panel. Depending on what you called yourself in the Identify section, you will now have a window open with two users, yourself and Guest. To set up a new user with access to your Macintosh, go to the File menu and choose New User. Make a couple of these, and label them with names of people you work with as shown in Figure 10-4.

Figure 10-4. *Adding new users*

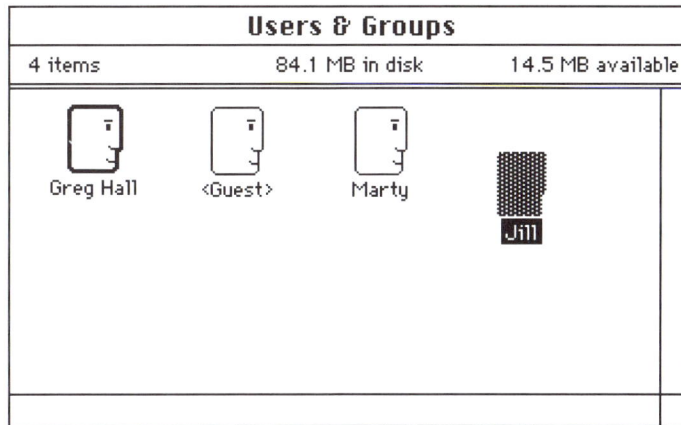

Select a new user from the ones you just created and open it by double-clicking. You should see something like Figure 10-5. Note that the default setting allows the user to connect to your Macintosh. If you want to, type in a password for this person. Why a password? If you are concerned that other people may want to get on your Macintosh and do nefarious deeds, then the password is a good idea. But if all the users are trusted friends, you can leave the password section blank.

Notice that the bottom half of the user's information box also contains a box for program linking. As stated earlier, when programs become available, program linking can be turned on, and other computers can share in your idle CPU resources. But for now, leave it off.

One more icon to look at is the Guest icon. Double-click it to open the information box and notice that the Allow Guests to Connect check box is already checked as you can see here:

10

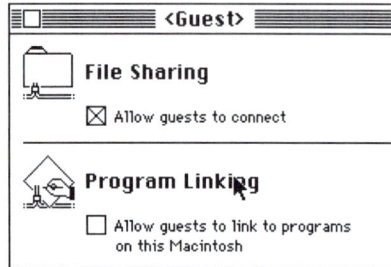

By default, anyone can connect to your Macintosh, and have access to those folders where "everyone" has privileges. If this is a concern, now is the time to turn off this option.

Look at the File menu again and note the New Group command. This is used to define broadly who has access to specific parts of your computer. Go ahead and make a new group now, and name it something like "My Group" as shown in Figure 10-6. To add users to this group, select the ones you want to add, and simply drag them to the group icon. When you open the icon,

Figure 10-5.   *New user information*

Figure 10-6. *A new group created*

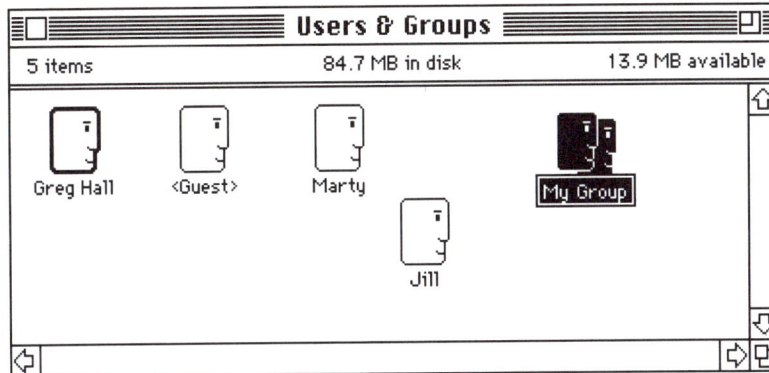

you'll see a window somewhat like Figure 10-7, with your own "rogues galley" of pictures on the wall.

To add or remove members from your group, drag their icons in or out of the group window. If you want to deny completely any users accessing your Macintosh, simply don't create icons for them. If you want to deny access to a user who is already in your "rogues gallery," just drag their icon to the trash. This will automatically remove them from any group.

Identifying Folders to Share

At this point, you have turned on file sharing for your Macintosh, and have identified some users you will allow to access it. Now define something for them to access, by setting up some shared folders. Follow these steps:

1. Make a new folder on your hard disk (not in another folder), and name the new folder "My Shared Folder."

2. Open the File menu and select Sharing from the menu.

3. Select the box "Share this item and its contents" and the rest of the dialog box will become visible. It should look like the Sharing dialog box shown in Figure 10-8.

10

Figure 10-7.   *Members of the new group*

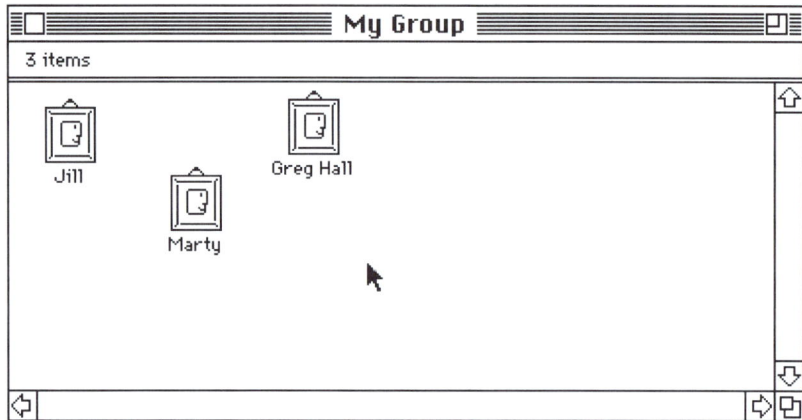

Figure 10-8.   *The Sharing dialog box*

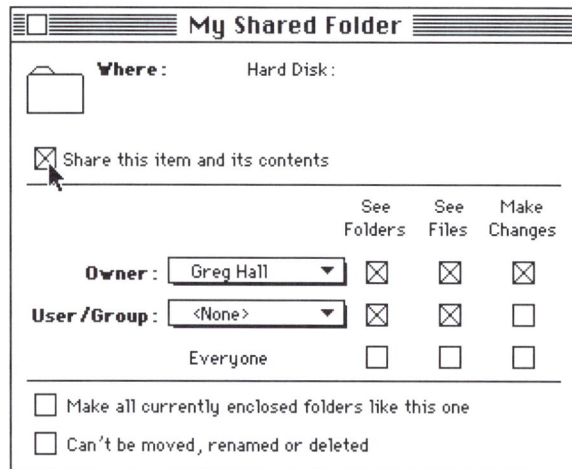

There are three levels of access in this box: Owner, User/Group, and Everyone. Click the pop-up menu just to the right of Owner, and you'll see all the users including yourself listed, as shown here:

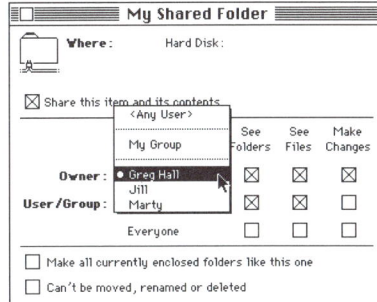

Below this is another pop-up menu with the same list of users. These two boxes allow you to assign who has ownership of this folder, and who can work with the contents.

Across the top of the columns of check boxes are the words "See Folders, See Files, Make Changes." When you first make a folder shared, the access level is again set at the lowest level (Everyone), to allow everyone to work with the files and make changes to them. Usually this is what you want, but you can define how much access specific users or groups can have. As an example, you could set the access privileges so that you could do everything, your New Group could only see files and folders, but make no changes, and everyone else would not be able to open the folder at all. The check box configuration shown in Figure 10-9 displays this setup.

When you close the dialog box, a dialog box like this one asks if you want to save the changes:

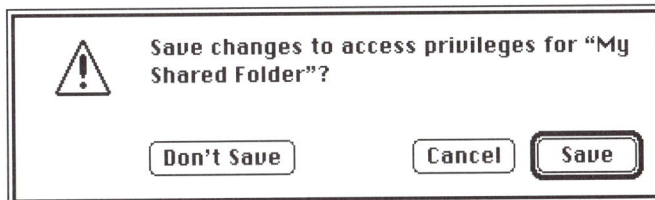

10

If you click the Save button the changes will take effect, and the My Shared Folder folder icon will appear like the one shown here:

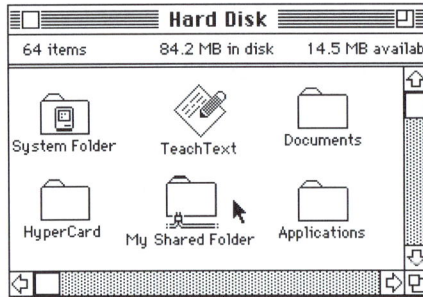

If just a few trusted people are going to be accessing your Macintosh, you can turn your entire Macintosh into a shared resource. Just select your hard disk icon, then select Sharing, and go through the same steps you just took.

Figure 10-9.   *Privileges set for Owner, User/Group, and Everyone*

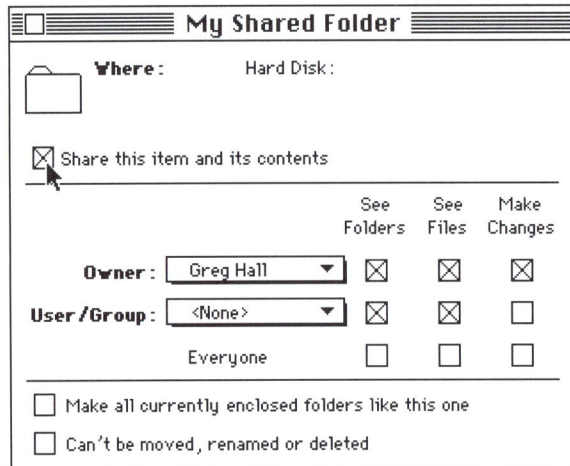

Using a File Server

Now that you have your system set up so others can share your files, let's look at how you can use someone else's files and how someone else accesses your files. A computer that makes folders on its disk (or an entire disk) available to the network, it is called a *file server*. Thus you turned your Macintosh into a file server in the preceding section.

Since the release of System 4.1 in 1987, all Macintoshes have had the ability to connect with file servers. Before System 7, though, Macintoshes had to be *dedicated* file servers, which meant they had to be running special software to share their disks, and they couldn't do anything else at the same time (or at least the range of tasks they could do at the same time was severely limited). With System 7, however, any Macintosh can be a file server when you select folders and share them.

The best way to show you how to connect to a file server is to show you how to connect to your own machine, assuming that you enabled sharing with the steps given in the previous section. Go to a second Macintosh connected with yours on the network, and follow these steps:

1. From the second Macintosh, select the Chooser from the Apple menu.

2. Click the AppleShare icon to see all the available servers. (If the Macintosh you are using to access your Macintosh doesn't have an AppleShare icon in its Chooser, then the AppleShare extension needs to be installed from the System software disks.) Assuming that your computer is the only file server on the network, your Chooser window should look something like the one in Figure 10-10.

3. Select your Macintosh as the file server by double-clicking your computer's name in the right side of the Chooser window. This will open a dialog box that requests your name and password.

   If you type your name and password (see Figure 10-11), you will see Hard Disk as the only selection, (see Figure 10-12) not your Shared Folder as you might expect. This is because, as owner, you have full rights to the entire disk.

10

Figure 10-10.   *AppleShare with one file server*

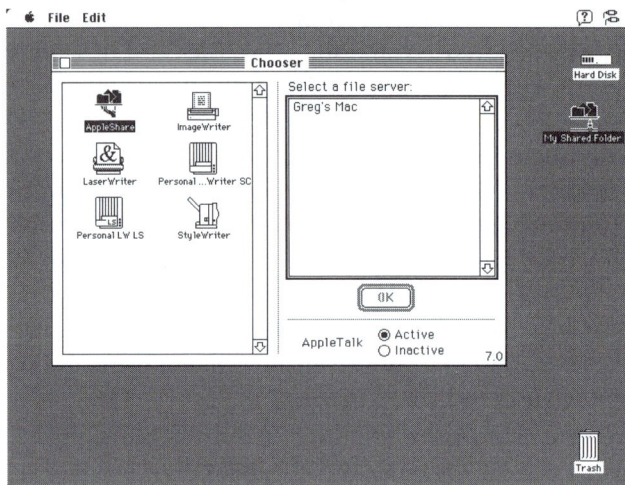

Figure 10-11.   *Connecting as a registered user*

Figure 10-12. When you connect as the owner you get the full hard disk

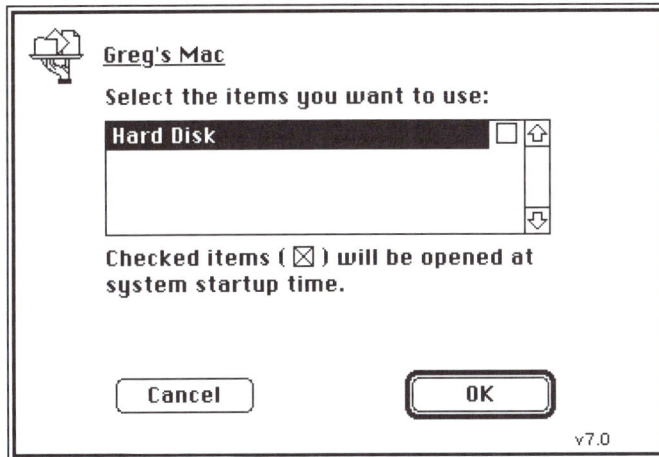

```
┌──────────────────────────────────────────────┐
│   ┌─┐                                          │
│   └─┘   Greg's Mac                             │
│         Select the items you want to use:      │
│        ┌──────────────────────────────┬──┬──┐  │
│        │ Hard Disk                    │☐ │⬆ │  │
│        │                              ├──┤  │  │
│        │                              │  │  │  │
│        │                              │  ├──┤  │
│        │                              │  │⬇ │  │
│        └──────────────────────────────┴──┴──┘  │
│         Checked items ( ⊠ ) will be opened at  │
│         system startup time.                   │
│                                                │
│                                                │
│        ┌──────────┐      ┌─────────────────┐   │
│        │  Cancel  │      │      OK         │   │
│        └──────────┘      └─────────────────┘   │
│                                        v7.0    │
└──────────────────────────────────────────────┘
```

As you type your password, it appears as asterisks or bullets, not as the text you actually type. This is a security feature; it prevents others from determining your password by watching over your shoulder as you type it. The password is also sent in an encrypted manner over the network, so that there is no way to eavesdrop on the network and determine user passwords.

4. Click OK, and the hard disk on your computer will be attached to the desktop of the second computer you are using, as shown in Figure 10-13. If you open the new hard disk, you'll be able to see all of its contents just as you can with the hard disk that's physically attached to the computer you are using.

One useful aspect of having file sharing turned on is that you can always gain full access to your Macintosh from anywhere on the network simply by logging in as the Owner. Give your personal password, and you'll be able to access all files and folders, even those that haven't been selected as "shared," just as if you were there at your Macintosh. If you make an alias of your Macintosh from another Macintosh while you have file sharing on, you can carry a copy of your hard disk around on a floppy: Just insert your floppy, double-click your hard disk icon, enter your password, and you will automatically have your hard disk opened in front of you. However, because file sharing is such a memory drain, you must weigh how much memory you have against the benefits of keeping file sharing on.

Logging On as a Normal User

Now see what others would see if they were to log on to your system. Follow these steps:

1. Select your attached hard disk by clicking the Hard Disk icon and choose Put Away from the File menu. This will disconnect your Macintosh.

2. Go through the steps of opening the Chooser and selecting your Macintosh as the file server. This time enter one of the user's names, as shown in Figure 10-14.

3. Click OK and notice that now only your folder, "My Shared Folder," is visible, as shown in Figure 10-15.

Figure 10-13.   *Your hard disk on the desktop of another computer*

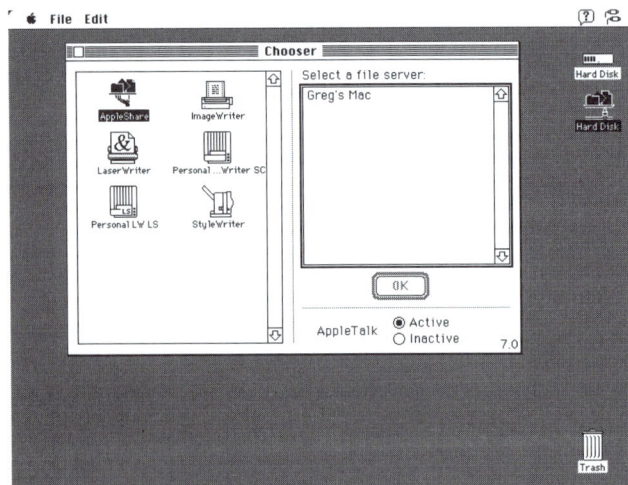

Figure 10-14. *Connecting as a normal user*

Figure 10-15. *Normal users only see shared items*

10

4. Click OK again and "My Shared Folder" shows up on the desktop just like the hard disk did before, but when you open it, only the folder's contents are accessible.

If you would like to have a file server connected each time you turn on your Macintosh, select the check box to the right of the name of the volume as shown in Figure 10-16. This allows the system to remember your name or your name and password if you select the second option at the bottom of the dialog box.

Connecting to a Large Network

All of the examples so far have assumed that you are connected to a simple network. But if you are connected to a large network, where there may be many file servers and many *zones*, or logical sections of the network, then the Chooser will look different, as shown in Figure 10-17.

Figure 10-16.   *The Access server at start up*

Figure 10-17. The Chooser with multiple zones and servers

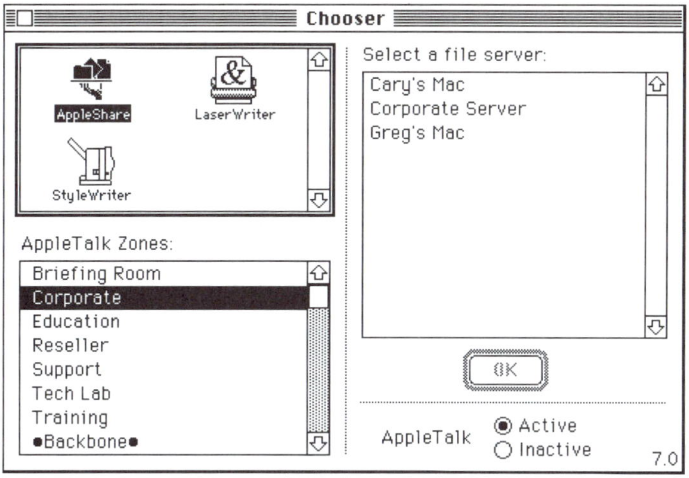

The bottom-left corner of this Chooser screen shows a scrolling list called AppleTalk Zones. These zones allow the network traffic to be separated into smaller groups, so that a large print job, for example, won't slow the entire network down.

Because there are more zones to search through, finding the devices you want to work with may take longer; you may have to search the various zones to find the servers, printers, or other devices you want to work with. A larger network might also differ from a simpler network by having different types of file servers. Because personal AppleShare is dependent on a given Macintosh having file sharing turned on, many companies use a dedicated file server that is not a workstation that people use.

AppleShare 3.0 is designed for a dedicated Macintosh file server, and is meant to be kept running all the time. It contains administrative functions, such as forcing a user's password to be changed every 30 days, and the ability to generate a list of who owns what on the file server—useful functions for a centralized Macintosh to have.

Another example of dedicated file server software comes from Novell, which is the dominant networking software publisher in the PC world. This

10

file server software is used in large PC and Macintosh environments, and offers more security and administrative functions than AppleShare. You connect to a running Novell server exactly the same way that you do for a personal file server, or an AppleShare 3.0 server.

Finally, Digital Equipment Corporation (DEC) makes another popular file server software package, Pathworks. Pathworks turns the hard disk drives and file structures of a Digital Equipment mainframe computer into a file server that is accessed just like any other file server.

The real magic of the Macintosh stems from the fact that each different file server software uses a different file structure and different file types, but all of the files are accessible to you just by clicking them. You can copy files from a floppy disk to a hard disk drive to a file server all in the same way, without needing to learn the different file commands for the various applications.

AppleTalk Remote Access

There is one more facet of networking that needs to be explored. Imagine you work on one Macintosh at home and another at the office. While working at home one weekend, you realize that you need a document that you left on your Macintosh at work. One alternative is to drive to work, get the file, and drive home. But if you've set up both home and work computers with modems, you also have the option of using a telephone line to fetch the file. (Simply put, a *modem* is a device that allows computers to communicate using telephone lines. You'll learn more about modems in the "Remote Communications" section next in this chapter.)

You can retrieve the file from your work Macintosh using software from Apple, called AppleTalk Remote Access. This software was first introduced with the PowerBook computers, and is installed just like any other system software on the Macintosh. The Installer will place the various extensions in their correct folders and modify other areas of your system software. Some of the differences between Local Access and Remote Access appear in the User & Groups dialog box where settings are needed for both a new user and the owner. There is also a new control panels device, called Remote Access Setup (shown in Figure 10-18), where you select the type of modem you will use and whether or not you want to have your Macintosh answer incoming calls. (You would set the Macintosh that's in your office to answer incoming calls.)

Figure 10-18. *The Remote Access Setup control panel*

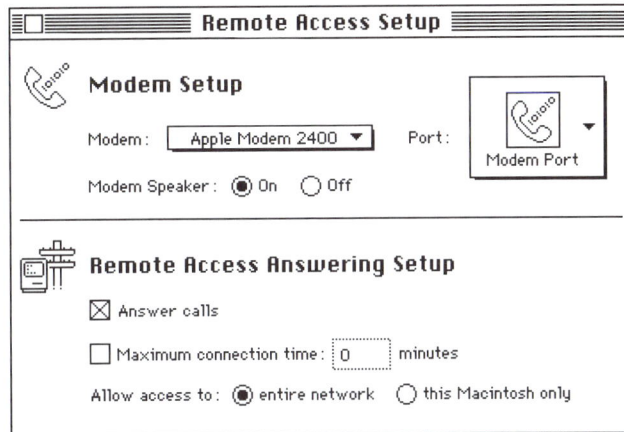

To connect, you'll need a modem on both the calling and receiving Macintosh, and both Macintoshes need to have AppleTalk Remote Access installed and running. This is the application that actually answers the phone when you call. In addition, you need to leave your office Macintosh set up to allow dial in. Finally, you need to enter your name, password, and telephone number into the Remote Access dialog box and select Connect to start the connection, as shown in Figure 10-19. Once connected, another dialog box will open and let you check periodically how long you've been connected.

When you are connected, you have full access to all the resources that are available on your Macintosh at work. This includes all the zones and services in the Chooser, including access to your hard disk (if you turned on file sharing), file servers on your network, electronic mail systems, and even LaserWriter printers. Everything is the same as if you were actually there, except that the access to these services is slower. A faster modem helps, but there will always be a time lag between actually being connected to a network, and dialing into the network with a modem.

There are other products that allow remote dial in, the most notable being Farallon's Liaison and Shiva's NetModem. These products allow more capa-

Figure 10-19.   *The Remote Access Status dialog box*

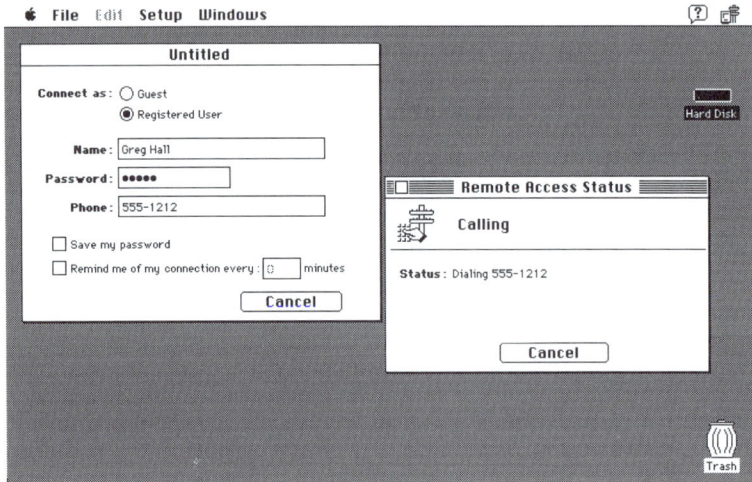

bilities or different ways of achieving these same capabilities. Liaison allows a Macintosh to be a *router*, so that network traffic on one zone can cross over to another zone. Shiva's NetModem allows any Macintosh to access a modem over the network, without needing a modem and telephone line for each individual Macintosh user.

Remote Communications

Remote communications means using devices (like the modem) to let computers send data to one another over telephone lines. You have just seen one way to set up remote communications with AppleTalk. This section explores other remote options.

Modems

A modem is a device that translates sounds, which can be sent via phone lines, to and from data which computers know. Modems come in various speeds, with 1200-, 2400-, and 9600-baud models being the most common ones used with a Macintosh.

Baud rate relates the numbers of bits that are transmitted. The higher the baud number, the faster the speed of communications. A 1200-baud rate is equivalent to 1,200 bits per second (bps). Each character takes 8 bits to store in the computer, but additional communications overhead (used to make sure the data was received correctly) increases this, so that one character usually takes 10 bits when transmitted through modems. Thus a 1200-baud modem is roughly equivalent to 120 characters per second and a 9600-baud modem is equivalent to nearly 1000 characters per second.

Several factors determine the speed of the modem you buy. First, since most online services support 2400 bps communications, and since the price of these modems is reasonable, there's no reason to purchase a 1200 bps modem. Although a 9600 bps modem is much faster than a 2400 bps modem it's also much more expensive, and you can only reap the benefits of its speed if your online services support it. In other words, it won't do you much good to pay a lot more for a 9600 bps modem if your online services can only register 2400 bps.

Both these factors—the high cost of modems and the limitations of online services—are likely to change, and in the next two or three years the prices of 9600 bps modems are likely to fall to the price range of 2400 bps modems today. So, the best advice for today is to purchase a 2400 bps modem.

On the other hand, if you plan to use a modem primarily with AppleTalk Remote Access, you should consider a 9600 bps modem both for home use and for the office. These modems can also operate at 2400 bps for connections to other services.

Besides working as data modems, some modems can also be used to send and/or receive faxes through the Macintosh. Examples of these include Teleport by Global Village and The Dove Fax by Dove. If you don't have a fax machine, and can see the need for this, it might be worth checking out.

10

Communications Software

Besides a modem, you need software to control it. There are two classes of this software. First, there's the generic communications program, which lets you connect to virtually any online system. Examples of this include Microphone II, SmartCom II, and ZTerm. All these (and others) provide good basic communications functions.

Another class of software is specific to certain services. For example, the popular America Online and Prodigy services use their own programs to allow you to connect and use a variety of their services—for example, with these information services you can use your Macintosh to order flowers, arrange the best price for plane tickets, shop at a variety of stores, and access your bank account (you'll learn more about information services shortly). These online service systems hide from you some of the dirty details of communications, and provide a friendly front-end to the service. CompuServe uses Navigator and CompuServe Information Manager as the software for its online service.

There are many uses for remote communications. The most prevalent is the simple transfer of files from one computer to another computer—whether the computers are separated by a few feet or several thousand miles. The two computers can be any mix of Macintoshes, PCs, minicomputers, and mainframes. Both communicating computers require a modem, communications software, and a telephone line between them, but given that, any two computers can exchange information. Two other major uses of remote communications are electronic mail and information services.

Electronic Mail

Electronic mail uses one computer as a mail server. Each user can receive messages and files and can leave similar "mail" for other users. Electronic mail is both a remote and a network communications facility. There are several companies that make electronic mail software, but two of the more prominent applications are Microsoft Mail and CE Software's QuickMail. To use electronic mail you install and start the software and connect to a computer that is running the mail server software. Then you can write a note, address it to others using the server, and even enclose files that will be sent to those users. An example of this is shown in Figure 10-20 where a message is being prepared with QuickMail.

Information services such as CompuServe, America Online, and Prodigy also provide electronic mail services, which let you communicate with others across the country or around the world. Of course, the person to whom you are sending mail must also use the same service.

Information Services

Information services have been around for many years and have evolved from services that required a computer genius to access them, to their present day incarnations, which are fairly easy to use.

One of the oldest services is CompuServe. This service charges you a connection fee based on the amount of time you are connected plus a service fee for the type of service you use. CompuServe probably has the best overall

Figure 10-20. *Preparing a message in QuickMail*

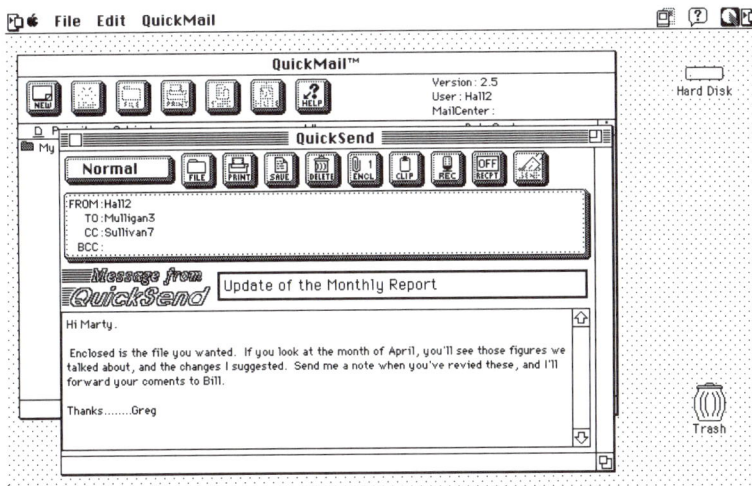

selection of services available, from booking your own travel reservations and checking the weather in the city of your choice, to buying discounted items through an online shopping service.

Another service, Prodigy, takes a different approach. To receive Prodigy you pay a very reasonable fixed monthly fee that allows you to connect for as long as you want, without additional charges. The disadvantage of using Prodigy is its very weak user interface, which has almost no Macintosh capabilities. Also, because they are sponsored in part by Sears and IBM, there is a fair amount of advertising that you have to get past to reach the services you want to use.

CompuServe requires you to purchase some kind of communications software (though you can purchase products such as Navigator and CompuServe Information Manager), while Prodigy comes with its own software. This means CompuServe is more complicated to learn, (you have to master the communications software as well as the service), but is more flexible because you can access other services with it. Prodigy is easier to use, but only runs on its own software. You have to make the decision on what you want to accomplish with these packages. There are also several other information services that you may want to investigate. These include GEnie (the General Electric Network for Information Exchange), Delphi, DIALOG, BRS/After Dark, Mead, and LEXIS.

The future of communications in the U.S. is moving toward ISDN (Integrated Services, Digital Network). ISDN provides pure digital communications. Also, ISDN can transport video images such as computer graphics and family videos, as well as sounds and computer data. This requires fundamental changes in the telephone equipment at your home and at your local telephone company, but it will allow many more enhancements to your computer system. Chief among these is the ability to have a 56,000-baud connection to other computers (or 5,600 characters per second).

Even today communications plays a large and growing part in computing. As more people work at home or in dispersed offices, the need for communications grows. As more people work on computers, the need to transfer information among them grows. As clerical costs increase, the need to use inexpensive messaging provided by electronic mail grows. You could almost say the future of computing is communications, but that would ignore the many other frontiers that the computer is racing toward.

With your Macintosh you are armed and ready with one of the most capable and definitely the most user-friendly tools with which to meet those new frontiers.

Communicating with IBM PCs

As a Macintosh owner, let's face it: you're outnumbered. There are more PC owners in the world than there are Macintosh owners. If you are working in a business, chances are that there are PCs at the site next to Macintoshes.

There are a couple of solutions for transferring data between the two machines. First, you can send files to PCs using information services as mentioned in the previous section. Also, some network-based electronic mail systems allow you to connect both PCs and Macintoshes to the same network, and run the same mail packages. But connecting both PCs and Macintoshes to the same network is no easy trick. Finally, if the two machines are close enough to one another physically, you can connect them using special cables, and use programs such as LapLink Macintosh or MacLink Plus/PC to exchange the files.

But chances are you can also use a floppy disk to share your files with PC users. All Macintosh computers currently being sold include disk drives capable of reading and writing to 720KB and 1.44MB 3 1/2-inch disks that are common to many PCs. This floppy disk on its own, however, is not enough, for two reasons. First, you need special software to let the Macintosh actually use the disk, and second, the manner in which the programs for the two machines store information in files (such as formatting in a word processing file) is different. In some cases, these two problems are solved in one software package.

With your Macintosh system software, Apple provides a utility called Apple File Exchange (AFE). This program can actually read PC-formatted disks that you insert in the Macintosh, and does some file translation. It also formats PC disks. However, it has a user interface that is very confusing to learn, and hard to remember how to use. If you plan to do a lot of translation, you should use another program, such as MacLink Plus/PC, which is discussed in the following paragraphs.

10

There are two system extensions available that let the Macintosh use PC disks just as if they were Macintosh disks: AccessPC from Insignia Software (shown in Figure 10-21), and DOSMounter from Dayna Communications. With either of these programs installed in your System folder, you can work with PC disks just as if they were Macintosh disks. They also provide ways of letting you open some files on those disks just as if the files were created on the Macintosh (if no file translation is involved).

The warhorse of enabling Macintosh to PC communications is MacLink Plus/PC. This program includes DOSMounter, to let you work with the disks, but also provides means of transferring the files between Macintoshes and PCs that are directly connected, or that communicate with a modem. Its sterling feature, though, is its translation power. It can turn nearly any kind

Figure 10-21.   *The AccessPC control panel*

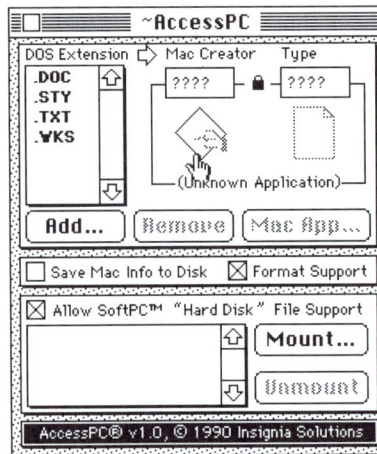

of PC file (including those produced by word processors, spreadsheets, databases, and graphics programs) into a file that can be used on your Macintosh. For example, a WordStar or WordPerfect document from the PC translates into either a MacWrite or Microsoft Word document on the Macintosh. If you plan to do file transfers between the two types of machines with any regularity, you need this program.

Many of the newer applications for the Macintosh include translators that allow you to work with the PC version of that same application. For instance, both WordPerfect and Microsoft Word are capable of automatically translating files for the Macintosh from the PC versions of (respectively) WordPerfect and Microsoft Word—and vice versa. If you have WordPerfect on your Macintosh and on a PC, all you need is the ability to read the PC's floppy disk, and copy the files to your Macintosh to work on them. The Apple File Exchange does this very well.

Working with floppy disks is fairly simple, but if you need to transfer files that are larger than 1.44MB, then the next best option is to use an external and possibly removable hard disk. These plug into the SCSI (Small Computer Systems Interface) port found on all Macintoshes. Hard disk drives vary from 20MB to more than 2000MB (2GB or gigabytes).

To use a non-removable hard disk to transfer data, plug the disk into first one computer, write the data to be transferred, unplug the disk, and plug it into another computer where you will read and work with the data. With a removable hard disk, you carry it between computers without having to change the cabling on the drive.

There is one special instance where the SCSI interface is used uniquely with the Macintosh: the PowerBook 100 has a special version of ROM that allows it to become an external SCSI drive to another Macintosh when a special cable is used. The screen that allows you to select which SCSI address to use is shown in Figure 10-22. Once the cable is inserted, and the PowerBook 100 restarted, it will automatically behave as a hard disk to another Macintosh. Since the PowerBook 100 uses an external floppy drive, connecting it as an external hard drive may be the simplest way to transfer files.

10

Figure 10-22.   *The SCSI hard disk address of a PowerBook 100*

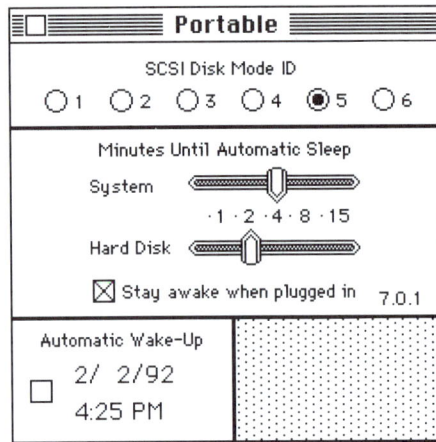

Summary

Even if you don't plan to do any communications today, chances are you will in the future. The Macintosh is especially capable of communicating with other computers—not just with other Macintoshes and PCs but with mainframes and minicomputers as well.

Appendix

Installing System 7

The rest of this book assumes that System 7, the current Macintosh system software, has already been installed on your computer. If you have a new Macintosh, it came from the factory with System 7 already installed. The other possibility is that you are using a Macintosh with an older version of the system software and have decided to install System 7 on your Macintosh to get some of its benefits.

Even if you do not have to install the system software, knowing about the process can give you some self-confidence about using your Macintosh. Knowing how to install system software on your Macintosh is like knowing how to change the tire on your car. Although you may belong to an automobile club, and have your car serviced regularly, knowing the basics of how to change a flat tire will get you where you need to go when you don't have other alternatives. When you realize that installing the system software is a lot simpler than changing a tire, and the worst that can happen is you'll need to insert a series of floppy disks, the procedure becomes less threatening.

You need to go through the installation process for only two reasons: you don't yet have System 7 installed, or you have decided to reinstall System 7 because of some problems you may be experiencing. For example, you may believe that the system software is corrupted from a previous hardware problem or a virus infection. However you reached this point, the process of installing the system software is the same.

Installation Steps

Before you start the actual process of installing the system software, take stock of your situation. Does the disk you are installing onto have information already on it, and do you want to erase or keep that information? Does this disk have a valid, bootable system software on it already that you want to update? Does the installation disk have a corrupted system that needs to be replaced? Each of these three scenarios requires a different set of steps to accomplish the installation of System 7 but some of the steps are similar. The basic steps are as follows:

- *Checking the compatibility of items on your hard disk*   If you are upgrading from a previous version of the Macintosh system software and plan to keep the application programs currently on your hard disk, you should use the HyperCard stack that comes with System 7 to see if the programs, especially the Inits, are compatible with System 7.

- *Backing up your hard disk*   If you have programs and information on your hard disk that you do not want to lose, you should back them up by making a copy of them on a floppy disk, even if you are not planning to initialize your hard disk.

- *Initializing your hard disk*   Initializing or formatting your hard disk (they mean the same thing) permanently erases everything on the disk and establishes or reestablishes the *sectoring* or pattern that determines how information is written on the disk. You need to initialize your hard disk if you have a new disk that has never been used, if you believe that your hard disk has been corrupted, or if you want to clean up your hard disk and start anew.

- *Updating your hard disk driver*   If you do not initialize your hard disk and you have had an earlier version of system software on it, you need to update the hard disk driver so that it is compatible with System 7.

- *Installing System 7*   The actual installation of System 7 is anticlimactic—it is little more than putting floppy disks into your computer when you see a message to do so on the screen.

If you have a new hard disk without system software on it, you only need to initialize it and install System 7. If you have a hard disk with existing system software on it along with application programs and information, you need to run the Compatibility Checker if possible, back up the information and maybe the applications, initialize or update your hard disk, and install System 7. Each of these steps will be discussed in detail in the following sections.

The following discussion assumes that Apple disk drives are being used. Some third-party drives will not be "seen" by the Apple HD SC Setup program. Use the utility program that came with your hard disk instead. The general steps remain the same.

Compatibility Checking

If you have existing application programs on your hard disk that you want to continue to use, your first step is to run the Compatibility Checker, a HyperCard stack that comes with System 7. This stack is designed to search your hard disk drive, and to report to you all of the applications that you have, their version numbers, and then to compare them to the list that is built into the stack and tell you which applications will or will not work with System 7.

The Compatibility Checker is only as good as the information that went into it. Most of the software vendors tested the current versions of their applications with System 7. Most did not do extensive testing of older versions of applications. Depending on when you bought your application, your program may work fine, or it may only work in 24-bit mode, or it may not run at all. It's left up to you to either upgrade your existing applications to their current level, or to do your own testing to find out if the application is compatible with System 7.

To use the Compatibility Checker you must have HyperCard 1.2.2 or later installed on your hard disk. (Apple has been shipping HyperCard with all of its Macintosh computers since late 1987. Although ownership of HyperCard has been transferred to Claris, the software subsidiary of Apple, a reduced or "slimmed down" version is still being included with most Macintosh computers.)

The Compatibility Checker is on a disk named Before You Install System 7. You must locate it and put it in your computer. Follow these steps:

1. Double-click the Before You Install System 7 floppy disk icon to open it.

2. Double-click the HyperCard stack named Before You Install System 7. If you have HyperCard installed, the stack will open and you will see the screen shown in Figure A-1. If you do not have HyperCard installed, you need to locate the HyperCard disks that came with the current system software you are using and copy HyperCard and the Home stack to your hard disk. Then click the Before You Install System 7 stack.

3. Click the Compatibility Checker button. If you have only one hard disk, you will be asked to copy the Compatibility Checker to your

Figure A-1.   *Before You Install System 7*

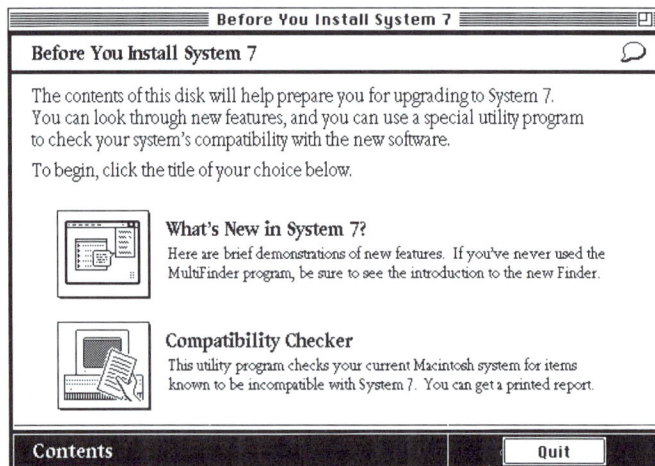

hard disk. Click Copy. If you have several hard disks, you will be asked to run Setup and then choose the hard disks you want to check.

4. You see the Compatibility Checker screen shown in Figure A-2. Click Start Checking.

The Macintosh is surveyed for all applications on its disks, then all Inits. You will see both a thermometer bar and a spinning beach ball to tell you the status. Those Inits that are "suspect" can be placed in a folder labeled May Not Work With System 7, as shown in Figure A-3. These Inits should be left out of your System folder until you feel comfortable using System 7. Once you're confident, put them back in your System folder.

Put only one suspect Init in your System folder per day. If you use your Macintosh for normal activity, and nothing adverse happens, then it's probably fine to leave that one in your Macintosh, and add another one. If it turns out that you do have a conflict, and you need to restart your Macintosh, hold down the (shift) key when the Macintosh is starting up, and all Inits and extensions will be disabled. You'll then be able to open your System folder, and remove the offending file.

Figure A-2. The Compatibility Checker screen

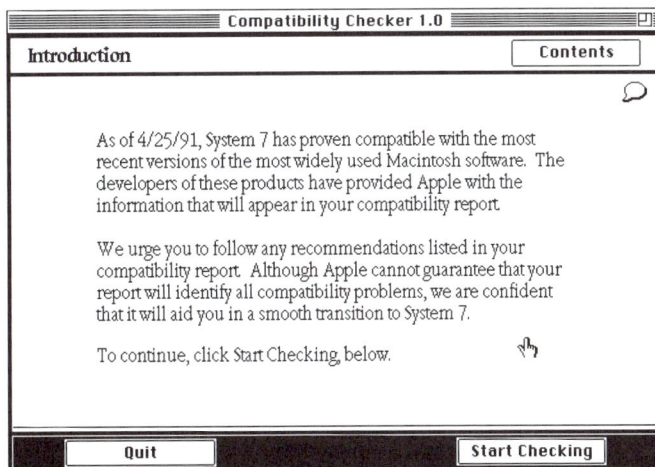

Figure A-3.   *Inits that are potential problems*

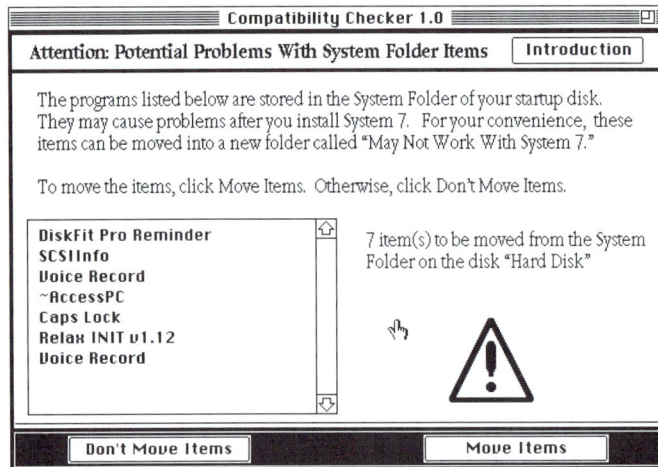

When the Compatibility Checker is done, it will prepare a report that lists all of the applications on your hard disk, giving you the status of each. You can use the scroll bar to review the report, as shown in Figure A-4 or you can print it. It makes sense to print it for future reference.

The Compatibility Report is very conservative. It tells you that there may be a problem if it doesn't know that there isn't one. Except for Inits, which can cause start-up problems, go ahead and try your applications with System 7. If you find one that has a glitch, contact the publisher of it and see what they suggest—probably that you upgrade it.

Backing Up Your Hard Disk

Backing up your information files by copying them to floppy disks is something you should do regularly. Usually you have the original distribution floppy disks for your application programs so you do not need to back them up. But if you have not backed up your information files, you need to do that before continuing with the System 7 installation. No matter how safe an

A

Figure A-4. *The Compatibility Report screen*

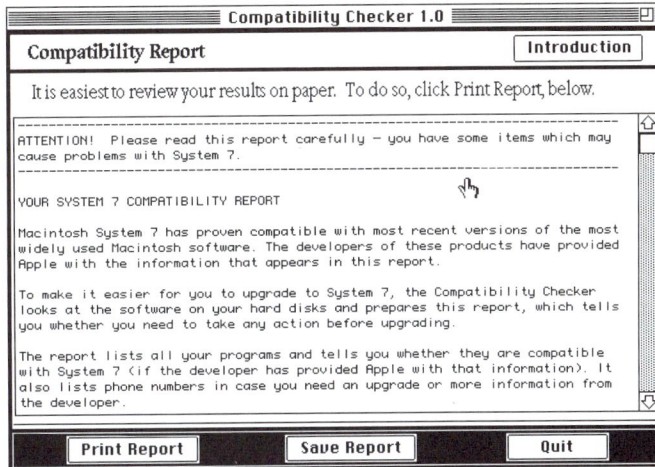

```
 ▤▤▤▤▤▤▤▤▤▤▤▤▤▤▤ Compatibility Checker 1.0 ▤▤▤▤▤▤▤▤▤▤▤▤▤ ⌐
 ┌──────────────────────────────────────────────────────────────────┐
 │ Compatibility Report                           [ Introduction ]   │
 │                                                                    │
 │   It is easiest to review your results on paper.  To do so, click Print Report, below.│
 │  ┌──────────────────────────────────────────────────────────────┐ ⇧ │
 │  │ ------------------------------------------------------------ │ │ │
 │  │ ATTENTION!  Please read this report carefully – you have some items which may │ │
 │  │ cause problems with System 7.                                │ │ │
 │  │ ------------------------------------------------------------ │ │ │
 │  │                                            ᶜᵐ                │ │ │
 │  │ YOUR SYSTEM 7 COMPATIBILITY REPORT                           │ │ │
 │  │                                                              │ │ │
 │  │ Macintosh System 7 has proven compatible with most recent versions of the most │ │
 │  │ widely used Macintosh software. The developers of these products have provided │ │
 │  │ Apple with the information that appears in this report.      │ │ │
 │  │                                                              │ │ │
 │  │ To make it easier for you to upgrade to System 7, the Compatibility Checker │ │
 │  │ looks at the software on your hard disks and prepares this report, which tells │ │
 │  │ you whether you need to take any action before upgrading.    │ │ │
 │  │                                                              │ │ │
 │  │ The report lists all your programs and tells you whether they are compatible │ │
 │  │ with System 7 (if the developer has provided Apple with that information). It │ │
 │  │ also lists phone numbers in case you need an upgrade or more information from │ │
 │  │ the developer.                                               │ ⇩ │
 │  └──────────────────────────────────────────────────────────────┘ │
 │ ┌──────────────┐       ┌──────────────┐       ┌──────────────┐    │
 │ │ Print Report │       │ Save Report  │       │    Quit      │    │
 │ └──────────────┘       └──────────────┘       └──────────────┘    │
 └──────────────────────────────────────────────────────────────────┘
```

installation process may be, there is always a chance that something unforeseen may happen, causing the loss of all information on the disk. An example would be if a power outage occurred just as you began to write to your disk—the Macintosh would scribble nonsense all over your information files. Don't take chances.

The best way to back up files is to use the specialized third-party backup programs such as those included with SUM II or the Norton Utilities for the Macintosh, both distributed by Symantec. If you do not have one of these programs (and they do a lot more than just backup), simply copy the files you want to back up by dragging them to a floppy disk.

Initializing Your Hard Disk

The ideal situation is to install system software on a new or blank hard disk. If you have information on your hard disk, but you have backed up all of it on floppies, then initialize your hard disk. This gives you a clean slate to work with, and is the best starting point. If you will not be initializing your hard disk drive, skip to the next section, "Updating Your Hard Disk Driver."

To initialize your hard disk drive on the Macintosh, you need to run a program called Apple HD SC Setup. This application is located on the Disk Tools disk that comes with System 7. If you are going to be formatting your only hard disk drive, you need to restart your Macintosh with the Disk Tools floppy disk in your computer. This is because the Macintosh will not erase the disk that it started up from. Follow these steps:

1. Place the System 7 Disk Tools disk in your computer and choose Restart from the Special menu. Then double-click the Apple HD SC Setup application and you'll eventually come to the screen shown in Figure A-5.

   It has five buttons on the left, and one in the center. You use the center button to select which hard disk drive you want to work on, and the left series of buttons to select the task you want to perform. The center button asks you for the drive number. There are seven available drive numbers, numbered from 0 to 6, which correspond to the drives' SCSI (Small Computer System Interface) addresses.

Figure A-5.   *The Apple HD SC main screen*

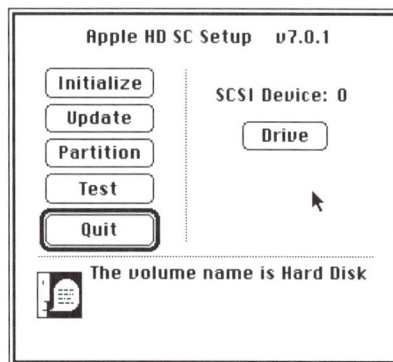

A

SCSI address 0 is most often the internal drive of your Macintosh. You will need to select the correct drive to format. Make sure you look at the name that is displayed at the bottom third of the dialog box. If your drive has a name, this is where it will show up.

2. When you are certain that you have selected the correct drive, select the Initialize button in the upper-left corner. Your computer will ask if you are sure, as shown here:

```
┌──────────────────────────────────────────────┐
│    ⚠    Initializing will erase all of the data│
│    /!\  on "Hard Disk" (SCSI Device: 0).  Do   │
│         you want to initialize this disk?       │
│                                                 │
│              ▶                                  │
│                   ┌────────┐   ┌────────┐       │
│                   │ Cancel │   │  Init  │       │
│                   └────────┘   └────────┘       │
└──────────────────────────────────────────────┘
```

If you press the button marked Init, all of the contents of your hard disk will be erased, and the drive reformatted.

Initializing a disk and formatting a disk are the same process, and the terms are often interchanged. They both create new sectors on your disk, destroying all information previously on the disk, with little hope of recovery.

Erasing a hard disk drive is not the same, however. If you select Erase Disk from the Special menu, the system software will simply erase, or "zero out" the directory structure of your hard disk. This leaves all the information on the disk, but tears up the road map to that information, essentially taking the information out of your reach. However, disk utilities such as Norton Utilities for the Macintosh and Symantec Utilities for the Macintosh II (SUM II) are capable of reading the tags that the system software leaves attached to each file, and can usually reconstruct the directory.

While the disk drive is being initialized, there is no gauge to indicate progress, except a spinning beach ball that simply tells you that something is happening. Depending on the size of your disk, this may take from a few to a number of minutes. When the Macintosh finishes, you'll be returned to the same dialog box that you started with.

3. Select Quit to end the program. If your disk had never been formatted for the Macintosh, you would be prompted to name your hard disk, as shown here:

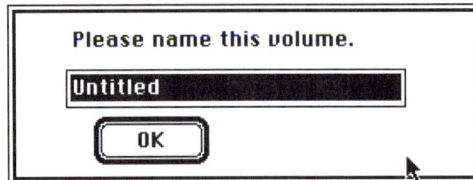

```
┌─────────────────────────────────────────┐
│                                         │
│        Please name this volume.         │
│                                         │
│   ┌───────────────────────────────┐     │
│   │ Untitled                      │     │
│   └───────────────────────────────┘     │
│       ┌─────────────────────┐           │
│       │        OK           │           │
│       └─────────────────────┘           │
│                              ▶           │
└─────────────────────────────────────────┘
```

Although you won't need them, the other three buttons on the Apple HD SC Setup screen allow you to update the driver from an older initializing, to allow it to work with the new System 7 features such as virtual memory; to partition the hard disk drive, which is useful on the Macintosh LC, where part of the hard disk can be used by the optional Apple //e card; and finally to test the hard disk drive for *bad sectors*—areas on the hard disk that do not accurately store information.

If you initialized your hard disk, your preparations are complete; you're ready to install System 7. To do that, jump ahead to the section "Installing System 7."

Updating Your Hard Disk Driver

If you did not initialize your hard disk for this installation process, you need to update the hard disk driver on your computer before you can install System 7. This is done with the same Apple HD SC Setup program on the Disk Tools disk used earlier for initializing. Use it now for updating your hard disk driver. Follow these steps:

1. Insert the System 7 Disk Tools disk into your floppy drive. Double-click the disk's icon to open it and then double-click the Apple HD SC Setup program icon to start that program.

2. When you get to the Apple HD SC Setup screen shown in Figure A-5, click the Update button.

    The Update command removes any earlier versions of the driver for your hard disk, and replaces it with one that is compatible with System 7. The major change is the driver's ability to support virtual memory, which uses part of the disk as an extension of memory.

3. When the Update is completed, select Quit from the Apple HD SC Setup screen.

Installing System 7

You use five disks to install the current version (7.0.1) of System 7 on a Macintosh. These disks are labeled Install 1, Install 2, Printing, Fonts, and Tidbits. (Disk Tools is not used during normal installation, but is very useful since it is a bootable disk and contains the Disk First Aid, and Apple HD SC Setup applications.)

Some of these disks contain information or files that are only usable with the Installer program. Other disks, such as the Printing disk, contain drivers and their own Installer, so that you can update or add drivers to another computer, without needing to run the complete System 7 install process. Depending on which version of System 7 you are installing, you may have more or fewer disks than the five discussed here. In any case, your Installer will ask you to insert one of the disks in your package and all you need to do is follow the instructions you see on the screen.

To begin the installation, it is best to start your Macintosh using the Install 1 floppy disk. Do that now with these steps:

1. Insert the Install 1 disk in your floppy drive and either turn on your Macintosh, or select Restart from the Special menu. (If your floppy disk is ejected when the Macintosh restarts, reinsert it.)

    The Install 1 disk is a special bootable floppy disk. Because it was necessary to cram as much information onto the disk as possible, some information used to make this disk boot was put on the boot tracks of the floppy disk. Under System 7, however, the boot tracks do not normally get copied when a disk is copied with the normal Finder disk copy process. If you received a set of System 7 floppy disks from someplace other than Apple, there is a possibility that the Install 1 floppy disk will not boot. If this is the case, use the Disk Tools floppy disk to boot your Macintosh, then insert the Install 1 disk, and start the Installer application located on the Install 1 disk. (This will entail a lot more disk swapping to get the Installer to run, but you will achieve the same results.)

It is possible to run the Installer from a Macintosh that is already up and running, but this requires more disk space on your hard disk than if you launched directly from the Install 1 floppy disk. This is because the Macintosh makes a copy of your active system folder, modifies the copy, then deletes the original. Booting from the Install 1 floppy disk is a little easier to illustrate, so discussion here focuses on that procedure.

When the Macintosh starts the Installer, your screen should look like Figure A-6. This screen welcomes you to the Installer program,

Figure A-6.   *The Welcome to the Apple Installer start-up screen*

and gives you the instructions you need to run the Installer. If you do not get this screen, or if the Macintosh generates an error condition, then your Install 1 disk is not a bootable disk, and you will need to reboot using the Disk Tools floppy disk, as noted earlier.

2. Select OK from the Startup screen and you will be taken to the screen shown in Figure A-7.

The Installer assumes that you want the Easy Install part of the program and for almost everyone this is true. Notice in the Easy Install screen that the Installer has checked the hardware configuration of your Macintosh, and has come up with some default items to install. For example, if your Macintosh includes an Ethernet interface card, the Installer will automatically add the software drivers needed to access Ethernet.

If you have more than one hard disk attached to your Macintosh, make sure the correct one is selected. If necessary, select Switch Disks to get to the hard disk to which you want to install. For most people, the default selections are fine. If the default selections are not appropriate, you can modify what the Installer will add, by going

Figure A-7.   *The Easy Install screen*

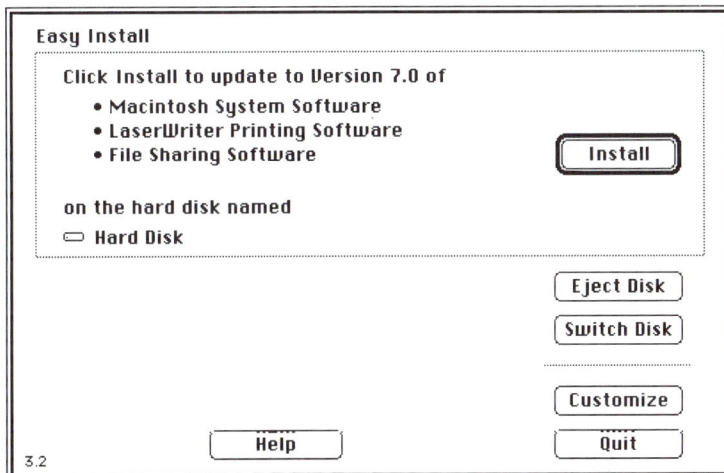

into the Customize section. This is described in more detail in the next section, "Customizing the Installation."

3. Click the Install button to begin the installation of System 7 and insert the appropriate floppy disks, as they are requested.

4. When all the disks have been read, the Installer will ask for the Install 1 disk again and then display the screen shown in Figure A-7. Click Quit to leave the Installer.

Your installation process is complete! Put the floppy disks away in a safe place, in case you need to do the installation process again.

Customizing the Installation

Customizing is useful if you add an interface card or printer after you've installed System 7. Doing a custom install is also useful if you don't have room for all the various items that the normal installation adds to your hard disk. Finally, if you know you will only need one printer driver, you can bypass installing the full selection of printer drivers and install only the one you need (you can always come back and install the others later).

If you want to do a customized installation, you'll need to follow steps 1 and 2 in the previous section to get to the main Installer screen shown in Figure A-7. Then, follow these steps:

1. Click the Customize button. This will take you to the screen shown in Figure A-8.

   The left side of the screen gives you a list of options that you can scroll and select from, and the right side of the screen displays buttons that you can use to start the process. (Note the button in the lower right, called Easy Install, shown in Figure A-8. This is the "escape route" back to the simpler Installer.)

   You have many choices. If you select one of the options, such as the System Software for any Macintosh, as shown in Figure A-8, you'll get a description of what will be installed in the lower part of the screen. It shows the size of the finished files, the date it was created, and the version of the software. Another example of this is

A

Figure A-8. *The screen for customized installation*

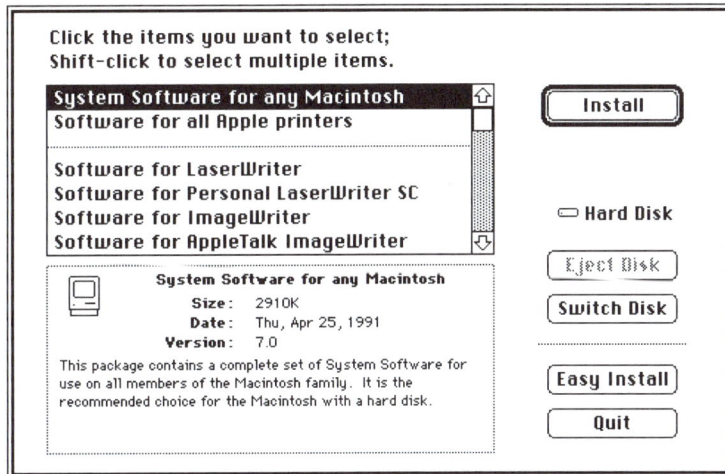

Click the items you want to select;
Shift-click to select multiple items.

System Software for any Macintosh
Software for all Apple printers
Software for LaserWriter
Software for Personal LaserWriter SC
Software for ImageWriter
Software for AppleTalk ImageWriter

System Software for any Macintosh
Size : 2910K
Date : Thu, Apr 25, 1991
Version : 7.0

This package contains a complete set of System Software for use on all members of the Macintosh family. It is the recommended choice for the Macintosh with a hard disk.

[Install]

⊂ Hard Disk

[Eject Disk]
[Switch Disk]

[Easy Install]
[Quit]

Figure A-9. *File Sharing selected*

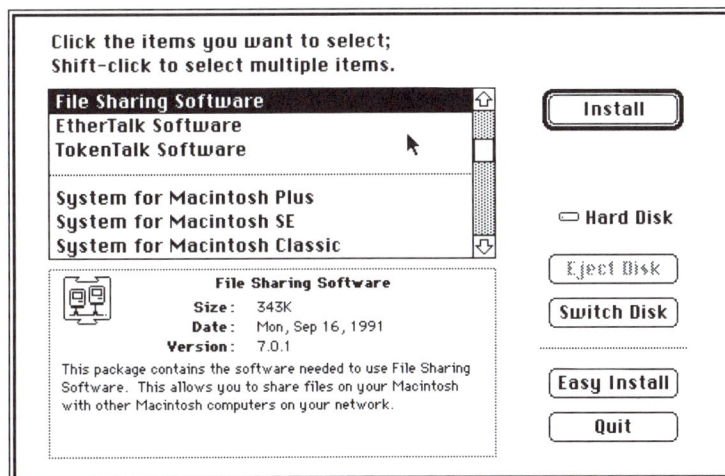

Click the items you want to select;
Shift-click to select multiple items.

File Sharing Software
EtherTalk Software
TokenTalk Software
System for Macintosh Plus
System for Macintosh SE
System for Macintosh Classic

File Sharing Software
Size : 343K
Date : Mon, Sep 16, 1991
Version : 7.0.1

This package contains the software needed to use File Sharing Software. This allows you to share files on your Macintosh with other Macintosh computers on your network.

[Install]

⊂ Hard Disk

[Eject Disk]
[Switch Disk]

[Easy Install]
[Quit]

shown in Figure A-9, where File Sharing has been selected.

Continue scrolling up and down the list to take a look at what each of the options will do for you.

2. When you know what you want to install, start at the top, and select the various options, remembering to hold down the (shift) key throughout if you want to select more than one option.

3. When you finish selecting the options, click the Install button in the upper-right corner. The Installer will then go through the process of asking you to insert the disks it needs.

4. When this process is finished, you will again be asked to insert the Install 1 disk. When ready to leave the Installer, click Quit.

What Else Comes with System 7?

Although the Installer is very complete in copying the files that you'll need to make your Macintosh run, you might find some of the other files included with it to be very useful. These files reside on the various floppy disks used by the Installer, but because many people don't need them they are not part of the default installation process. The following lists what's extra on each disk of the current version of System 7 (7.0.1), and what each does.

To use any of these extras, all you have to do is insert the appropriate disk in your drive, and then drag the program icon onto your System folder. The Macintosh will automatically put them where they belong.

Extras on the Install 1 Disk

The Install 1 disk contains files only used by the Installer, including the Network Extension.

Extras on the Install 2 Disk

The Install 2 disk contains files only used by the Installer, including the Finder, AppleShare, EtherTalk, and TokenTalk drivers.

Extras on the Printing Disk

The Printing disk contains its own Installer, as well as drivers for all of Apple's current printers. You can use this disk alone, to update other people on a network to the same version of the printer driver you are using.

Extras on the Fonts Disk

The Fonts disk contains all the fonts that you would normally have on a Macintosh, plus some fonts that have historically been included on the Macintosh, including Athens, Cairo, London, Los Angeles, San Francisco, and Venice.

Extras on the Tidbits Disk

The Tidbits disk contains the most unusual files. Here, you'll find the following files:

- *CloseView*   With CloseView, users who have trouble seeing the screen can enlarge all of the characters on the screen, much as a magnifying glass would.

- *Easy Access*   With Easy Access, users who have difficulty controlling a mouse or using a keyboard can make full use of the Macintosh with only one finger. Easy Access includes sticky keys, where the (shift), (⌘), (option), and (control) keys can be held down, as if you were using two fingers and Mouse Keys where the numeric keypad can replace the Macintosh mouse. Easy Access and its keys are discussed in more detail in Chapter 6, "Customizing with Control Panels."

- *Apple File Exchange*   With Apple File Exchange, you can transfer files to and from MS-DOS formatted floppy disks, as well as ProDOS Apple // formatted disks.

- *TeachText*   TeachText is a simple word processing program.

You'll also find on the Tidbits disk all the control panels and desk accessories.

Extras on the Disk Tools Disk

Disk Tools is a bootable System 7 floppy disk, with the absolute minimum Finder and System files necessary to be a bootable floppy disk. You'll also find Disk First Aid and Apple HD SC Setup programs here.

How to Get More Support

Apple has done a number of things to support System 7 users. If you purchased System 7 from an Apple Computer dealer, you are eligible for 90 days of free technical support with their toll-free telephone number. If you got System 7 from some other source, then Apple has a 900 phone number, which uses your touch tone phone to help you select the right category and question from a series of choices.

Another good choice for support is to use the dealer where you purchased your Macintosh. Most dealers will discuss your problem, and depending on the scope of it, they will offer a solution right there, or they will put you in touch with their support staff or outside consultants who can actually come to where your computer is and help you solve your problem. There is usually a charge for this service, but it's often worth the money to get your system up and running quickly.

Another excellent source of help is your local Macintosh user group. These groups are voluntary organizations of people who get together to discuss questions and solutions on their Macintosh computers. They come from all walks in life, and range from very technically oriented, to those who just want to know more about their own Macintosh computers.

Here are the telephone numbers for these sources:

- Free System 7 support for those who purchased the software from an Apple dealer: 1-800-RUN-7777 (you will need to enter your serial number to use this)
- System 7 support, charged by the minute: 1-900-535-APPL
- To locate your nearest dealer: 1-800-538-9696
- To locate your local user group: 1-800-538-9696, Ext. 500

A

- Apple Computer's Customer Assistance Center: 1-800-776-2333
- Apple Computer's main office: 1-408-996-1010

The Future of System 7

What can you expect in the future with System 7? Well, System 7 is the beginning of a whole new way of working with your computer, so Apple is committed to improving this product. Some of the more recent additions, detailed in the following sections, demonstrate Apple's commitment to it.

Remote AppleTalk Access

Remote AppleTalk Access, first introduced in late 1991, allows a remote Macintosh to connect and communicate with another Macintosh. This software is bundled with all the PowerBook computers, and was designed to allow the business person to call into their office while on the road, and to give them access to their office's network, file servers, electronic mail systems, and even their own Macintosh computer to get that one critical file that they left back in the office. Using software compression schemes, this software makes even slow 2400-baud modems effective when connecting into a network.

QuickTime

QuickTime allows any color-capable Macintosh to display full-motion video and animation in any application, without any additional software. This remarkable software extension is free to all users of the Macintosh, and makes working with time-based events, such as video, as simple as pasting a graphic into current applications. Also included in QuickTime are compression schemes that compress graphics from 10:1 up to 100:1, and the ability to cut and paste sound along with visual images. Applications such as computer-based training, educational story books with full-motion characters, and enhanced business communications are all being done with more impact and quality, due mainly to QuickTime.

How to Make Your Disk Look Better

Now that you have all the System 7 files on your computer, it may be getting hard to find things. There are probably as many ways to organize a hard disk as there are people. One sensible way to organize your hard disk is to group files functionally. For example, group all application files in one folder, all utility files in a second, and all information files in a third. The next section tells you how it works.

Storing in the System Folder

First, you must have the System folder. It doesn't have to be called the System folder, but since all the other applications will refer to it in their manuals as the System folder, you might as well call it that too. Inside the System folder you'll put everything that your applications need but weren't smart enough to store themselves. You already know that Inits, control panels, and other extensions belong here. But you can put more in here—lots more.

You can put in the System folder dictionaries for your word processor, modules for your graphics program (SuperPaint calls these "Tools in a pouch"), settings files for your applications, all your help files, and in general, things that your applications will need to have access to. Some companies, such as Claris and Aldus, create a folder inside your System folder, and dump most of their necessary files inside of it automatically. Expect to see more companies doing this as they create more complicated applications.

Storing in the Applications Folder

Make a folder called Applications. (From the Finder File menu, choose New Folder, then type **Applications** to rename it.) This is where the actual applications go. Don't get fooled by all the little utility programs that might have come with the application. This folder should *only* contain applications that match the name on the boxes, and that you plan to use on a regular basis.

Storing in the Utilities Folder

Next, make a folder called Utilities. This is where all the little applications go that don't have a home anywhere else. This includes the Dialog Box Editor from Excel, the Conversion Utility from Word, all that stuff that came with PageMaker to send files to a slide house, and so on. You get the idea. It's an accessory application, you paid for it, but you don't use it very much. Those things belong in the Utility folder. This is also a great place for the Apple HD SC Setup program that is used with the Installer.

Do not copy any Installer application programs into the Utilities folder. Those files are very specific on where they think they ought to be located, so they only work from a floppy disk. Don't waste your hard disk space copying them here.

Finally, if you have Norton Utilities for the Macintosh, or a similar program, copy all their files into a folder with an appropriate name, and put the entire folder in this Utility folder.

Storing in the Word Folder

Make a Word folder, and dump all those demos, tutorials, mailing labels, English dictionaries, and so on into it.

Storing in the Other Data Folder

Now make a folder called Other Data. This folder gets all the demo and tutorial files that came with all those applications. Make sure you try to keep the tutorial files together by application, and generally the way they were on the floppy disk you got from the manufacturer.

Now make a folder for each of the other applications you have, put all their demo files in their appropriate folder, and then put that entire folder into the Other Data folder. You should end up with a folder for each application you have in the Applications folder. This will allow you to quickly find a file if the application requests it. (If the application keeps asking for a file every time you launch the application, then put that offending file in the System folder. The application will stop asking you for it.)

Storing in the Games Folder

Do you have any games? If not, you probably will. Make a folder called Games. If you share this Macintosh with several others, leave the Games folder at the top level—not inside another folder. This will keep them from looking around on your hard disk for something fun to do. If the Macintosh belongs solely to you and nobody else uses it, then put the Games folder in the Applications folder. Other people will be impressed with how well organized and professional you are. Just don't show them this folder.

Storing in Your Folder

Now make a folder using your name as its title. If you put a period in front of it, it will always be at the top of View sorted by name. If you put a • ((option)-(8)) in front of your name, it will be at the bottom of this list. This is where things that are really personal go. Make folders inside of this folder that allow you to quickly find that name, telephone number, or recently sent correspondence that is important. This is *your* folder.

But wait, there's more. Why did you buy this Macintosh? Was it for work? For school? Make some folders that relate to your key topics. These should be by job, not by application type. Let's say you do construction. You are bidding on a house, and have created drawings, expense estimates, correspondence, and so on. All of these documents would go in the same folder. Don't worry, the Macintosh will keep track of which application created which document, and will automatically start these files with their correct application. You now have a logical place to store all the interrelated files. It's as easy as using a file in a file drawer.

If you follow these recommendations, your Macintosh will be neat and the information will all be organized in a manner that makes sense for you. Just remember that when you use an application to create a new document (such as writing a new letter), save the file to the Desktop; when you quit that application, you'll see a file that needs to be put away. Or you can save it in the correct folder to start with, by selecting the appropriate folder when you do the initial Save command.

Aliases

Another helpful feature is an *alias*. An alias lets you place your application and information files anywhere you want and still be able to function. For example, make aliases of your favorite applications, folders, or documents, and put them in your Apple menu. They'll always be available, no matter which application you're working in. (Chapter 4, "Files, Folders, and Disks" more fully explains aliases.)

Another suggestion is to make a folder called Work in Progress. Put this in the lower-left corner of your desktop, then put an alias of the files you are working on inside this folder. The originals will stay in their correct folders, but you'll have instant access to those files, in an easy-to-maintain system. As you finish working on the document, you can just throw the alias away.

You have probably used a fair amount of hard disk space. If you need more space, take a hard look at the Other Data folder. It's likely that you can get rid of a lot of what is in this folder and never miss a thing.

Index

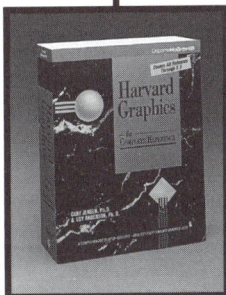

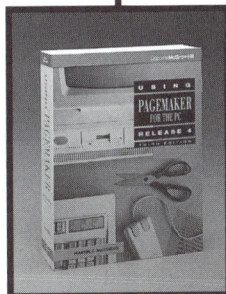

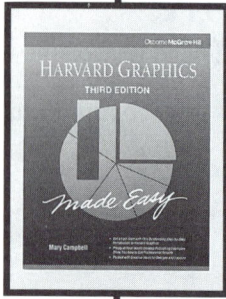

Harvard Graphics 3.0 Made Easy
by Mary Campbell

Campbell covers the basics of the latest version of Harvard Graphics before showing you how to create a variety of charts and demonstrating new drawing features. You'll also learn the latest presentation techniques for producing professional slide shows.

$24.95, ISBN: 0-07-881746-3, 358 pages, 7 3/8 x 9 1/4

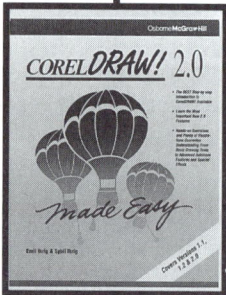

CorelDRAW! 2 Made Easy
by Ihrig & Matthews

This Made Easy guide offers both step-by-step instruction to this popular graphics program for IBM PCs and an easy reference to menus, keyboard shortcuts, available fonts, and clip art. A wealth of illustrations guarantee quick understanding of everything from basic drawing tools to advanced features.

$24.95, ISBN: 0-07-881726-9, 7 3/8 x 9 1/4

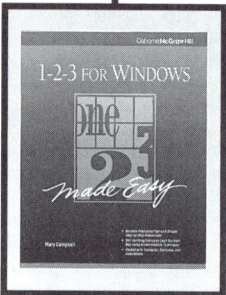

1-2-3 for Windows Made Easy
by Mary Campbell

With Mary Campbell's latest book you'll learn all about using this popular spreadsheet in the Windows graphical environment. Whether you're a first-time 1-2-3 user or experienced in 1-2-3 but new to Windows, Campbell takes you through the basics and carefully describes the special features of this new program.

$19.95 ISBN: 0-07-881731-5 450 pages 7 3/8 x 9 1/4

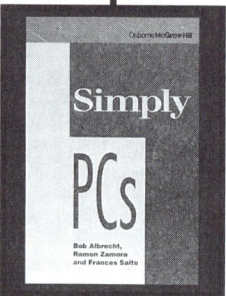

Simply PCs
by Bob Albrecht

First-time computer users won't want to miss this short, beautifully illustrated guide that thoroughly explains what a computer system is and how to use it. Simply PCs provides a clear overview of software, hardware, peripherals, and systems.

$14.95 ISBN: 0-07-881741-2 208 pages, 5 3/8 x 8 3/4

Covers All IBM PCs and Compatible Computers

Osborne **McGraw-Hill** ■ **Available at local book and computer stores.**

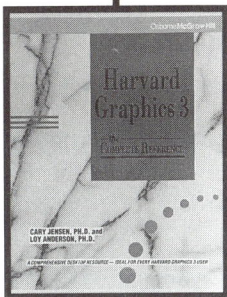

Harvard Graphics 3: The Complete Reference
by Cary Jensen & Loy Anderson

Bestselling authors Jensen and Anderson have written this comprehensive reference covering Harvard Graphics' powerful Release 3 providing detailed explanations of every Harvard Graphics feature, including its enhanced drawing tools and expanded interactive presentation capabilities.

$29.95, ISBN: 0-07-881749-8, 672 pages, 7 3/8 x 9 1/4

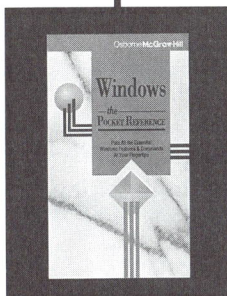

Windows: The Pocket Reference
by Allen Wyatt

This is the best Windows memory jogger you can buy! Rely on this handy reference anytime you need to remember a Windows command or function. All listings are briefly described with examples and are arranged alphabetically so you can turn to the command you need fast.

$9.95 ISBN: 0-07-881750-1 224 pages 4 3/4 x 8 Covers Windows 3.0

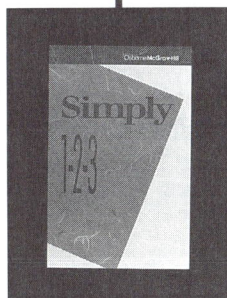

Simply 1-2-3
by Mary Campbell

Lotus 1-2-3 beginners will welcome this quick guide to the basics of the world's most widely used spreadsheet. Filled with illustrations and computer screen displays, you'll quickly learn the basics of creating worksheets and performing calculations.

$14.95 ISBN: 0-07-881751-X 208 pages, 5 3/8 x 8 3/4

Covers All Releases of Lotus 1-2-3

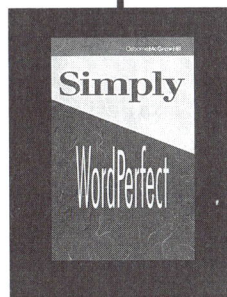

Simply WordPerfect
by Kris Jamsa

If you're new to computers and WordPerfect, this book is for you. Simply WordPerfect is a short guide that gives you the basics of this popular word processing program in a user-friendly format, accompanied by practical illustrations.

$14.95 ISBN: 0-07-881752-8 208 pages, 5 3/8 x 8 3/4

Covers All Releases of WordPerfect

Osborne **McGraw-Hill** ■ **Available at local book and computer stores.**

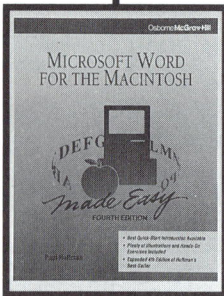

Microsoft Word 5 for the Macintosh Made Easy
by Paul Hoffman

With Paul Hoffman's outstanding Made Easy guide, you'll learn all the basics as Hoffman leads you through short hands-on exercises. All the newest features and capabilities are explained, including features for handling the new Macintosh System 7 operating system.

$19.95 ISBN: 0-07-881769-2 450 pages, 7 3/8 x 9 1/4

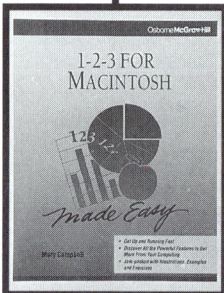

1-2-3 for the Macintosh Made Easy
by Mary Campbell

Internationally recognized Lotus expert Mary Campbell has now written another classic to cover the newest version of the Lotus 1-2-3 spreadsheet that runs on the Macintosh. The book is designed to help beginners learn everything from building a spreadsheet to graphing data.

$19.95 ISBN: 0-07-881774-9 512 pages, 7 3/8 x 9 1/4

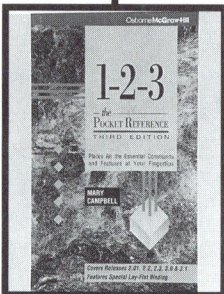

1-2-3: The Pocket Reference, Third Edition
by Mary Campbell

Next time you're wondering how to format a 1-2-3 calculation, set up a print option, or copy a column, reach for your indispensable copy of the third edition of this handy, bestselling guide. This Pocket Reference features a special lay-flat binding allowing you to keep the book open to any chosen page.

$9.95 ISBN: 0-07-881777-3 224 pages, 4 1/4 x 8

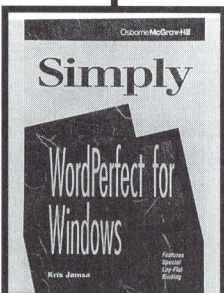

Simply WordPerfect for Windows
by Kris Jamsa

Kris Jamsa is back with a new book for beginning users of WordPerfect for Windows. Prior computer experience is not necessary to understand Jamsa's clear instructions. A wealth of illustrations clarify your understanding while a special lay-flat binding keeps this book open to any page.

$14.95 ISBN: 0-07-881781-1 209 pages, 5 3/4 x 8 3/4

Osborne **McGraw-Hill** ■ **Available at local book and computer stores.**

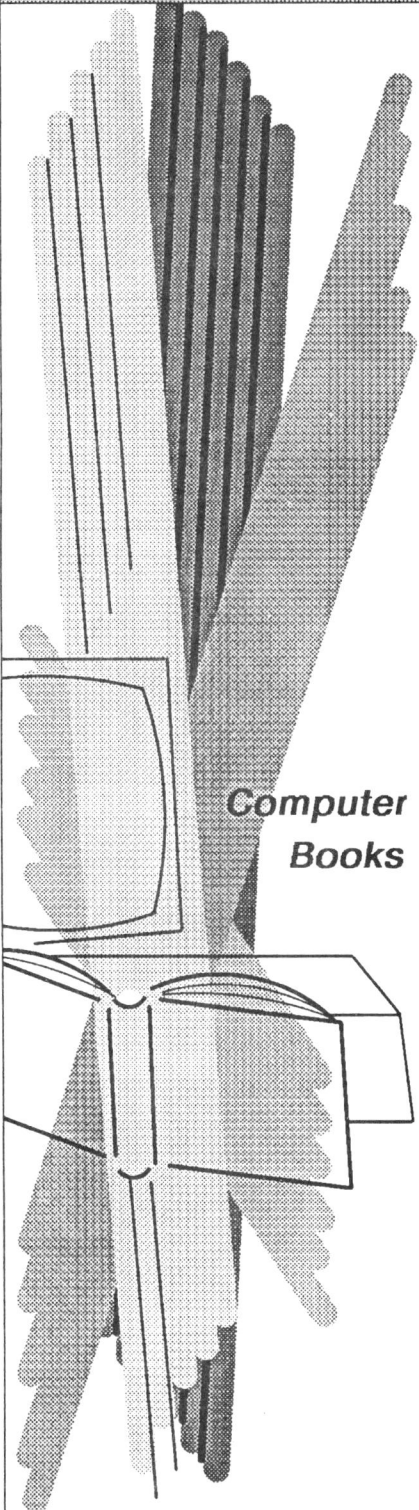

▼

You're important to us...

We'd like to know what you're interested in, what kinds of books you're looking for, and what you thought about this book in particular.

Please fill out the attached card and mail it in. We'll do our best to keep you informed about Osborne's newest books and special offers.

► *YES, Send Me a FREE Color Catalog of all Osborne computer books*
To Receive Catalog, Fill in Last 4 Digits of ISBN Number from Back of Book (see below bar code) 0-07-881 _ _ _ — _

Name: _____ Title: _____

Company: _____

Address: _____

City: _____ State: _____ Zip: _____

I'M PARTICULARLY INTERESTED IN THE FOLLOWING *(Check all that apply)*

I use this software
- ☐ WordPerfect
- ☐ Microsoft Word
- ☐ WordStar
- ☐ Lotus 1-2-3
- ☐ Quattro
- ☐ Others _____

I use this operating system
- ☐ DOS
- ☐ Windows
- ☐ UNIX
- ☐ Macintosh
- ☐ Others _____

I rate this book:
- ☐ Excellent ☐ Good ☐ Poor

I program in
- ☐ C or C++
- ☐ Pascal
- ☐ BASIC
- ☐ Others _____

I chose this book because
- ☐ Recognized author's name
- ☐ Osborne/McGraw-Hill's reputation
- ☐ Read book review
- ☐ Read Osborne catalog
- ☐ Saw advertisement in store
- ☐ Found/recommended in library
- ☐ Required textbook
- ☐ Price
- ☐ Other _____

Comments _____

Topics I would like to see covered in future books by Osborne/McGraw-Hill include:

_____

IMPORTANT REMINDER
To get your FREE catalog, write in the last 4 digits of the ISBN number printed on the back cover (see below bar code) 0-07-881 _ _ _ — _

Osborne **McGraw-Hill**

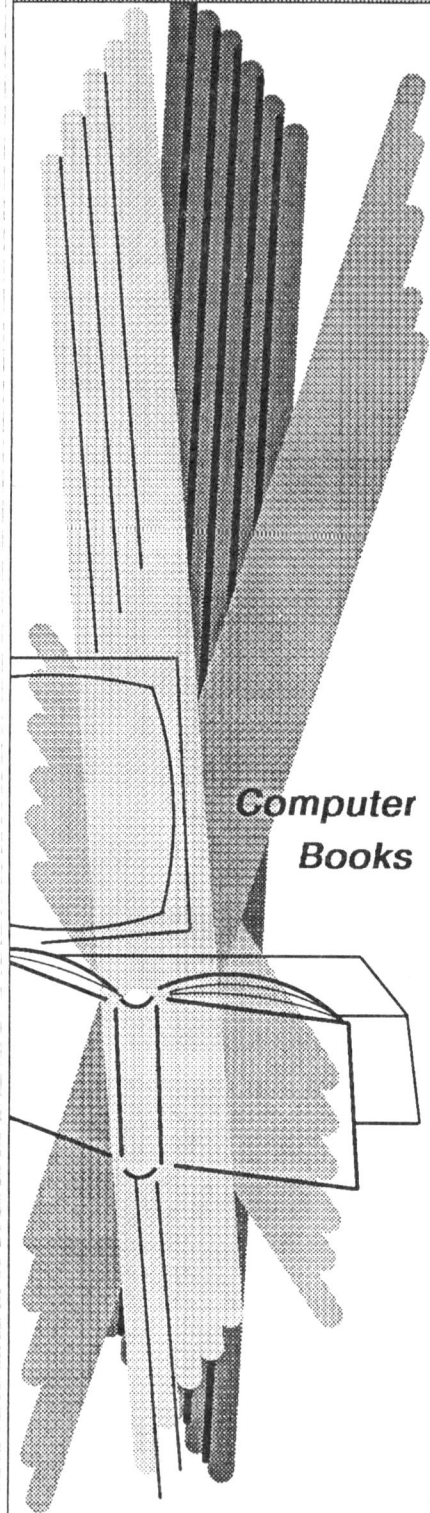

Computer

Books

(800) 227-0900